[JAIL SENTENCES]

Stages

[JAIL SENTENCES]

Representing Prison
in Twentieth-Century
French Fiction

ANDREW SOBANET

University of Nebraska Press : *Lincoln & London*

A portion of chapter 1, "Everyman in
Prison," previously appeared as
"Ideology and Fictional Construction:
Victor Serge's *Les Hommes dans la
prison*," in *Romance Quarterly* 50.1
(Winter 2003): 43–55. "For a Trivial
Motive" by Jean-Paul Vigneaud,
from *Sud Ouest* of 10 December 1996,
is reprinted by permission.

*Library of Congress
Cataloging-in-Publication Data*
Sobanet, Andrew.
Jail sentences : representing prison
in twentieth-century French fiction /
Andrew Sobanet.
p. cm.
Includes bibliographical references and
index.
ISBN 978-0-8032-1379-1 (cloth : alk.
paper)
1. French fiction—20th century—
History and criticism. 2. Prisons in
literature. I. Title.
PQ673.S6 2008
843'.91093556—dc22
2008000411

Set in Sabon by Kim Essman.
Designed by A. Shahan.

For my parents, Diana and Henry

If sensational "revelations" about some dark side of our life occasionally find their way into the daily Press; if they succeed in shaking our indifference and awaken public attention, we may have in the papers, for a month or two, excellent articles and letters on the subject. Many well-meant things may then be said, the most humane feelings expressed. But the agitation soon subsides; and, after having asked for some new regulations or laws, in addition to the hundreds of thousands of regulations and laws already in force; after having made some microscopic attempts at combating by a few individual efforts a deep-rooted evil which ought to be combated by the combined efforts of Society at large, we soon return to our daily occupations without caring much about what has been done. It is good enough if, after all the noise, things have not gone from bad to worse. If this remark is true with regard to so many features of our public life, it is especially so with regard to prisons and prisoners.

PETER KROPOTKIN, *In Russian and French Prisons* (1887)

[CONTENTS]

[ACKNOWLEDGMENTS]

THIS BOOK FIRST EXISTED as my doctoral dissertation, completed at the University of Pennsylvania under the direction of Gerald Prince. I would like to thank Professor Prince wholeheartedly for his continued generosity and kindness. I could not have completed this project without his assistance. I would also like to extend thanks to the other members of my thesis committee, Joan DeJean and Jean-Marie Roulin, for their valuable assistance. Moreover, I would like to express gratitude to the University of Pennsylvania for funding my graduate studies.

I transformed my doctoral thesis into this book while teaching at Georgetown University. Georgetown's Faculty of Languages and Linguistics generously supported this project through two summer grants, for which I am very grateful. Publication of this book was also assisted by a competitive grant-in-aid from Georgetown University's Graduate School of Arts and Sciences. I would also like to thank all of my colleagues in the Department of French for their support, both moral and academic. I would especially like to express gratitude to my department chair, Deborah Lesko Baker, for her continued support.

Special thanks also go to Shelley Temchin for her very kind and generous assistance in proofreading the entire book manuscript. Jean-Max Guieu, David Andrew Jones, Amadou Koné, Denis Provencher, and Susan Terrio also read portions of this book, and I appreciate their helpful feedback. I am grateful to Alissa Webel for her assistance in translating particularly thorny phrases and also to Roger Bensky for many enjoyable brainstorming sessions.

A sincere thank-you to Warren Motte for his continued support and mentorship.

François Bon was very generous with his time and information, and I would like to thank him for providing me with unpublished source material that was invaluable for my fourth chapter.

Thanks also go to all those at the University of Nebraska Press who made this book possible.

The patient, loving, and understanding support of my wife, Amanda Sobanet, helped me write each page of this book, and I am very grateful to her.

I could not have written this book without the unfailing and unconditional support of my parents, Diana and Henry Sobanet, to whom I owe a lifetime of education. This book is dedicated to them.

[JAIL SENTENCES]

[INTRODUCTION]

Prisoners are storytellers. Whether their tales take the form of a message tapped in code through concrete, graffiti traced on a cell wall, a conversation through the pipes of an archaic plumbing system, a lament spoken through bars in a visiting room, or written testimony left behind by the condemned, storytelling is an integral part of imprisonment.[1] Incarceration lends itself to telling, and narratives of crime and punishment take many forms and serve myriad functions on both sides of prison walls. A prisoner assimilates into the hierarchies and cliques of the society of captives by telling a heroic tale of rebellion or a pathos-ridden fall from grace.[2] Inmates ruminate on their legal cases and their appeals, determining precisely *how* to present their crime to the authorities (Who is to blame? Should I confess? How should I plead?). Isolated in their cells, prisoners seek pen and paper to record their thoughts and come to terms with their social relegation.[3] Convicts are often compelled to write in order to convey to the uninitiated on the outside what transpires on the inside. Stories of brutality, dehumanization, and radical deprivation are counterbalanced — often in the same narrative — by accounts of solidarity, salvation, and enlightenment.

The prison narratives with which readers are likely to be

most familiar are stories told by and about inmates that expose the horrors, the ephemeral joys, the entrenched bureaucratic processes, and the mind-numbing routines of incarceration. In those narratives, commonplaces inevitably recur, from themes (rehabilitation, corruption, rebellion), to images (high walls, bars, slamming doors), to events (entry, riots, liberation), to character types (abusive guards, angry inmates, merciful chaplains). The cultural influence of those narrative topoi is strong, a fact noted by contemporary novelists. The protagonist of Chester Himes's novel *Yesterday Will Make You Cry* (1998), for example, struggles in the first moments of his imprisonment with his received ideas about prison life: "Jimmy couldn't get used to any of it, any of the entire dormitory scene. It wasn't real—convicts walking about and mingling with each other. The real prison was the one which kept coming back—a prison of dark, dank dungeons with moldy bones in rusted chains, the prison that held the Count of Monte Cristo, Jean Valjean, Saint Paul—the real prison was the prison in his mind" (25–26). Similarly, as Jean-Baptiste Clamence—the world-weary narrator and "judge-penitent"[4] of Albert Camus's *La chute* (*The Fall*, 1956)—tells the story of his detention in a desert prison camp, he elects not to describe its physical characteristics. There is no need, he laments, because his contemporaries are already far too familiar with "the lyricism of the prison cell." "I'll leave it to you," he states. "You need add but a few details: the heat, the vertical sun, the flies, the sand, the lack of water" (123–24).

The frequent reiteration of the commonplaces of prison life and the public's familiarity with them is, in part, attributable to the nature of incarceration. The prison is a "total" institution distinguished by a high degree of bureaucratic regularity.[5] Modern penal practices began to take shape in the second half of the eighteenth century in England, Europe, and the United States when imprisonment came to be defined, to use Michel

Foucault's phrase, as "the penalty *par excellence*" (*Discipline* 267).[6] As a consequence of the international development of the practice of punishment, prison experiences throughout the industrialized world bear striking similarities.[7] Organizational and procedural similarities contribute to general familiarity with the plight of prisoners: the tale of one inmate is, in a number of ways, representative of what all inmates endure. The proliferation of prison narratives written by inmates during the twentieth century—itself a noteworthy phenomenon commented on by historians and social scientists alike—is no doubt a significant contributing factor to a general understanding of the experience of incarceration.[8] Furthermore, testimonies by guards, doctors, and teachers who work or have worked in prison are frequently published.[9] The propagation of media reports, feature films, television shows, and documentaries about prison life has also played no small role.[10] We should be careful to note, however, that the public's intimate knowledge of the commonplaces of prison life antedates the recent proliferation of media reports and testimonies, not to mention the maturation of the prison as the modern total institution we are familiar with today. Indeed, through his references to Saint Paul, Alexandre Dumas, and Victor Hugo, Himes underscores the fact that narratives of incarceration are far from a novelty in the Western tradition. As Victor Brombert writes in his study on prison literature from the era of Dumas and Hugo, "Prison haunts our civilization" (3).

The long list of canonical writers who were incarcerated and subsequently wrote about the imprisoned and the condemned—Silvio Pellico, Fyodor Dostoyevsky, Oscar Wilde, and Jack London, to name just a few—attests to the cultural and literary significance of the prison and prison narratives, not to mention the relationship between imprisonment and storytelling. The present study is an investigation into a specific form of prison narrative: fictional texts that purport to document conditions and relations behind bars. *Jail Sentences* examines the narrative mechanics, the thematics, and the ideological impulses of such "prison novels," as I will refer to them.[11] The authors studied here—Victor Serge, Jean Genet, Albertine Sarrazin, and François Bon—had direct experience with prison and composed texts about incarceration that artfully straddle, cross, and blur the line between fiction and nonfiction. For reasons explained in more detail later in this introduction, *Jail Sentences* limits itself to texts about prison, as opposed to other spaces of confinement in widespread use during the twentieth century, such as penal colonies, concentration camps, and Nazi extermination camps. The novels studied here claim to document, rather than simply represent, the specificities of the "prison-institution" defined by sociologist Corinne Rostaing as a "place of detention, materialized by a fixed space and a bureaucratic organizational apparatus" (4).[12]

Although "prison writing"—a term that encompasses journals, letters, autobiographies, and novels—has received some attention in scholarly studies and anthologies, scant critical work has been done on the prison novel as a literary form. *Jail Sentences* explores the narrative particularities of the prison novel, investigating the use of fiction as a documentary tool. This study thus aims to analyze techniques that are employed in fictional and autobiographical literature as well as in hybrid genres (such as autofiction) that attempt to obfuscate the distinction between the two. Furthermore, this book examines critiques of the prison promoted in these fictions, underlining the relationship between form and ideology. *Jail Sentences* focuses on novels published in French that describe life in French prisons during the twentieth century. However, as we will see over the course of this book, study of French prison novels sheds light on prison literature from a number of other national traditions because of a host of shared narrative, thematic, and ideological characteristics.

"My Hand Is Severe but My Intention Benevolent"

Given the brutality that has come to characterize modern prison life, it is perhaps difficult to envision the well-intentioned severity promoted by Seneca's motto, which was carved in stone above the doorway of the Amsterdam Rasp House. The rehabilitation methods in use during the late 1700s at that Dutch jail (such as regimented meal, work, and prayer schedules) led British reformer John Howard to admire it as a model of criminal punishment.[13] Howard, the most prominent figure in the early penitentiary movement in England, was not alone: a trend toward "benevolent" treatment of criminals was evident in Europe and America in the late eighteenth and early nineteenth centuries. In France it was the hope of many reformers that post-revolutionary prisons would constitute a shift from the filth, danger, and promiscuity of ancien régime holding cells to more efficient, more fair, and more rehabilitative modes of punishment.[14] The prison came to be envisioned as a site for reflection, inspiration, edification, and transformation. Indeed, the very concept of the penitentiary is based on the notion that inmates will be rehabilitated and transformed into decent, law-abiding citizens through a combination of solitude, silence, work, discipline, and religious instruction—a monastic existence of sorts.[15]

Although prisons are most often notorious for endemic violence, the notion that incarceration lends itself to reflection has persisted throughout its history, particularly in the literary realm. One of the most famous episodes of intellectual awakening in twentieth-century literature takes place in a prison, as Malcolm X sits in his cell, honing his reading and writing skills by copying the pages of his dictionary one by one.[16] That scene, along with the prodigious and often radical intellectual activity of many other prisoners, led critic H. Bruce Franklin to hypothesize in his 1978 book on American prison narratives that "in our society the two main competing intellectual centers may be the universities and the prisons" (*Literature* 235). Although vastly overstated, Franklin's comment is worthy of note as it illustrates an enduring perception of the prison as a privileged center for thought. The notion of the prisoner-turned-intellectual goes beyond simple personal enrichment and radicalization: prisoners are commonly seen as having a special relationship with art. Martin Esslin, for example, opens his widely cited book *Theater of the Absurd* by telling the story of San Quentin penitentiary inmates' fascination with an in-house production of *Waiting for Godot* (1952). Esslin writes that Beckett's masterpiece made an immediate and profound impact on the convicts (who were intimately familiar with empty time and alienation), whereas its meaning escaped supposedly highbrow audiences on the outside.[17]

Prison has proved to be a site not just for personal enrichment and edification but also for writing. To be sure, inmates who are able to write in prison or who testify to the experience of incarceration are exceptions: illiteracy, the difficulty of writing under harsh conditions, censorship, and seizures of property often inhibit prisoners from writing. In some cases, imprisonment can destroy a prisoner's will to witness. Jack London, for instance, writes that he felt so "meek and lowly" upon his release from jail that his once-strong determination to tell the story of his unjust arrest and detention simply dissolved (49).[18] In spite of those many obstacles, however, many well-known texts were produced in prison, such as Wilde's *De Profundis* and Gramsci's celebrated prison notebooks.[19] Imprisoned writers, not to mention writers who produced texts about their experiences with incarceration, are found on the French literary-historical landscape from the medieval era through the twentieth century. The tradition of the prisoner-turned-writer dates as far back as François Villon, whose reputation as a fifteenth-century *poète maudit* is based on the extent to which his literary production was informed and enriched by his legendary criminal exploits, exiles, wanderings, and multiple incarcerations.[20] Prison is integral to descriptions of the literary career of the Marquis de Sade, who wrote *120 journées de Sodome* (*120 Days of Sodom*) in 1784 and 1785 while locked in the Bastille.[21] Similarly, while jailed in Saint Lazare prison before being guillotined in 1794, André Chénier wrote his last *Iambes* on strips of paper used for wrapping dirty laundry (Scarfe 323). It was in that prison, moreover, that he wrote "La jeune captive," the famous ode written in the voice of an incarcerated young woman awaiting execution. Several decades later, a prison in Belgium proved to be the site of Verlaine's (at least temporary) religious awakening, not to mention the composition of some of his most famous poems, which he describes in detail in his 1893 text, *Mes prisons* (*My Prisons*).[22] A generation after Verlaine, Apollinaire was compelled to put pen to paper after his imprisonment: his short stanzas of "A La Santé" in *Alcools* (1913) provide a glimpse of the lives of prisoners in that notorious Parisian prison in the early part of the twentieth century. Perhaps the most legendary of all prison writers, Jean Genet, whose 1946 novel *Miracle de la rose* (*Miracle of the Rose*) is the primary focus of chapter 2 of this study, was canonized a literary saint by Sartre in the middle of the twentieth century. Alongside Genet in this same long tradition, Victor Serge, Albertine Sarrazin, and François Bon are the most prominent twentieth-century writers in France who have used their experiences in prison for literary inspiration.

Among studies of the literature of incarceration, *Jail Sentences* is the first to isolate and describe the characteristics of the prison novel, a form of documentary and testimonial literature. Previously, critics have underlined the importance of the theme of imprisonment (both literal and metaphoric) in a number of periods, genres, and traditions, going as far back as early Greek drama and the Platonic dialogues, not to mention a host of biblical tales.[23] Book-length studies of American and British prison literature have also been published in recent decades, focusing on authors such as Daniel Defoe, Malcolm Braly, and Chester Himes.[24] In French studies, among the most prominent critical works is Victor Brombert's *The Romantic Prison*, an analysis of incarceration, both literal and figurative, as a dominant preoccupation in nineteenth-century literature. Highlighting the dialectical nature of representations of the prison, Brombert argues persuasively that nineteenth-century French literature consistently depicted spaces of detention—no matter how horrid—as privileged sites for reflection and edification. In *Imagination in Confinement*, Elissa Gelfand analyzes, through a "socioliterary feminist" lens (23), the figure of the female criminal-prisoner in French women's writing from the Revolutionary era through the twentieth century.[25] In *Existential Prisons*, Mary Anne Frese Witt studies the theme of confinement (in prisons, bedrooms, and cities, among other sites and situations) in mid-twentieth-century French literature, with chapters on Malraux, Sartre, Camus, and Genet. Those noteworthy book-length studies have underlined the significance of the prison not only as a site for the production of culture but also as an important literary and philosophical device in nineteenth-and twentieth-century texts.[26] *Jail Sentences* fills lacunae left by those studies, as it is the first to focus on the narrative and ideological characteristics of twentieth-century French prison novels.

Prison literature—whether in the form of a personal journal, an autobiography, a novel, or reportage—is a compelling form of writing due in part to the nature and design of the prison-institution, not to mention its complex history.[27] The modern prison is a penal instrument whose mechanisms are hidden from public view. That fact is well demonstrated by Foucault in the opening segment of *Discipline and Punish*, which contrasts the public spectacle of the corporal (and, ultimately, capital) punishment of a regicide with the intensely regulated daily routine of a youth detention center in Paris (3–7). The latter, of course, unfolds exclusively behind the walls of the institution. Prison novels expose the details of life behind bars to an outside public that is ostensibly uninitiated in the bureaucratic practices and the sociological and psychological processes of the carceral universe. Prison literature reveals, often in highly personal and politicized terms, how individuals respond to a hostile and foreign environment.

In the modern prison system, inmates are collectively subjected to systematic and radical deprivation.[28] They are stripped of freedom, contact with loved ones, and normal daily routines. Upon incarceration, after being examined, photographed, and measured, prisoners must trade their own clothes for regulation uniforms and their names for numbers. Inmates are then exposed to surveillance, power structures in a rigid bureaucracy, and a strictly regimented schedule.[29] The world of the inmate is a subculture with distinct mores and methods of communication.[30] Prisoners have a slang that is all their own and exhibit distinct signs of community living, such as the embrace of specific value systems (solidarity among inmates, resistance to the power of the administration, etc.), tattooing, and black marketeering. They must integrate into hierarchies in inmate populations and must cope with what Erving Goffman calls "batch living," that is, situations in which individuals who are not members of the same family share living space. Guards are often corrupt and cruel. Riots, the pain of solitary confinement, sexual abuse, vermin, filth, and inadequate nutrition represent other legitimate hazards. Finally, after being subject to the dehumanization of incarceration, prisoners find themselves stigmatized upon their release.[31] To tell the story of a prison sentence is therefore tantamount to telling the tale of a person exposed to a universe with distinct risks, humiliations, values, and rules and regulations.

As we will see in the chapters that follow, prison novels portray, in great detail, daily life behind bars and use the prison as a vehicle to question and critique socioeconomic, cultural, and political power structures. While such works constitute neither histories of the prison nor sociological studies of prison life, they do proffer testimonies and stories that complement and inform a variety of scholarly, scientific, and philosophical investigations of the prison. This is especially the case with recent historiography of the prison, which has sought to examine the everyday lives of prisoners and, moreover, to study the prison as an expression of economic power, state priorities (some say obsessions), and chronic social ills.[32] Prominent examples of such historical examination of incarceration in the French context include Patricia O'Brien's *The Promise of Punishment*, an excellent study of prison and the living conditions of prisoners in nineteenth-century France. Jacques-Guy Petit's highly informative *Ces peines obscures* (These Mysterious Punishments) examines penal reforms, philanthropy movements, and daily life in prison from 1780 to 1875. Petit also contributed to a collaborative study with Claude Faugeron and Michel Pierre, *Histoire des prisons en France (1789–2000)* (History of Prisons in France), which is, to date, the best and most concise history of twentieth-century French prisons. Also noteworthy is former justice minister Robert Badinter's *La prison républicaine* (The Republican Prison), which delves into the political machinations of prison reform between 1871 and 1914.[33] Outside the French context, other prominent social histories include David Rothman's study of the birth of the American asylum and prison, *The Discovery of the Asylum*, and Michael Ignatieff's book on the prison reform movement in England, *A Just Measure of Pain: The Penitentiary in the Industrial Revolution, 1750–1850*.[34] A number of those historians credit Foucault's

Discipline and Punish as being a greatly influential study of the evolution of discourses of punishment from the ancien régime to the modern era. Foucault's seminal work demonstrates convincingly that the prison is an institution whose development, internal organizational processes, architecture, and goals are profoundly linked to the formation of other social institutions and the spaces in which they practice their disciplines and assert their normative power. His work is distinct from the histories of the prison cited above, as it does not emphasize the chronological development of specific reforms, legislation, prison construction, philanthropy movements, and so on.[35] However, his insights on changes in discourses on punishment, the body, and the soul in the modern age, as well as his examination of the modern state's power apparatus, have indeed proved influential in recent social and cultural historiography of the prison.

The link Foucault emphasizes between the prison and other important social institutions is reflected in many sociological studies, even those published before the recent wave of social histories. Goffman's definition of total institutions in *Asylums*, for example, encompasses not simply prisons but also concentration camps, mental institutions, tuberculosis sanitaria, army barracks, naval ships, and religious cloisters. In his book on maximum-security prisons, *The Society of Captives*, Gresham Sykes notes that in order to study the prison it must be interpreted not as an isolated institution (as its physical separation from the outer world would suggest) but rather as an instrument of the state: "The prisons of the 18th and 19th centuries replaced the dungeons and detention rooms of prior years. The criminal was no longer simply to be killed, tortured and dismissed, or thrust beyond the pale in the exile of transportation. Now he was to be encapsulated in the body of the State" (xii).[36] Given the widespread perception of the prison as an institution linked to state power structures and to institutions that are central to social order, it is not surprising that when prisons fail to rehabilitate prisoners (as they often do) and when abhorrent conditions behind bars are exposed (as they often are), their failures are interpreted as failures of society at large. Faugeron, Petit, and Pierre, for example, conclude their collaborative history with the following bleak observation: "Everything that diminishes the dignity of the guarded has an effect on the guard, humiliates the Republic and contributes to the development of the feeling of insecurity in society" (239).[37] In a similar vein, Winston Churchill, in an oft-quoted observation made before the House of Commons on 20 July 1910, stated: "The mood and temper of the public in regard to the treatment of crime and criminals is one of the most unfailing tests of the civilization of any country" (1598). As we will see, prison novels tell the story of the difficulties of incarceration—which are often linked to larger social and economic forces—from within the institution.

Modes of punishment and the plight of the punished have long attracted the attention of French intellectuals and have been the subject of innumerable studies, inquiries, and polemics. As Foucault remarks in *Discipline and Punish*, "The prison has always formed part of an active field in which projects, improvements, experiments, theoretical statements, personal evidence, and investigations have proliferated" (235). In the earliest days of eighteenth-century reform, changes in the treatment of criminals were advocated by the likes of Mirabeau, Malesherbes, Voltaire, Montesquieu, and Rousseau.[38] Early reformers hoped that imprisonment could represent an enlightened and humanitarian form of punishment, especially when compared to the treatment of criminals during the ancien régime. Later in the nineteenth century, humanitarians, early social scientists, and state workers—true to the ideals of their predecessors—often described the prison as a source of individual and social corruption and sought remedy through the penitentiary model of punishment, which included varying degrees of work and solitary confinement.[39] Gustave de Beaumont and Alexis de Tocqueville, perhaps the most widely known advocates of penal reform in France, took a nine-month trip to the United States to study methods of prison reform in 1831 and 1832.[40] They were attracted above all by the American penitentiary, which was at that time considered a revolutionary and model instrument whose central goal was prisoner rehabilitation.[41] As Beaumont and Tocqueville note in their classic 1833 report, *On the Penitentiary System in the United States and Its Application in France*, French prisons not only failed to reform criminals but succeeded in completing the corruption of the "working classes who are in want of bread and labor" (34).

Similar critiques of the prison in its early decades as the form of punishment *par excellence* surfaced in the literary realm. Victor Hugo, for example, wrote passionately about the nature of punishment in his era in works such as *Le dernier jour d'un condamné* (*The Last Day of a Condemned Man*, 1829) and *Claude Gueux* (1834). Although never an inmate himself, Hugo visited prisons, interviewed prisoners, and wrote about their living conditions. He championed above all the abolition of the death penalty and sought to raise public awareness of its inherent cruelty.[42] Like other reformers and humanitarians of his era, he discerned a clear role for the state in eliminating what was perceived as a hardened criminal class. For example, *Claude Gueux*, which is based in actuality, emphasizes the importance of social support and education of the poor while denouncing the treatment of prisoners and the death penalty. The story's eponymous protagonist is a capable but impoverished worker driven to theft by need and imprisoned for his crime. Gueux is productive in the prison workshop and displays excellent leadership skills, surviving the vagaries of carceral life by forging strong bonds with his fellow inmates. His closest relationship is with a younger man named Albin, who generously shares his food ration with Gueux. For no reason other than harassment, a cruel workshop superintendent has Albin removed from the cell block in which Gueux resides. The latter sees this as a life-threatening action, as he has come to depend on Albin for friendship and food. The protagonist kills the guard in revenge and is then executed. The ultimate lesson Hugo emphasizes is that society is responsible for the atrocity, not Gueux. He writes: "Take the common man's head, cultivate it, weed it, water it, sow it, enlighten it, moralize it, and put it to good use; then you will have no need to cut it off" (129). *Claude Gueux* serves as a precursor to the transformation of reality into fiction found in the prison novels studied here. The author fictionalizes a real-life murder trial and execution, as Geoff Woollen argues, thereby turning a habitual criminal and bully into an "apostolic martyr and victim of society" (xv). Woollen correctly notes that Hugo does not emphasize Gueux's cruelty and violence as a criminal and prisoner; rather, he underlines "the environmental causes determining criminal behavior" (xv).[43] Hugo uses his skills as a writer of fiction to transform actuality into a compelling prison narrative that promotes a distinct sociopolitical message.

Serge, Genet, Sarrazin, and Bon represent a recent manifestation of the distinguished French tradition of prominent intellectuals who have commented on, investigated, and advocated reform of prisons and the treatment of criminals. Indeed, through the late twentieth century in France, the prison continued to serve as a vehicle for social critique for a diverse group of thinkers, including politically committed writers and philosophers. Sartre and Foucault, for example, were active in the Groupe d'information sur les prisons (GIP) from 1972 to 1974. The goal of the GIP, as Foucault wrote in its manifesto, was to expand knowledge of prison, which he characterized as "one of the hidden regions of our social system" (43).[44] The prison novel, like other forms of testimony about prison, serves a similar function. The narrative particularities of the fiction studied here—which are detailed below—create a contract between text and reader such that referentiality and verifiability are emphasized. The actuality of prison, as we will see, plays a prominent role in these fictions.

The Prison Novel

Each of the prison novels examined in the following chapters—Victor Serge's *Les hommes dans la prison* (*Men in Prison*, 1930), Jean Genet's *Miracle de la rose*, Albertine Sarrazin's *La cavale* (*The Runaway*, 1965), and François Bon's *Prison* (1997)—claims to document, rather than simply represent, the experience of life behind bars. The manner in which the documentary value is postulated varies from text to text. Prison novels rely on a combination of textual and paratextual strategies to blur the line between fiction and nonfiction, and this ambiguous generic boundary establishes a contract between text and reader that opens the possibility for both referential and fictional interpretations. This fluid contract influences readings of the texts in two ways. On the one hand, the autobiographical inclinations enhance the documentary effect of the novels.[45] *yes* The heightened referential implications indicate to the reader that the experience portrayed is not simply the product of the author's imagination but rather is representative of actual conditions of captivity. On the other hand, the fact that the texts are works of fiction allows writers to manipulate their source material without a breach of contract between text and reader. The authors use the flexibility afforded to them by the production of fiction to achieve a variety of ends. In some instances their version of the reality of incarceration can be designed specifically to promote an ideological agenda, such as an anti-capitalist or anti-bourgeois stance. In others, writers simply use their creative license to construct a more thematically balanced portrayal of life behind bars than the constraints of other genres and media—such as personal diaries, letter writing, or memoirs—have allowed.

To be sure, manipulation of source material is not limited to the realm of fiction writing. Selective editing is elementary to narrative construction, be it in a fictional or nonfictional text. As Hayden White remarks, "Every narrative, however seemingly 'full,' is constructed on the basis of a set of events that might have been included but were left out; this is as true of imaginary narratives as it is of realistic ones" (10). Editing is a creative process that also involves the prioritization of selected events through ordering, elaboration, abbreviation, and so on. It is, moreover, a process that is motivated by authorial intent, be it ideological, documentary, artistic, or otherwise.[46] Content can be thus manipulated by the context in which it is placed.[47] In other words, whether or not the events in a narrative are invented, a text's discourse is crafted by its author. However, while fictional and nonfictional texts share that very important "creative" quality on the level of discourse, manipulation on the level of story is a different matter. Whereas producers of nonfiction—historians, autobiographers, biographers, documentary filmmakers, and so on—may create or manipulate the discursive context in which they couch events, they do not, if they wish to remain faithful to the referentiality to which their works aspire, invent the events themselves.[48] In the realm of fiction, however, as a simple matter of a generic contract, authorial creation is subject to fewer boundaries. As Dorrit Cohn writes in *The Distinction of Fiction*, "The novelist's relation to his sources is free," and he or she therefore has more freedom of expression than the writer of a nonfictional text (114).

While the texts examined in this study are works of fiction, they are by no means novels in the classically realist sense of that term. Prison novels are testimonial and documentary literature. Each text examined in this study eschews its status as a work of fiction in order to emphasize its referential grounding. At the same time, the texts embrace fictionality so the authors may freely manipulate their source material and their stories, complementing the referential aspects of their narratives with fictive material. It is this artful interplay of invention and actuality that sets prison novels apart from the traditional realist model. A novel about prison is not necessarily subsumed under the category of a documentary prison novel, however. To take one prominent example, prison plays an important role in Albert Camus's *L'étranger* (*The Stranger*, 1942), as the entire second part of the book takes place after Meursault's arrest. However, the novel does not attempt—either textually or paratextually—to blur the line between fiction and nonfiction. There is no deliberate conflation of the identities of narrator-protagonist and author: Camus does not seek to represent the experience of his narrator-protagonist as his own. Critical reception of *L'étranger* reflects the work's straightforward and unambiguous status as a nondocumentary novel. Unlike the reception of prison novels examined in this study, there is no broad spectrum of fictional and referential interpretations of *L'étranger*. Although it is understandable that a critic might be swayed to read Genet's *Miracle de la rose* as an autobiography, an autobiographical reading of Meursault's experience would constitute a gross misapprehension of the generic status of Camus's novel. To be sure, *L'étranger* is not the only fictional text about prison life with no claims to referentiality or documentation. Jean Cau's *La pitié de Dieu* (*Mercy of God*, 1961) serves as an example of a novel whose action takes place entirely within the walls of a prison cell but which does not claim to be a documentary representation of life behind bars.[49] Cau is more concerned with rehashing Sartrian existential philosophy than with establishing his text's referential grounding. Dramatization of philosophical precepts takes precedence over documentation.[50] The goal of this study is therefore not to provide a comprehensive examination of representations of prison in the twentieth-century novel but rather to analyze the themes and narrative mechanics of a specific type of documentary fiction, the prison novel.

While an imaginary story such as *La pitié de Dieu* may indeed depict the radical separation from the outside world experienced by prisoners also portrayed in a documentary fiction such as Serge's *Les hommes dans la prison*, the two texts constitute different means of achieving that end. Articulating the difference between those two types of narratives sheds light on the form and function of documentary fiction as a literary modality distinct from realist fiction. Prison novels are driven by an implicit question: What is prison life like? They attempt to treat—albeit through widely divergent strategies—every facet of life behind bars, borrowing their authority from lived experience. The blurring of the boundary between fiction and autobiography is a necessary element in the establishment of discursive authority, for the novels' autobiographical facets underline their referential grounding. Unlike traditional memorializing autobiographies, however, prison novels do not recount a life; they focus on telling the story of a specific experience. The telling of the story is necessitated by the brutality of that experience, and the narration is motivated by a desire to expose what the narrator-author witnessed in prison.

The referentiality exhibited by prison novels is designed to heighten their ideological currency and urgency. If the reader is given indications that what is presented is strongly based in and representative of actuality, the texts—given their pronounced ideological slant—could be interpreted by the reader as a call to political or social action. One can, of course, easily imagine a text with no claims to a basis in actuality that motivates the reader toward similar ends. However, documentary fictions have a social function that is distinct from the function of classically realist texts, and they mimic some of the formal techniques and traits of nonfictional texts. A contract between text and reader is established, and the reader approaches the text with a set of expectations and conventions based on the nature of that contract.[51] The writers studied here employ a variety of strategies, both textual and paratextual, to assert that their stories are rooted in actuality. Publication information, subtitles, generic designations, dedications, epigraphs, prefatory notes, warnings, material on the front or back book covers—all such paratextual information influences reception and readings of the text. Moreover, a number of textual strategies (examined in detail in the chapters that follow) can further encourage the reader to interpret a text as a nonfiction. Examples include confessional autobiographical strategies, such as the use of an author's own name for the narrator-protagonist (a tactic also commonly used in autofictional texts); the prioritization of extended documentary description over the elaboration of plot; and verifiable details that reference historical figures, events, places, and phenomena.[52] Such strategies may be found in other documentary fictional forms, such as the historical novel, but I contend that, when examined and taken together as a whole, those strategies in carceral novels combine to create a distinct kind of documentary fiction.

As first-person narratives that recount an experience in which the narrator-author appears to have participated, prison novels have a testimonial impulse and share a number of characteristics with other forms of witness literature. Over the course of the twentieth century—an era in which literature became increasingly democratized—testimonial literature acquired a variety of functions as writers sought to document a wide array of circumstances and experiences.[53] Furthermore, testimony has been linked not simply to the documentation of specific experiences but also to urgent goals such as individual and group survival, remembrance, and moral duty. A fundamental aim of testimonial narratives is to impart the telling of an individual or group experience to an audience that is ostensibly unfamiliar with what is recounted. Indeed, a number of Holocaust testimonies, war narratives, Latin American *testimonios*, and AIDS diaries—all forms of witnessing that have garnered recent critical attention—share that basic function with prison novels. The static, brutal, and generally otherworldly qualities of the prison are presented in great detail in prison novels. It is clear, moreover, that the imagined readership needs to be informed of even the most basic matters of daily life in prison, ranging from the types of food served to the complex relations among prisoners and guards. The function of prison novels is similar to that of *testimonios* in that they tell the story of an individual who is representative of a group characterized by marginalization. John Beverley writes: "The situation of narration in testimonio has to involve an urgency to communicate, a problem of repression, poverty, subalternity, imprisonment, struggle for survival, and so on, implicated in the act of narration itself" (26).[54] That Beverley mentions imprisonment is no coincidence, as incarceration is a situation of extremity. A vehicle for detainment and punishment rather than rehabilitation, the prison acts as a barrier between the outside world and the harmful criminal by stripping the latter of his or her freedom. Because incarceration is intended to benefit society rather than inmates, it is no surprise that prisoners describe conditions that, as a whole, amount to an extreme situation, proving to be an agent of corruption rather than reformation. Moreover, testimonies by prisoners often emphasize the social stigmatization and marginality that result from incarceration. Writing provides a type of agency and authority to the inmate that he or she lacks in mainstream society, and, as with *testimonios*, it is often the case that the text gives voice to the many who have none.[55]

The importance of survival, of telling the tale for those who have been silenced, and of telling what is—or at least purports to be—a truthful account are themes common to many narratives of confinement and incarceration. However, in spite of their many similarities, it is important to make a clear distinction between prison novels and confinement narratives that take place in other spaces of incarceration, for that distinction has an impact on the limits of this study. The prison is an institution both historically and sociologically distinct from concentration camps, penal colonies, and Nazi extermination camps. Concentration camps, as Philip Williams and Yenna Wu have noted, "intern political prisoners or others defined as undesirable, and do so outside the normal channels of a legal system" (2). The experience of the common-law prisoner is distinct from that of the political prisoner, even when the latter is held in a prison designed and destined to hold the former.[56] Penal colonies, which the French used in the nineteenth and twentieth centuries, also had a social function distinct from that of prisons. Those faraway territories served as sites of transportation (for forced-labor sentences) and relegation (of hardened recidivists).[57] Sociological and historical distinctions are even more pronounced in the case of Nazi extermination camps. The horrors of the latter constitute phenomena of a markedly different order and magnitude than the conditions endured by common-law inmates in twentieth-century France. While the prison experience entails difficulties of its own—difficulties that will be examined carefully in the following chapters—death does not hover over an ordinary prisoner as it does the lager inmate.[58] Prisoners who await execution are exceptions and are treated as such.[59]

The documentation of experiences of incarceration in those diverse spaces of detention in many cases necessitates the use of specific textual forms and narrative strategies. To take one example, a number of Holocaust survivors emphasize the ineffable in their tellings of the extermination camp experience, a trait absent from prison narratives. Elie Wiesel, Jean Améry, and Dori Laub underline the incomprehensible nature of camp life and the failure of narrative to convey what transpired. Wiesel, who is perhaps best known for his *Night* trilogy, writes: "Auschwitz negates all systems, destroys all doctrines. They cannot but impoverish the experience which lies beyond our reach. Ask any survivor and he will tell you, and his children will tell you. He or she who did not live through the event will never know it. And he or she who did live through the event will never reveal it. Not entirely. Not really. Between our memory and its reflection there stands a wall that cannot be pierced" (7). In his essay "At the Mind's Limits," Auschwitz survivor Jean Améry evokes his difficulties in comprehending the logic of destruction employed by the ss in the camps. It was a logic that forced the lager inmates into accepting that which was illogical: "You always had to be clean-shaven, but it was strictly forbidden to possess razor or scissors, and you went to the barber only once every two weeks" (10). Similarly, Laub writes: "Not only, in effect, did the Nazis try to exterminate the physical witnesses of their crime; but the inherently incomprehensible and deceptive psychological structure of the event precluded its own witnessing, even by its victims" (Felman and Laub 80).[60]

Differences in inmates' testimonies and experiences—combined with the divergent functions, sociopolitical purposes, bureaucratic procedures, and histories of the spaces of detention described—justify the limits of this study to narratives about the experience of prison *as punishment*. However, the existence of important differences among spaces of confinement and testimonial discourses and forms does not mean that comparisons among various types of literature of witnessing are not fruitful. Indeed, such comparisons—which will be evoked when applicable in the following chapters—sharpen the specificity of the prison novel as a literary modality with its own traditions and conventions. Comparisons also contribute to the description and analysis of narrative strategies used in many types of documentary and testimonial texts.

The establishment of testimonial discourse—like a number of other textual and paratextual strategies—contributes to what I referred to above as the documentary effect of prison novels. There are also a number of elements, however, that blur the contract between text and reader, such that the documentary effect is counterbalanced by what Cohn calls "signposts of fictionality." Certain textual and paratextual strategies indicate to readers that what they are reading is indeed a fictional text. In *The Distinction of Fiction*, Cohn argues that some textual properties are the exclusive province of fiction writing, such as probing descriptions of the psychological interiority of fictive characters: "the minds of imaginary figures can be known in ways that those of real persons cannot" (118). Shifts in narrative voice, from a limited first-person perspective to a third-person omniscient view, can therefore be an indicator of fictionalization. In the chapters that follow I will highlight other such signposts as they become relevant to my analysis, such as the blending of multiple voices into a single voice, or certain systems of reference to fictional traditions. Furthermore, research shows that there is not simply narrative construction in these texts but also *invention*. Even though prison novels make claims to referentiality and verifiability, the authors have taken advantage of their blurred contract with their readers and have altered their narratives on the level of story. The texts are therefore further differentiated from nonfictional forms—such as testimony, autobiography, and history—that have similar claims to referentiality and verifiability. Fictionalization is highlighted in part by comparing prison novels to biographies, autobiographical texts (such as memoirs and personal journals), and, when possible, source material (notes, correspondence, etc.). Reception of the works examined in this study reflects the blurred contract between text and reader: the corpus of critical writing reaches across an entire spectrum of fictional and referential interpretations. One goal of this study is to underline the limitations of exclusively referential readings of these texts. In the case of each novel examined here, a purely nonfictional reading constitutes a misapprehension of the text's generic status.

Chapter Overview

Victor Serge's *Les hommes dans la prison* serves as an excellent starting point for the study of the twentieth-century French prison novel in part because it provides a literary-historical link to the nineteenth century. *Les hommes dans la prison* is modeled on one of the great European works of prison fiction, Dostoyevsky's *Memoirs from the House of the Dead* (1861–62). With its first-person narration, its attempt to document all facets of the carceral realm, and its testimonial impulse, *Les hommes dans la prison* serves as a bridge between Dostoyevsky's touchstone and twentieth-century French prison literature.[61] Serge's text is also representative of its subgenre in that its credibility as a testimonial narrative is bolstered by its strong documentary slant: the novel furnishes a great deal of referential and verifiable detail about prison rules and regulations, power relations between prisoners and guards, and inmate behavioral tendencies. In the first chapter of *Jail Sentences*, I analyze the prison experience of the narrator-protagonist of *Les hommes dans la prison* in the light of Serge's personal memoirs and notebooks. Furthermore, I examine the discursive and documentary traits of Serge's depiction of processes and procedures that were common to French prisons in the early twentieth century. Contrary to other critics, I argue that, in spite of the strong documentary thrust of Serge's work and the author's inclusion of a vast amount of accurate detail about French prisons, it is important to read *Les hommes dans la prison* as a fictional text. I show that Serge's novel bears a number of signposts of fictionality and, moreover, that the events therein are not entirely representative of what occurred during the author's five-year incarceration in France. Indeed, my analysis demonstrates how Serge fictionalized his experience behind bars in order to accentuate his critique of European capitalist power structures.

Unlike Serge, Jean Genet wrote no memoirs unambiguously detailing his life's key events. Genet made a career out of blurring the boundary between his life and his fiction, and his prison novel *Miracle de la rose*—the focal point of my second chapter—is marked by a constant tug-of-war between referentiality and fictionality. So unclear is the novel's contract between text and reader that an entire spectrum of critical interpretations of Genet's work exists: much like criticism of Proust's *A la recherche du temps perdu* (*Remembrance of Things Past*), interpretative readings of *Miracle* range from the purely autobiographical to those that insist that there is a high level of fictionalization in the text. Like Serge, Genet uses specific narrative strategies to bolster the referential and documentary facets of his work. He borrows a number of confessional autobiographical conventions, and the narrator (who is named "Jean Genet") remains almost exclusively within the limits of his first-person, eyewitness perspective, thereby lending a testimonial quality to the novel. In spite of the testimonial and documentary impulses of Genet's text, its referentiality is anything but straightforward. Indeed, close examination of Genet's strategies reveals that *Miracle de la rose* appears to be a referential text simply because it borrows the conventions of referential texts. While various formal aspects of the narrative indicate that *Miracle* documents the prison experience of one real individual (the author), the text also bears a variety of signposts of fictionality. I underline those signposts in order to show that the text—in spite of its legitimate documentary value—should be read as a work of fiction. As we will see, Genet heightens the documentary effect of his work by including much referential and verifiable detail about prisons and agricultural penal colonies. At the same time, he takes advantage of the creative license afforded by fiction writing to construct a vision of the carceral realm that advances his critique of mainstream bourgeois culture and accentuates his position as an outcast.

Due to similarities in their domestic and criminal backgrounds, there is an overwhelming temptation to draw parallels between the literary production of Jean Genet and Albertine Sarrazin. Both writers were abandoned by their biological parents, only to find themselves in unhappy situations with adoptive families. Both began to dabble in crime as adolescents, were placed in reform schools at an early age, and were chronic recidivists well into their adult years. Genet and Sarrazin perpetually gravitated to the margins of society, and each found the same means of financial support in prostitution and theft. However, in spite of the numerous affinities that exist between the lives of the two authors, the parallel does not extend into the realm of their writing. Beyond the strong autofictional tendencies present in both writers' major prose texts, their fictions share few similarities. Differences in style, form, and ideological slant distinguish their depictions of the prison sentences of their fictional alter egos, "Jean Genet" and Anick Damien. Whereas Genet's depiction of the prison wavers between documentary precision and lyrical remembrances, Sarrazin's autobiographical prison novel, *La cavale*, is a detailed and consistently realistic depiction of Anick's everyday life as an inmate. Indeed, the text's strong documentary impulse and its focus on the minutiae of daily life behind bars reflect Sarrazin's original goal: to write a series of nonfictional news articles about incarceration that would be complemented by photos documenting conditions in "the lousiest prison in France."[62] Still, like the other works examined in this study, *La cavale* is marked by considerable generic tension, and the line between fiction and autobiography is artfully blurred. In the third chapter of this study I analyze the autobiographical and fictional aspects of *La cavale* and examine how incarceration, as Sarrazin depicts it, is a debilitating rather than a rehabilitative experience. Indeed, her novel illustrates that the prison and legal systems, rather than preparing inmates for a return to mainstream society on the outside, gradually transform them into submissive and anonymous creatures.

Like Sarrazin's project as it was first conceived, François Bon's *Prison* entails a form of reportage. Instead of the photographs envisioned by Sarrazin, however, Bon interpolates texts produced by inmates in the writing workshop he conducted at the Bordeaux-Gradignan Youth Detention Center. A compelling mixture of documentary and imaginary details, *Prison* is a fictionalized account of the author's seven-month experience directing that workshop. Bon conducted twenty-one separate writing sessions with a total of sixty-two inmates, many of whom were homeless or resided in low-income housing before being arrested. A number of them were also either immigrants or from the first generation of their families to be born in France. As workshop director, Bon proposed a number of themes and introduced the prisoners to well-known literary texts from which they were expected to find the beginnings of a narrative thread. The themes and literary texts imply engagement with a set of marginalizing socioeconomic factors, as the author sought to elicit testimonies from the inmates about delinquency, racism, and the vicissitudes of urban and suburban life. As he depicts the inmates' trajectories from the streets to the detention center in *Prison*, Bon includes quotes of varying length from the prisoners' texts—spelling and grammar mistakes included. The result is a literary work that is peculiarly hybrid in its structure, alternating between observations of the workshop director and the slang-filled commentaries of the prisoners. In the fourth chapter of *Jail Sentences*, I not only examine the innovative literary aspects of Bon's work (its hybrid structure, its creative obfuscation of the line between fiction and autobiography) but also show that Bon uses his creative license in crafting what appears to be a documentary depiction of prison life. Bon strategically avoids casting the inmates in the same menacing mold used by the mainstream press in France, even if it means altering the inmates' texts to suit his sociopolitical purposes. Indeed, as my research into his source material for the novel shows, Bon manipulates the prisoners' prose in order to humanize his depiction of them, thereby rendering their experiences and their texts more palatable to a mainstream and ostensibly law-abiding readership.

Prison novels are a distinct kind of documentary fiction, a specific form of witness literature that exposes and critiques phenomena in a vital social institution. Readers of *Jail Sentences* will gain a keen understanding of the twentieth-century legacy of highly prominent French social critics—like Alexis de Tocqueville and Victor Hugo—who advocated system-wide reform when the penal prison was still a relative novelty in France. As we will see, twentieth-century social critique and calls for reform target facts and phenomena unimaginable in Hugo and Tocqueville's era: an anticipated worldwide clash between Marxism and capitalism; a critique of the systematic abuse and neglect of prisoners in juvenile penal colonies; a proto-feminist portrayal of the debilitative effects of incarceration in institutions segregated by sex; and, finally, a depiction of the marginalization of disadvantaged young men in sprawling late-twentieth-century French suburbs. In spite of the fact that contemporary social criticism has taken on a variety of new forms, it should be no surprise—as Peter Kropotkin's comments in this book's epigraph suggest—that noteworthy writers continue to diagnose systemic problems in the treatment of prisoners. In the chapters that follow, therefore, readers will find echoes of age-old injustice in the modern French prison system, and, at the same time, will discover the innovative means through which intellectuals document that injustice and critique the society at its source.

[ONE] EVERYMAN IN PRISON

Ironically for a man who spent the majority of his adult life writing and whose output is as diverse as it is vast, Victor Serge's closest brush with the French canon is an appearance aboard the *Capitaine Paul-Lemerle* in the opening pages of Claude Lévi-Strauss's *Tristes tropiques*. That is not to say that Serge's lengthy bibliography is devoid of merit. But the marginal status of the author in posterity's memory certainly recalls the peripheral quality that his life took on as he experienced exile after exile in country after country, until he was legally stateless at the time of his death in November 1947.

Victor-Napoléon Lvovich Kibalchich (alias Victor Serge) was born in Belgium to impoverished Russian émigré parents fifty-one years prior to that maritime encounter with Lévi-Strauss in 1941. Despite his Slavic roots and his constant meanderings (after leaving Belgium he resided in France, Spain, Russia, Germany, Austria, and Mexico), Serge wrote all of his major historical, autobiographical, and literary works in French.[1] Lévi-Strauss's paragraph-long snapshot shows us the author as he was traveling with his son, Vlady, and André Breton en route to Mexico from Marseilles, leaving Nazi Europe behind for good. Lévi-Strauss admits being taken aback at what he refers to as Serge's monk-like appearance, given his past as a Russian revolutionary and the expectations one might have of an alleged subversive. Oddly enough, in accordance with Lévi-Strauss's observations, after that transatlantic voyage the former revolutionary did indeed spend his final years in Mexico leading a monastic existence in poverty and isolation, writing, as he dejectedly remarks in his *Carnets* (Notebooks), "for the desk drawer" (117).[2]

Given the marginality that characterized Victor Serge in life and that has unfairly marked his place in literary history, it seems fitting that the Library of Congress placed his first novel, *Les hommes dans la prison*, as well as its English translation, *Men in Prison*, in the HV section of its classification system, a section normally reserved for works on social pathology and criminology. Such an erroneous categorization of Serge's 1930 novel is perhaps not surprising if we take into consideration not only the author's marginal status in the French literary tradition but also the text's blunt and often documentary depiction of the penal system in early-twentieth-century France. The affinities shared by *Les hommes dans la prison* and sociological works that deal with penology are not limited to the realm of style. Serge covers many of the same subjects as his sociologist counterparts, such as the dehumanization of inmates, power relations between the prison administration and the detainees, and the difficulties of living in isolation. Clearly aware of the potential for misreading created by his novel, Serge voiced his concern for the reception of his text in a letter to the Romanian writer Panaït Istrati, author of the novel's preface: "I stress that it is a novel, for the use of the first-person singular, while convenient, can lend itself to misunderstanding. I do not want to write memoirs. This is not about me. It is about men" (*Les hommes dans la prison* 20).[3] The Library of Congress's reception of Serge's text suggests that *Les hommes dans la prison* sends a different message from the one so adamantly expressed by its author. Still, regardless of the documentary value of Serge's novel and the affinities it shares with penological tracts, one cannot ignore the generic choice of the author when classifying and interpreting his text. In this chapter I argue that Serge crafts his documentary prison narrative by taking advantage of the creative liberties furnished by his chosen genre, the novel. Through analysis of specific narrative techniques, the author's memoirs, pertinent biographical information, and the text's critical reception, I underscore the distinct fictional, testimonial, and ideological traits of *Les hommes dans la prison*. As we will see, although the novel is based on Serge's own prison sentence, the text's primary goal is not to provide an exact representation of life behind bars as the author experienced it but rather to promote a virulently anti-capitalist sociopolitical agenda.

The Library of Congress is not alone in reading *Les hommes dans la prison* as an accurate portrayal of conditions and relations in both the prison system and society at large. Istrati reads Serge's text as a credible depiction of life behind bars and, moreover, a strong denunciation of Western greed. Throughout his preface to the first edition of Serge's novel, Istrati rails against both writers who produce art for art's sake and a corrupt public eager to consume their vain and precious work. Their art, he states, "reeks of perfume, toiletries, and soap" (*HP* 14). For Istrati, that is not surprising, given the values of both authors and readers alike. He writes: "Cars, sports, clothes, jazz, drunkenness, debauchery: *that* is the life for which almost the entire modern world salivates" (14). Istrati embraces only intellectuals, such as Serge, who are willing to confront the "savagery of our time" and whose work addresses in a forthright manner the problems of oppression and hunger (12, 18). He ends his preface with a call for unification and liberation inspired by the cry for freedom at the end of Marx and Engel's *Communist Manifesto*: "Friends of those who are crushed in the dark corners of society, unite with those who are fighting for a free humanity!" (21). Istrati's reading implies that Serge's novel accurately depicts the daily life of those forced to live "in the dark corners of society." *Les hommes dans la prison*, in the context of that sociopolitical discourse, serves as damning evidence of the exploitative and destructive forces of capitalism.[4]

In his 1969 preface to the English translation of Serge's novel, Richard Greeman, like Istrati, does not shy away from the antiestablishment rhetoric of his era. He writes: "Our jails are full of victims, 'innocent' or 'guilty'—war resisters, black militants, student protesters, migrant workers, narcotics users, and all the poor and disaffected who are driven to 'riot' or 'crime' by a society that promotes and lives by violence while preaching 'law and order.' This book is also about them, their suffering and their incredible courage and humanity. If it does not make you angry, nothing will" (MP xxvi). One need only count the number of terms Greeman places between quotation marks to grasp the extent of his disdain for the American criminal justice system. He reads Serge's novel in the same light that Istrati does: as a condemnatory account of Western civilization's abuses of its downtrodden and its underclasses. Moreover, Greeman implores readers of *Men in Prison* to emulate his own reading and see the novel as documentary evidence of what happens every day in the contemporary American penal system.

Readings by Istrati, Greeman, and the Library of Congress all emphasize actuality in Serge's novelistic representation of the French penal system. Their interpretations neglect the text's fictionality and view it as a document that is true to life, a factually precise rendering of the experience of prisoners in the Western world—a heavy burden for a text whose author has overtly declared it as fictional. Perhaps, given the affinities between Serge's text and sociological tracts, the three interpretations we have mentioned are understandable. Other paratextual information, however, shows that those strictly referential readings are in need of recalibration. In a brief statement that is granted its own page in both the French and American editions (a page that precedes the main body of text), Serge writes: "Everything in this book is fictional and everything is true. I have attempted, through literary creation, to bring out the general meaning and human content of a personal experience" (*MP* v; *HP* 9). The initials "V.S." that appear directly under the assertion enable the reader to differentiate between the author's voice and that of the anonymous, first-person narrator. In view of that distinction, both aspects of Serge's assertion—the documentary *and* the fictional value of the text—should be taken into account in reading *Les hommes dans la prison*.

Les hommes dans la prison and *Mémoires d'un révolutionnaire*

Serge was imprisoned in France from 1912 to 1917, first at La Santé prison in Paris and later at Melun. He was arrested, tried, and convicted for being associated with a group of notoriously violent criminals known as the Bonnot gang. At the time of his arrest he was working as the editor of *L'anarchie*, a weekly paper in which he defended the activities of Jules Bonnot and his accomplices, activities that included armed robbery and even murder. In an editorial dated 4 January 1912, for example, he wrote: "I am on the outlaws' side. . . . [A]mong them, I sometimes see real men. Elsewhere, I see nothing but louts and puppets" (*Rétif* 162). A few weeks after the publication of those comments, police searched the offices of *L'anarchie* and arrested Serge upon finding two revolvers. Serge was singled out during the trials of the various members of the Bonnot gang as the intellectual author of their crimes; he was convicted and sentenced to five years in prison (Weissman 18).

In his *Mémoires d'un révolutionnaire* (*Memoirs of a Revolutionary*), written in the early 1940s, Serge provides few details on his prison term. As if to say that he has already told the story of his incarceration, he opens the discussion of his prison time with the phrase "Of prison I shall say only a little here" (*Memoirs* 45; *Mémoires* 53). He then directs his readers to his first book, which, by his own estimation, "is reasonably well known in France and Spanish-speaking countries" (45; 54). Explaining his motivations for writing *Les hommes dans la prison*—which, he is quick to point out, is a novel—he writes that prison "burdened me with an experience so heavy, so intolerable to endure, that long afterwards, when I resumed writing, my first book (a novel) amounted to an effort to free myself from this inward nightmare, as well as performing a duty towards all those who will never so free themselves" (45; 53). Serge's discourse of witnessing resembles that of Holocaust writers—Primo Levi being the most prominent example—who time and time again insist on the need to tell their stories in order to liberate themselves from a heavy burden. Telling one's own story not only proves to be personally cathartic but, as Serge suggests, allows one to act as a witness to the oppression of others who cannot (for whatever reason—death, illiteracy, continued incarceration, etc.) tell their own stories. He describes his feeling of responsibility toward his fellow inmates in his letter to Istrati: "Among the thousands of miserable men broken by prison—a prison few have heard about!—I was no doubt the only one who could one day attempt to tell all" (*HP* 19–20). For Serge, using fiction as a medium to tell the truth—indeed, to "tell all"—was not an inherently contradictory act.

Greeman claims that Serge's status as a novelist is advantageous in that it allows Serge to reproduce actuality effectively and accurately: "That ineffable quality of 'what things were really like'—the aspect, tone of voice, emotional context of a human event, personal or historical—that is what the novelist's eye and ear can catch and what makes of his fiction a truer record of living reality than the historian's data or the dogmatist's abstractions" (*MP* xx). In his evaluation of the advantages fictional production provides an author, Greeman ignores the fact that it is *because* Serge's text is fictional that one must evaluate critically its representation of that which is supposedly "true." Serge's decision to tell the story of his incarceration in a novel (rather than only in his memoirs) is ideologically motivated. His choice of genre enables him to conflate the truth of his own carceral experience (i.e., what really happened) and the "truth" of his political agenda (i.e., his interpretation of the functioning of the prison system within a specific socioeconomic context). The contract established in his prefatory statement allows him to decide the degree to which representation will correspond with reality.

The truth Serge depicts in his novel must be distinguished from the "record of living reality" that Greeman sees in Serge's fiction. The term "record" suggests that there is no bias in Serge's account and that the raw, objective reality of his prison sentence is conveyed to his readers without the influence of a subjective intermediary. The truth Serge imparts to his readers is far from an objective record of his carceral experience. That truth is fictional (not fictitious) in that its depiction relies upon the flexibility of the novel form. As Michael Riffaterre remarks, "The only reason that the phrase 'fictional truth' is not an oxymoron, as 'fictitious truth' would be, is that fiction is a genre whereas lies are not" (1). Unlike the historian or the sociologist, a novelist may manipulate narrative on the level of both discourse and story. A fiction writer, contrary to the producer of nonfiction, is not bound by a contract between text and reader to sacrifice creative freedom in the name of accuracy. What Serge refers to as a truthful depiction of life behind bars is, in fact, a bitter critique of power relations within the French prison system and a deeply politicized rendering of the abuses fostered by capitalism and industrialized modes of production. To read his novel and interpret it as legitimately representative of society's ills is thus an inherently politicized act.

One can therefore understand Istrati's and Greeman's referential readings of the text, given their own self-expressed ideological convictions.

Les hommes dans la prison details—with great precision—nearly every major aspect of an anonymous narrator-protagonist's incarceration from arrest to release. The story's trajectory is quite simple: the reader witnesses the plight of that "Everyman" prisoner for the duration of his entire prison sentence. At the beginning of the novel, the narrator-protagonist is arrested and is first placed in a jail in the Palais de Justice. He is then moved to La Santé prison in Paris to await prosecution and sentencing. After spending an unspecified amount of time in that notorious institution, he is transported back to the Palais de Justice, where he is sentenced to approximately four years in a central prison of detention (*maison centrale*). In his descriptions of life at La Santé and the *maison centrale*, the narrator provides a detailed account of how prisoners interact with each other as well as how they eat, sleep, work, and struggle to survive the various stages of incarceration. Major components of the story include elaborate descriptions of conditions in prison cells, workshops, the exercise yard, and the infirmary, as well as portrayals of a host of inmates and various employees of the prison administration. The novel comes to a close as the narrator anxiously prepares for his liberation, and the final scene depicts his dramatic release from prison into a world at war.

Les hommes dans la prison shares numerous affinities with the author's terse account of his prison sentence in his memoirs. Indeed, the novel is to a great extent based on Serge's term of penal servitude—assuming, of course, that the memoirs are a truthful representation thereof. A general vision of the prison as an efficient and bureaucratized machine for "breaking" men is consistent in both texts, as is the portrayal of the capacity of the human spirit for survival through strength of will. Moreover, Serge's treatment of World War I in his memoirs closely resembles the novel's depiction of the repercussions of the conflict. Like the narrator of the novel, Serge the memoirist expresses disbelief and disappointment at the knee-jerk nationalism displayed by many of his fellow prisoners at the outset of the war: blind patriotism diminishes solidarity among the men in prison, who are of diverse national origins.

While information in the memoirs reveals that the novel is partly based on Serge's experience, it also shows that the fictional narrative aims to promote the author's ideological message forcefully and convincingly. This is especially the case at the end of the novel, when the narrator-protagonist is released from prison during wartime. The first encounter he mentions is a crucial one: "This first man I meet at the threshold of the world is a man of the trenches" (251; 308). One of the novel's major themes is the struggle to survive life behind bars, and readers see the narrator fight his way through the difficulties of solitude, depression, and serious physical illness. His personal resistance and strength of will are nourished, in part, by a conviction that the conflict outside the prison walls is toppling the powers of the "old world" (178; 226). Resistance on a personal level is thus intertwined with political resistance. The conflation of the struggles of the prisoner and of the denizens of the outside world is made explicit at the end of the novel, when, upon his release, the narrator-protagonist passes from one battleground—the prison in which he struggled to survive—to another. The narrator comments that as he and the man of the trenches approach each other, "Our ringing footsteps fall in together" (251; 308). The merging of the sounds of their steps highlights the similarities of their battles, their solidarity, and the common path that they will follow as they fight for a new political order. That optimistic final note is characteristic of Serge's fiction in general, for while his novels often depict human suffering in a variety of circumstances (such as war, exile, and revolution), their endings tend to focus on idealistic hope for the future. In the case of *Les hommes dans la prison*, the inspirational chance encounter between the inmate and the soldier befits the struggle of the narrator-protagonist, who, against unfavorable odds, survived a disease-infested prison for many years.

In his memoirs, Serge's portrayal of his release is without question more pessimistic and seeks to convince his readers of a different ideological reality than does his novel. Serge describes his encounter with the soldier quite tersely: "The first man I had met, in the mist of a gloomy bridge, had been a soldier with a mutilated face" (*Memoirs* 49; *Mémoires* 58). Compare that description with the following excerpt from the novel: "This first human figure suddenly transforms into reality the unreal landscape I have been moving through. He emerges in front of me, very tall and very strange, like a barbarian in his shadow-colored overcoat, leather-belted, crisscrossed by the straps of the heavy musette bags hanging at his hips. The soldier's bony face, his piercing eyes glowing in their dark sockets, surges up before me for an instant under the dented helmet which bears, gray against gray, an incendiary grenade" (251; 308). Clearly, that dramatic, portentous encounter scarcely resembles Serge's allegedly true-to-life meeting with the mutilated soldier. The man who evokes a captivating worldwide struggle in *Les hommes dans la prison* is portrayed simply as a victim of the brutality of war in Serge's memoirs. Moreover, whereas the novel ends on that ominous yet ultimately hopeful note, the memoirs go on to describe in detail Serge's alienation from society and its excesses. Frenchmen were dying in the trenches, and meanwhile Paris "was leading a double life" (50; 58). The war economy was booming: the French capital was graced by low unemployment, high salaries, and plenty of foreign soldiers spending money while on leave. In the novel, the first encounter that is depicted is with the man of the trenches; in the memoirs, the first meeting Serge describes is one with an "oily procurer" (49;

58) who bluntly tells him where to find the nearest brothel. The giddy, schizophrenic society depicted in the memoirs does not come close to mirroring the somber, desolate landscape that Serge portrays at the end of his novel. Each rendering serves a different discursive and rhetorical purpose.

The story of the release from prison and the encounter with the man of the trenches, told in different ways and in different contexts, illustrates how Serge's novel is constructed to convey a specific ideological vision of a world in transformation. Serge's depiction of the soldier in the novel corresponds to his idealized perception of the political changes that a struggle against established order can bring into effect. The artful omission of details irrelevant to (and, in this case, counter to) the narrator's optimistic vision of a revolution in progress is emblematic of the politicized nature of *Les hommes dans la prison*. Serge neglects to inform the readers of his novel that Paris was in the midst of an economic boom resulting from the war that was supposedly going to rid the world of such nefarious capitalistic forces. "Was it always to be the world-without-escape? What good was the war doing? Had the dance of death taught nothing to anyone?" writes the memoirist, expressing a level of alienation from the outside world that the novelist never reveals (50; 58). That omission has as potent a rhetorical effect on the fictional narrative as his portrayal of the man of the trenches. It is clear that Serge is not aiming to convey the same ideological message in his novel and his memoirs. Whereas in the novel Serge focuses consistently on depicting the validity of the struggle against the old capitalist order, he is more willing as a memoirist to acknowledge the disparity between his vision of the revolution and the actual state of the world at large.

Serge portrays the task of writing about men in prison as something he would have been unable to accomplish in his memoirs, given his perception of the egocentric nature of autobiographical writing. As he wrote in his letter to Istrati, "I do not want to write memoirs. This is not about me. It is about men" (HP 20). As the title of the novel indicates, the jail sentence Serge portrays is meant to be read as one that has bearing on all experiences with prison. The text is replete with generalizations about prisoners and the ways in which they react to certain situations and stimuli. The narrator-protagonist frequently makes sweeping assertions about "man imprisoned" ("l'homme enfermé") and often uses the pronouns *on, nous,* and *chacun* (*one, we,* and *each one*) to refer to what the prisoners collectively experience. The universalistic implications of *Les hommes dans la prison* are intimately tied to Serge's status as a witness: Serge conceives of himself as the spokesperson for his comrades. In his memoirs he writes about his preference for the use of the universal *we* over the egocentric pronoun *I*. "The 'I' disgusts me as a vain assertion of oneself," Serge notes, "containing one large share of illusion and another of vanity or unjust pride. Every time it is possible, that is, every time I can avoid feeling isolated, that my experience sheds light in some regard on the experience of the men to whom I feel linked, I prefer using 'we,' which is more true and more general. . . . [H]e who speaks, he who writes is essentially a man who speaks for all those who are voiceless" (*Mémoires* 53).[5] That preference for the first-person plural explains, to some degree, the extremely terse account of Serge's prison sentence in his memoirs—it is roughly six pages long—compared to the lengthy, generalized telling in the novel. The use of *we* allows Serge to act as a witness not only to his personal experience but also to the collective experience of his comrades, and the writing of a novel with universalistic implications affirms his belief in the solidarity among men involved in a common struggle.

The efficient and routine nature of life in prison facilitates the universalistic witnessing to which Serge aspires. Prison life, as it is depicted in both *Les hommes dans la prison* and Serge's memoirs, is dictated above all by bureaucratic forces known for their regularity and consistency. The sameness of the experience for all "men in prison" is literally inscribed into the edifice itself: "You have to examine the walls very closely to make out these graffiti; but they are always the same, in every prison cell. . . . A thousand hushed voices fill it with their changeless, unremitting murmurs. You soon grow tired of listening, tired of the constant repetition of the same miseries" (MP 9; HP 32). The graffiti serve as written proof for the narrator that the experience of prison is essentially the same for all men: a thousand prisoners have been able to express their misery in only one way. The paucity of expression on their part renders his universalistic prison novel politically necessary and validates Serge's position as a witness to the untold suffering of his fellow inmates. Serge's novel serves as an elaboration of that same quiet murmur of the prisoners. As is manifest in his description of the pronoun *we*, Serge found that literary creation, not memoir writing, was the most effective means through which he could tell the story of the multitudes of prisoners crushed by the penal system. The novelist's ability to play with his sources allows him to conflate the voices of thousands of inmates into one: that of the narrator. While Serge ostensibly describes in his memoirs what actually occurred during his prison sentence, in his novel he avowedly extracts "the general meaning and human content" of that lived experience and transforms it into a fictional narrative that is meant to be representative and typical of what all prisoners endure.

The universalistic slant of *Les hommes dans la prison* plays into Serge's belief in the importance of solidarity among all those who struggle against the "old world" (such as the man of the trenches encountered at the end of the novel). Indeed, the portrayal of that solidarity is so important to Serge as a novelist that he is merciful even in his depiction of the prison guards. Preferring to transfer all blame for suffering to the evils of the prison machine, Serge recognizes the guards as his fellow human beings: "The guards are no better and no worse than the men they guard" (MP 164–65; HP 211). Even the prison's most vicious and abusive guard, Latruffe, is depicted as having been corrupted by the carceral environment: "Latruffe gradually acquired his mountain of pale flab from his years in prison" (193; 244). While his portrayal of the guards is forgiving in the novel, they benefit from no such kindness in the memoirs, where Serge declares: "Generally speaking, with only a few exceptions, the warders, of whatever grade, were on a much lower level [than the prisoners]. They were criminals, respectably but obviously so, gifted with a guaranteed immunity from punishment and super-annuation at the end of their unspeakable lives" (45; 53). The contrast in the representations of the guards shows again that Serge's novel is a literary construct whose aim is to promote a politicized vision of the carceral universe and the society that spawned it. Serge uses his text's generic status to his discursive and rhetorical advantage, crafting a narrative that forcefully presents a specific ideological stance.

The story of the abusive Latruffe—told in a chapter that bears the guard's name—is emblematic of Serge's use of techniques that are the province of fiction writing to depict that which he deems truthful. In that brief segment of *Les hommes dans la prison*, the narrator recounts the disciplinary practices and systematic abuses of the chapter's eponymous central character. The narrator abandons the use of the first-person singular pronoun *je* for the duration of that chapter, and in one section of it he suddenly begins narrating from an omniscient perspective. Dorrit Cohn writes that such a manifestation of omniscience is one device that a first-person narrative may display to break with the norms of autobiographical discourse and mark its fictionality (60). While telling the story of Latruffe in an omniscient voice, the narrator is no longer limited to recounting his own experience and general truths about the carceral realm: he depicts Latruffe's thoughts and intentions, despite the impossibility of having firsthand knowledge thereof. Take, for example, the following description of Latruffe's interaction with an unnamed prisoner who is resting within his solitary confinement cell. Latruffe has just told the young inmate to wake up: "The boy gets up slowly. The wicket gate [le guichet] closes again. Latruffe pretends to leave. Actually he is watching at the door. He knows the boy has lain down again. The wicket clicks open again. Again the dazzling light whips the figure stretched out on the cement floor. This time Latruffe opens the door and walks toward the boy, who is standing motionless on his feet now, glued to the back of the wall" (MP 191; HP 241). By changing point of view, Serge exploits the liberties provided by the novel form. He does so in order to convey specific aspects of the carceral environment that his narrator does not claim to have experienced directly. That sort of narrative slippage is entirely absent from Serge's brief account of his prison experience in his memoirs. As a memoirist, Serge limits descriptions to that which he himself experienced and to his own impressions of the carceral universe. In the context of *Les hommes dans la prison*, however, Serge freely uses a fictionalized narrative voice to depict yet another aspect of life in the French prison system.

An Anti-capitalist Prison Narrative

Even at a very young age, Victor Serge had the mind of a revolutionary. If the opening pages of his memoirs are any indication, political activism and nonconformity were an integral part of his identity. Indeed, revolution seemed to be in his blood: in only the second paragraph of his memoirs, Serge mentions a distant relative of his father's who participated in the assassination of Czar Alexander II. Serge writes that his parents lived a bohemian existence, moving from town to town in search of jobs and good libraries. The young Victor was homeschooled because of his father's stance against "stupid bourgeois instruction for the poor" (*Memoirs* 7; *Mémoires* 14). They decorated their various humble dwellings with portraits of men who had been hanged, and discussions revolved around current issues and writings of the day, executions, trials, and prison escapes (2–3; 8–9).

After spending years in poverty and performing a variety of odd jobs such as printmaking and language tutoring, Serge began to write professionally as a journalist. While working at *L'anarchie* before his arrest—signing his articles "Le Rétif" ("the stubborn one")—Serge criticized society's power apparatus, not to mention the passive populations living in its servitude. His embrace of the cause of the Bonnot gang was in accordance with his praise of the virtues of individual and independent action. Upon his release from prison, Serge was required by court order to leave France and traveled to Barcelona, where he continued to write polemical articles and engage in political activism. He did not begin writing novels, however, until the mid-1920s, after he had spent a number of years in the USSR and central Europe working to foment revolution as a writer and propagandist.[6]

Over the course of the 1920s Serge grew increasingly alienated from the bureaucratization of the Communist Party, its totalitarian tendencies, and the increasing spread of capitalistic economic forces in the USSR. In 1928, after a brief interlude in a Soviet prison following his expulsion from the party as a left oppositionist, Serge decided to engage in writing of a different sort: "I had labored, striven and schooled myself titanically, without producing anything valuable or lasting. . . . I thought of what I would write, and mentally sketched the plan of a series of documentary novels [romans-témoignages] about these unforgettable times" (*Memoirs* 261; *Mémoires* 283). *Les hommes dans la prison* was the first of those "romans-témoignages."[7]

In spite of the fact that the author was suffering persecution at the hands of a Stalinist Soviet Union, anarchist inmates in the novel express optimism for the coming Russian Revolution. Indeed, long after it became apparent that Stalinism was corrupting the USSR and that the legacy of the revolution was tainted by brutality and repression of dissent, Serge remained committed to the ideals of socialist democracy. An integral element of that commitment was a firm rejection of the capitalist economic model, a stance Serge maintained until his death.

Given Serge's resolutely anti-capitalist position, it is not surprising that a discursive link between capitalism and penal processes is maintained throughout *Les hommes dans la prison*. Indeed, early in the novel, upon his transfer to La Santé from the *Palais de Justice* holding cell, the narrator explicitly links the modern prison to the capitalist society that produced it: "A modern prison is as different from an old crenelated castle . . . as today's all-powerful capitalist society is unlike the absolute monarchies of olden times, so limited in their real power" (27; 53). Serge uses the carceral universe as a locus for the delineation of societal mechanisms of power vis-à-vis the individual and the working class at large.

Serge's link between capitalism and the prison creates a larger context for his treatment of the efficient, bureaucratic, and industrialized operations of the institution. In depicting the institution's daily operations, Serge underscores the processes valued in systems of industrial mass production. A precise and routinized schedule, efficient use of space for surveillance and the assertion of power, and an assembly-line-like processing system are used to assimilate and discipline prisoners in order to transform them into productive and obedient workers. That process is evident as soon as the prisoners are incarcerated: "From window to window, from measurement to search, from search to shower, from shower to compartment, we move on" (15; 40). The narrator notes that the operations of the prison are so highly regulated that the inmates can tell time by the sounds in their environment (39; 66). It does not escape Serge that the very policies and laws that enable the *maison centrale*—or "la Meule" (the Mill), as the narrator dubs it—to operate were the direct product of capitalist concerns. Once assimilated into the prison, convicts find that their time is exploited by private enterprise: "Forced labor, usually piecework—that is to say, poured on to the limit of your strength—ten hours a day, from seven in the morning to seven in the evening, with two interruptions of an hour each for meals and exercise and two or three fifteen-minute breaks. Labor, industrial labor, at peon's wages, under concession to different firms by the penitentiary administration" (116–17; 156). Prisoners have been used as laborers since the late sixteenth century, and reformers have viewed work in prison—often erroneously—as a means of rehabilitating unruly and undisciplined inmates into law-abiding citizens.[8] In *Les hommes dans la prison*, forced labor is seen from the perspective of the inmates, and it is neither therapeutic nor rehabilitative; rather, it is simply another reminder of the exercise of power over the inmate and of the brutal capitalistic forces that dictate the operations of the prison.

Capitalist modes of production are routinely presented as destructive rather than creative. The prison is, for the narrator-protagonist, "a machine for grinding up lives slowly" (86; 119). "The system" notes the narrator, "tends, in a continuous manner, to weaken the mind, destroy the will, obliterate the personality, to depress, oppress, wear down, torture" (60; 90). The dehumanization of the prisoners is accentuated early in the novel, as they pass through the various steps of the process of entry. They are treated with the same brutal and impersonal efficiency as their dirty clothes: "While they were in the shower, the clothes they had been wearing were sent through the steam press: an instantaneous disinfecting from which—pulverized under the enormous pressure—they emerge like rags, honeycombed with wrinkles that can almost never be removed" (16; 41). Bureaucrats manage the flow of prisoners as they would material in any other organization. Serge underlines the vastness of the penal system's bureaucracy by portraying administrators languishing in their work and drowning in paper: "Their eyes have grown dim with the horrid dullness that emanates from the forms, receipts, registers and filing cabinets, where the same inanely bureaucratic descriptions of hopeless victims and miserable wretches pile up ad infinitum" (14–15; 39). Furthermore, prison employees are dubbed "automatons" ("hommes-machines") (11; 34) and seem to be part of the physical institution itself: "Guards and officials blend into the walls themselves, the Judases, bars and bolts. You can feel in the marrow of your bones that they are no more than cogs in the prison machine" (73; 105).

Incarceration destroys men, and the inmate population is viewed as if it were an enemy army (*MP* 113; *HP* 152). Although the prison is effective in its destruction of its foe, the narrator points out that other methods are more direct: "The blade's lightning efficiency grinds better" (86; 119). The guillotine plays a role in the same class war in which the prison is central. The narrator declares: "Masked or thinly veiled, from time immemorial, they have needed to use the death penalty against us—the working people" (85; 118).[9] As in his portrayal of the abusive prison guard Latruffe, Serge uses third-person omniscient narration—a signpost of fictionality—to articulate fully his critique of capital punishment and the suffering it inflicts on those awaiting execution. *Les hommes dans la prison* describes in detail the experiences of those on death row, even though the narrator reveals subtly that he was not housed in that section of La Santé.[10] Changing narrative stance to describe power relations between the condemned and the guards, he notes: "Every five minutes the round 'eye' cut into the Judas blinks its metal eyelid; a human eye glows within it, rests impassively for a moment on the condemned man. In the cell, nothing. The rough pottery bowl in which, in other cells, you can wash your face, is forbidden. The blunt iron penknife you used to be able to buy for three *sous* at the prison store is forbidden. Forbidden is the milk bottle which might be used to knock out a guard or, broken, provide a liberating piece of sharp glass to open your veins" (83; 115).

The notion that the prison houses its own enemies becomes increasingly pertinent in the context of Serge's critique of capital punishment. The narrator advocates a violent offensive attack so that the working class may resist destruction and rise above its oppressors. "Murder will close the circle of murder," he remarks, "for a war can only be ended by a victory; for the victors can be liberators—having liberated themselves. In the class war, which is like the other kind but stripped of hypocrisy, the greatest humanity must be combined with the most decisive use of force. The class that wants to build a new world, forever cleansed of killing machines, must learn how to kill in battle so as not to be killed" (85; 118). The narrator hopes that modern prisons and the totalitarian capitalist structures that spawned them will fall victim to the same fate as the castles and absolute monarchies of the past (27; 53).

Political resistance and violent, revolutionary uprising against the "old world" are the only solutions proposed by the novel to put an end to what the narrator sees as the destruction of the masses. Individual and group strength lie at the heart of Serge's vision of political resistance. To maximize the political capital of his vision of the penal system, Serge portrays imprisonment as an experience that tests the limits of the survival capacities of human beings. From the beginning of his incarceration, the narrator likens his experience to death: "I am already in a sort of tomb" (9; 33). His struggle to survive the destructive environment begins instantly upon his arrest, and the imprisonment-as-burial motif is consistent throughout the narrative.[11]

Certain prisoners are unable to muster enough resistance to survive and life is slowly sapped out of them. Others, from the narrator's point of view, fare better because of sheer strength of will. The narrator-protagonist has an unfailing faith in his own strength and has an optimistic and humanistic belief in the strength of others. "We all," he states, "have great powers of vitality" (60; 90).

The narrator's optimism is ultimately tied to a positive outlook on the potential of revolutionary uprising and victory for the working class. Near the end of the novel, the narrator and his comrades in prison engage in political complicity: "Long before Europe ever dreamt it, we were discussing, in whispers, the coming Russian Revolution. We knew in what part of the globe the long-awaited flame would be born. And in it we found a new reason for living" (181; 230). The solidarity of the prisoners, coupled with hope for the future, gives momentum to the active spiritual and intellectual resistance of the prisoners while they are still trapped behind the walls of the prison. The wider struggle that exists on a societal level gives their struggle to survive renewed energy.[12] Addressing his hopes for the war and a potential revolution, the narrator-protagonist declares, "I felt a sort of exaltation which gave birth to a great serenity. The old world was being smashed by the cannon. The Mill would be crushed by the cannon" (178; 226). The solidarity of the inmates feeds the narrator's hope that resistance, though potentially violent, will result in a future society without oppressive and destructive capitalist power structures.

The Documentary Effect

Although he wrote a number of historical works and biographies about the Russian Revolution and its participants, Serge notes in his memoirs that such work can prove limiting: "Historical work . . . does not allow enough scope for showing men as they really live, dismantling their inner workings and penetrating deep into their souls" (262; 284). While drawn to the novel, Serge specified in very precise terms the type of fiction he sought to write: his texts would speak for those who were silenced, be devoid of concerns for profit, and most importantly, be of a different order than the traditional French novel. "[T]he form of the classic novel seemed to me impoverished and outmoded," he writes, "centering as it does upon a few beings artificially detached from the world. The commonplace French novel, with its drama of love and self-interest focused, at best, upon a single family, was an example I was determined to avoid at all costs" (263; 285). In its structure and content, *Les hommes dans la prison* exhibits a number of characteristics of documentary fiction and testimonial autobiographies, scarcely resembling the Balzacian-style novel Serge so disdains. As we will see, plot, characterization, and setting—combined with the inclusion of much verifiable and accurate detail about life in prison—contribute to the novel's strong documentary effect.

The structure of *Les hommes dans la prison* closely resembles that of other documentary and testimonial narratives of confinement, such as Silvio Pellico's account of his incarceration in the notorious Spielberg, *My Prisons* (1832); Fyodor Dostoyevsky's narrative based on his years as a convict in Omsk, *Memoirs from the House of the Dead* (1861–62); Levi's *Survival in Auschwitz* (1946), and Armando Valladares's memoirs of political imprisonment in Cuba, *Against All Hope* (1985). Each of those narratives follows the same capture-to-freedom structure of *Les hommes dans la prison*. The texts' chapters are short and focus on specific subjects, characters, situations, and settings. With little variation, the first and last chapters are dedicated to entering and exiting the space of confinement.[13] Furthermore, as is the case with the narratives by the aforementioned Italian, Russian, and Cuban authors, the chapters of *Les hommes dans la prison* tend to be disparate in their subject matter, covering wide-ranging topics (as indicated by their titles, such as "Capital Punishment," "Discipline," "The Will to Live," or "The War"). Consequently, a chapter can have little or no relationship to the chapters that come before or after it. The result is a lack of continuity in the narrative and a striking absence of a steady, progressively developing plot line. Some of the chapters ("Architecture," e.g.) are so unconnected to the rest of the work that they could be read as brief, self-contained essays on specific aspects of the French penal system. That lack of cohesion among the chapters stems in part from the manner in which Serge composed his early novels. In his memoirs, Serge wrote about how his lifestyle as a revolutionary affected his writing: "I knew that I would never have time to polish my works properly. They would be worthwhile without that. Others, less engaged in combat, would perfect a style; but what I had to tell, *they* could not tell. To each his own task. . . . For my books I adopted an appropriate form: I had to construct them in detached fragments which could each be separately completed and sent abroad post-haste; which could, if absolutely necessary, be published as they were, incomplete; and it would have been difficult to compose in any other form" (263; 284–85). While Serge's writing process is no doubt an important factor, the text's structure and lack of a complex plot are also explained by its documentary thrust. Critic Evelyn Cobley writes that documentary accounts "lend themselves to extended analyses of description and narration rather than of plot" (12). Very little narrative energy in *Les hommes dans la prison* is devoted to plot development: the work is primarily concerned with providing a detailed account of surviving life in prison. The outside world is depicted only in relation to the narrator's movement in and out of prison, a characteristic that is typical of documentary prison novels. Furthermore, the nature of life behind bars influences the structure of prison narratives like *Les hommes dans la prison*: the defining characteristic of a prison sentence is stasis. Inmates' routines scarcely change for years at a time. Depicting the multifaceted nature of prison life is therefore facilitated by the use of chapters that focus on specific themes and groups rather than discrete time periods.

As he does with plot and structure, Serge avoids the use of traditional novelistic characterization in *Les hommes dans la prison*. The function of characters in the novel is often transparent, and for the most part, individual characters are neither elaborately developed nor present in the novel for more than a few pages. Even the narrator-protagonist, the novel's primary figure, ultimately serves as a vehicle to depict the various conditions and situations that a prisoner in any given prison might experience. The author uses a number of narrative techniques to render his narrator-protagonist an "Everyman" prisoner: anonymous throughout the text, he is given few characteristics that distinguish him from the other prisoners. Serge provides no physical descriptions of his narrator, and the reader is given very little information regarding his life story, apart from a few details about his activities as a rebel and his revolutionary aspirations. Serge's use of his narrator in such a role is emblematic of a larger tendency in the novel to avoid the use of traditionally constructed characters: individuals in the novel are better described as types who represent specific states of being. A broad sample of prison society is presented in *Les hommes dans la prison* through numerous brief portraits of inmates and descriptions of their behavior and habits. Examples include, among many others, depictions of a pedophile former priest; crazed, self-mutilating prisoners; a parricide; inmates facing transportation to penal colonies; and a homosexual prisoner with an active fantasy life.

Plot and character—two pillars of the traditional realist novel—are strikingly absent from *Les hommes dans la prison*. The same can be said about the specifics around the physical setting in which the bulk of the story takes place. Spaces of confinement contribute to both the documentary impulse of the novel and its universalistic tendencies. The carceral space is restricted to two prisons, with brief interludes in holding cells in Paris's Palais de Justice (in the Conciergerie and the Souricière). The first prison in which Serge places his protagonist is La Santé in Paris. By mentioning La Santé and the holding cells by name (all three of which are real-life jails used for short-term detention), the author inserts referential detail into the novel and thereby enhances its documentary effect. The second prison is unnamed and is simply referred to as a *maison centrale*. Serge devotes approximately two-thirds of the text to the years his narrator spends there as a convict. The omission of a specific name for the latter institution presents the narrator's jail term as one that is typical of all medium to long-term sentences, regardless of the place of detention.

Although Serge's text is a work of fiction, it is fiction of a different order from the realist novel. The use of plot, character, and setting in *Les hommes dans la prison*, combined with the text's strong testimonial discourse, contribute to its documentary thrust. Moreover, as is the case with other prison novels and other types of witness literature, Serge's text is replete with information that is referential and verifiable. And while that information is couched in Serge's anti-capitalist fictional narrative, it nonetheless has documentary value. The presence of such documentary detail is not surprising, as it is clear that *Les hommes dans la prison* was written for an imagined readership that is ostensibly uninitiated into the most basic rites and rituals of prison life. The inclusion of verifiable and referential information acquaints the reader with fundamental aspects of prison life and heightens the novel's ideological urgency and currency: the stronger the documentary effect of the text, the more effective its sociopolitical message becomes. Serge succeeds in capturing much evidence of a number of penal processes and policies in use in the prisons in which he was incarcerated—La Santé and the *maison centrale* in Melun—not to mention a great deal of information about inmates' daily lives. To underline the degree to which *Les hommes dans la prison* is a documentary depiction of prison life, I will begin by providing a bit of background information on the institutions in which the author was held.

The construction of La Santé prison in Paris was heavily influenced by the major penal reform movements of the nineteenth century. In the years following its inauguration in 1867, La Santé was hailed as a "model" prison.[14] In his book on the history of that prison, Michel Fize writes that the institution was "[b]uilt for a special purpose: cellular imprisonment. La Santé seemed to offer the best conditions for ventilation, health, cleanliness, light, and space" (*Ville* 31). The prison's architecture, of course, reflected not just concerns for sanitation but a security mission as well. To that end, its chief architect succeeded in building two prisons on one site: the first was designed according to the Pennsylvania system for half of the prisoners (the accused awaiting prosecution or release), the second for the remaining half (convicted prisoners) according to the Auburn system. The Pennsylvania system—named for the disciplinary methods in use in Pittsburgh and Philadelphia—was based on total cellular isolation of prisoners and one-on-one moral and religious instruction. The Auburn system, which was first designed for use at Sing Sing prison in New York, prescribed stringent corporal punishment, nighttime isolation, and collective work (conducted, theoretically, in total silence). The results of the combination of those two systems at La Santé were impressive: "All observers report the stunning modernity of the new prison. . . . Everything in it represented progress" (Fize, "Histoire" 707). Yet by 1912, when Serge first passed through its doors, the prison had taken a marked turn for the worse. In the 1860s La Santé had a reputation for being clean and comfortable and having conditions that sought to moralize and thus rehabilitate inmates. By the late nineteenth and early twentieth centuries, however, it was better known for corrupting inmates through harsh discipline, filth, overcrowding, and promiscuity.[15]

The *maison centrale* in Melun, where Serge spent the bulk of his sentence, is on prime real estate at the center of town on the eastern tip of the île Saint-Etienne, a fact bemoaned by the Melunais.[16] André Dumas, a visitor to the prison in 1907 (just a few years prior to Serge's incarceration), explains his interest in taking a tour of and documenting conditions at the *maison centrale*: "We have chosen the *maison centrale* of Melun, not only because of its importance, but because as one of the best built, planned, and equipped prisons of its kind, it will offer us a classic example of a 'modern prison.' . . . The workshops, most notably the printing shops, are furnished with the newest and most perfected machines. The detainees themselves who populate the prison are, for the most part, able and intelligent workers. One can, in a way, view the *maison centrale* of Melun as a model prison house" (qtd. in Plancke 128).[17] The adjectives "modern" and "model" stand out as strikingly similar to the original assessments of the design of La Santé. The Auburn system of punishment was in use at Melun, and therefore the prisoners (again, in theory) worked communally in silence during the day in a variety of workshops. Dumas notes that the lives of the inmates were predictable and routine and that few events, such as religious services, meals, and exercise broke up their days. Meals were meager and some prisoners were even able to supplement their rations with wine, which was to be consumed immediately upon its serving to prevent trafficking and bartering (Plancke 132).[18] The exercise routine consisted of two daily walks around the prison courtyard, which the inmates were required to do in file and which involved a repetitive, circular retracing of one's steps.

In his depiction of life at La Santé and the *maison centrale*, Serge highlights a number of processes that were in use in those prisons and that have, moreover, been commonplace through-out the Western world since the early nineteenth century. Some of those processes are so fundamental to modern conceptions of criminal justice that it is difficult to imagine their absence. The most basic of the characteristics—one Serge repeatedly empha-sizes—is the use of a precise timetable to dictate the function-ing of the prison.[19] While in La Santé, the narrator highlights the regularity of events, such as the exact times of meals, the twenty minutes of exercise allowed in the courtyard, and brief visits from doctors, family, and the prison chaplain. The prison-ers' daily schedule is even more regimented in the *maison cen-trale*. For the narrator, the pace is maddening: "The rhythm of life within this sequestered city follows a clockwork precision. . . . In the workshop, a few minutes are set aside for washing at the faucet. At 7:15 a bell gives the signal for work to begin. At 9 o'clock the bell again: stop work. The bell: line up. The bell: Indian file toward the mess hall. The bell: leave the mess hall; exercise, twenty-five minutes, from 9:30 to 9:55. The bell: back to the workshops. The bell: begin work again. The bell, the bell, the bell" (115–16; 155).

An important element of the efficient functioning of the prison involves a systematic process of integrating new prison-ers, a procedure basic to any penal institution. Serge's detailed portrayal of the process of entry into the prison is emblematic of the documentary tendencies of *Les hommes dans la prison*. During his passage through the various stages of his lengthy sentence (from cell to cell and prison to prison), Serge's narrator describes the process of entry twice: first, just after he has been arrested and is forced to await his trial, and second, upon entry into the *maison centrale* where he spends close to four years as a convict. In both cases, the narrator-protagonist is stripped of markers of his individuality. Upon his initial detention, he notes, "I was no longer a man, but a man in prison" (4; 26). He is searched and his personal items are taken from him: "Incarceration begins with the search. Necktie, collar, belt, suspenders, shoelaces, pocketknife, anything that might be used in secret to free a desperate man from the power of the law by stabbing or strangulation; papers, notebook, letters, snapshots, everything that characterizes a man, the little objects that accumulate around his private life—all this is taken from him" (8; 31). The entry procedures result in tangible, physical changes: "Man imprisoned differs from man in general even in his outward appearance" (8; 31). After being subjected to the initiation rites at the *maison centrale*, the narrator is left naked, shorn, and faced with the prospect of donning regulation prison clothes for the duration of his sentence. He glumly declares, "There is nothing left to distinguish me from the others" (110; 149). Indeed, he has no distinctive characteristics save his new number, which he is forced to sew onto his own regulation outfit himself: "Number 6731, that's me" (110; 148).[20] At the end of the novel, the narrator-protagonist's survival and newly regained liberty are in part emphasized by much-welcomed physical renewal: "My three months' growth of hair already gives me more individuality than Number 6731 ought to have" (243; 299).

The prisons in which Serge places his protagonist show the effects of changes in methods of criminal punishment, which were in perpetual transformation throughout the nineteenth century in France. *Les hommes dans la prison* provides a snapshot of a prison system whose rehabilitative ambitions and capacities have long since been in decay. Some policies Serge describes are clearly vestiges of the great period of reform of the first half of the nineteenth century and are still in place despite their failure to rehabilitate prisoners or deter crime. For example, Serge points out, as did many prison reformers during the nineteenth century, that the system of cellular solitary confinement provokes obsession and madness rather than the calm meditation its designers intended: "Depression tortures the tired brain" (*MP* 80; *HP* 112). Auburnian workshops are in place, but the narrator notes that the inmates surreptitiously break the rule of enforced silence: "The movements of their [the prisoners'] lips are barely perceptible" (119; 160).[21] The convicts' sole exercise, called "the Round," appears on the surface to be a fairly innocuous and perhaps beneficial process in which prisoners walk around a courtyard in a queue following a very rigid, repetitive pattern, but Serge's narrator deems it a "senseless ritual" (154; 199) emblematic of a cruel system of punishment: "One, two. One, two. There is no end to the round. There is no end to time. There is no end to crime. There is no end to misery. There is no end to the reign of the swine" (155; 200). Serge is not alone in depicting the deplorable nature of the prisoners' round. Verlaine comments on its harsh effects on the spirit of prisoners in his poem "En prison." The round also inspired Gustave-Doré's grim engraving of prisoners walking in a circle in his *Newgate: Exercise Yard* (1872), which in turn served as the basis for Vincent van Gogh's *Prisoners Exercising* (1890), in which inmates—one of whom has Vincent's face—glumly march around a dark, tightly enclosed square space.

Evidence of changes in punitive processes can also be found in the structural characteristics of the prisons Serge describes. The institutions portrayed by the narrator have facets that are decidedly archaic and others that are more modern. Such architectural hybridity is a hallmark of many French prisons, as financial constraints have dictated that older structures be adapted to conform to new methods of punishment.[22] Take, for example, the narrator's description of the room in which prisoners are measured and examined, an old space that is used for modern practices: "We climb a long spiral staircase. We are in one of the medieval towers of the Conciergerie, I discover. . . . In earlier times they used to put their victims 'to the question' on the rack in the cellars of this very tower. Today, they apply Bertillon's scientific system upstairs. This is the stairway of progress" (10; 33–34). The passage refers to Alphonse Bertillon, the founder of modern techniques of criminal identification based on anthropometrics. The Bertillonage system was adopted in France in 1888 in order to identify prisoners and keep records on them (O'Brien 289). Serge's description highlights not only the use of what was then considered a highly modern and technical phenomenon in criminology but also the fact that there is a long history of brutal incarceration in the Western world. The sardonic reference to the "stairway of progress" underlines that, for the narrator, criminal punishment humiliates, degrades, and disempowers the prisoner, whether one is interrogated in a dungeon or measured and photographed in a high tower.

Beyond bureaucratic and punitive processes, Serge heightens the documentary effect of his novel by providing an accurate and detailed depiction of inmates' daily lives. In *Les hommes dans la prison*, every day in prison is the same, with the exception of a few extraordinary events (which are also usually repeated), such as special meals and religious celebrations on Sunday, visits from outside the prison, and the receipt of correspondence. Breaks in the routine also include less felicitous events, such as being thrown into solitary confinement, taking trips to the infirmary, or witnessing a suicide. The essence of a prison sentence is the time spent in the cell, and Serge's narrator explicates the monotonous routine of cellular existence. And each time he changes locales, the narrator provides a description of his new physical surroundings, including minutiae such as the dimensions of his new cells and the types of toilets and sinks therein. For example, the narrator describes his living space in La Santé: "Three or four yards in length, the same in width. A little oak table, bolted to the wall; a heavy chair, attached to the wall by a chain to prevent it becoming a weapon in the hands of the unknown man whose despair and fury have been anticipated. A camp bed of satisfactory cleanliness folds up against the wall during the day and hardly takes up any room" (30–31; 56–57). There is not much to do in such an environment, and the inmates are in a state of sensory deprivation: minor details like rays of sunlight passing into a cell therefore take on great significance (56; 84). Even the work that is performed by the detainees is marked by the same monotony and simplicity: "sorting coffee beans, making paper bags, making paper fans, folding school notebooks. The same dull gesture to be repeated several thousand times a day" (33; 59). With no real form of diversion, prisoners are forced to confront their own minds, and the narrator describes the deterioration of the inmates' mental state while locked in isolation.

Other verifiable details in *Les hommes dans la prison* include information about the food given to inmates and the books they are allowed to read, again highlighting the documentary ambitions of Serge's novel. Food is distributed to the prisoners with the same parsimony as is space in the cells, and the types of meals bear a striking resemblance to historical documentation about prison alimentation in La Santé in the early twentieth century. In the morning, the narrator notes, prisoners receive seven hundred grams of bread, followed by soup (43; 70). Their second meal, taken around four in the afternoon, consists of the same soup, only with more vegetables, and on Sundays it contains meat (45; 72).[23] Undernourished and deprived of meaningful work, the inmates are left with few forms of intellectual distraction from their day-to-day monotony. Some diversion can be attained through reading clandestine newspapers, letters, or books. The narrator states that La Santé has a library that seems to consist mainly of bad adventure novels, a few moralistic tracts, and the work of a few good writers, notably Balzac and Jules Verne. While the books are filthy, defaced by the notations of the inmates, and missing pages, any reading material is a welcome distraction: "I learned, alone with these books, that the most mediocre printed page can have its value. Everything is in knowing how to read and how to make the book a pretext for meditations" (34; 61).[24]

Forced to cope with an abundance of empty time, prisoners are notorious for interacting creatively with their environment. Their creativity in finding ways to subvert the physical and procedural constraints of prisons is routinely highlighted in social histories, fictions, and testimonies about life behind bars.[25] *Les hommes dans la prison* is no exception: the narrator provides a number of details about the peculiarities of the inmate community and its unusual rituals. For example, the narrator portrays how prisoners communicate secretly through wall tapping (38; 66) and speak to each other clandestinely by using pipes in the plumbing system as a "telephone" (52; 81). Serge describes how prisoners use their linguistic skills to communicate in secret: "In covert language, half-slang, half-Javanese—Javanese being a language, unknown to philologists, formed by interposing made-up syllables between the syllables of each word" (24–25; 50).[26] The author often italicizes and defines jargon used by the inmates, thereby further indicating that one of his primary goals is to explain, analyze, and document even the most minor characteristics of a prison culture into which his imagined readership is uninitiated.[27]

Although *Les hommes dans la prison* has been relegated to the margins of the French literary canon, Serge's novel is an important work from the perspective of literary history, for it is, on many levels, an exemplary prison novel. The text shares a number of thematic and ideological similarities with other French narratives of confinement as well as those from a host of other national literary traditions. One of the mainstays of prison literature is an insistence not only upon the realistic quality of the narratives but also on the texts' capacities to document actual conditions in the carceral milieu. In its structure and content, *Les hommes dans la prison* seeks to tell the story of an Everyman common-law prisoner, and in doing so, Serge's novel captures much documentary detail about penal processes and procedures that were widely used in total institutions throughout the Western world early in the twentieth century. However, as I have argued, it is essential to recognize the fictional component of Serge's text in evaluating both its documentary value and its ideological stance.

As we will see in the following chapter, Jean Genet, like Victor Serge before him, melds actuality and fictionality in his prison narrative *Miracle de la rose*. Genet's novel depicts a narrator-protagonist (dubbed "Jean Genet") in two prisons: Fontevrault penitentiary and the Mettray agricultural colony. Analysis of the narrator's ruminations reveals a great deal not simply about prison life in twentieth-century France but also about Genet's artful construction of documentary fiction. Like Serge, Genet uses the prison as a vehicle for sociocritique: for his part, Genet targets the mainstream French bourgeoisie. In contrast with Serge's narrator, however, Genet's narrator-protagonist not only depicts the difficulties of life behind bars to sharpen that sociocritique but also embraces prison life in order to underline and exult in his status as an outcast.

[TWO] A PARIAH'S PARADISE

Jean Genet's 1946 prison novel *Miracle de la rose* leaves its
readers sifting through a trough of conflicting and ambiguous
information that both complicates and enriches critical interpretation. Although *Miracle* is most often cited for its pervasive
lyricism and nostalgic poeticity, Genet uses specific narrative
strategies to heighten the documentary effect of his work, leading readers to believe that information in the text is representative of conditions and relations in prisons and agricultural penal
colonies. The documentary value of Genet's novel is brought
to the fore through a referential pact initiated by the narrator
in the book's opening pages.[1] However, while the narrator of
Miracle appears to share with his imagined bourgeois readership information that refers to a reality outside the text, the
work's referentiality is anything but straightforward. Indeed,
close examination of Genet's narrative strategies reveals that the
referentiality of the text is, in many ways, nothing more than
artifice: *Miracle de la rose* appears to be a referential text simply because it borrows the conventions of referential texts. As
Jean-Paul Sartre wrote in his monumental study on Genet's life
and work, *Saint Genet, comédien et martyr* (*Saint Genet, Actor
and Martyr*), Genet in *Miracle de la rose* "splits his personality,

he is torn between truth and fiction" (340; 380).[2] In this chapter I will analyze the narrative characteristics of *Miracle*, arguing that it should be read as a work of fiction in spite of its referential pact and legitimate documentary value. Genet artfully cultivates the semblance of referentiality in his novel in order to enhance its documentary effect and heighten its ideological urgency and currency. At the same time, he constructs his representation of prison using a number of strategies and techniques that are normally the province of fiction. As we will see, Genet uses his fictional depiction of the experience of a chronic recidivist to accentuate his position as an outcast from what is presented to readers as a dominant bourgeois culture.

Published in 1946 by Marc Barbezat, *Miracle de la rose* is Genet's second novel. The text depicts the experience of the narrator, a thirty-year-old recidivist named Jean Genet, as he serves a sentence of unspecified length in the Fontevrault central prison of detention. The narrator begins his story with a description of his entry into that imposing *maison centrale*, and thereafter he focuses on his complex and often sexual relationships with fellow inmates, the physical conditions of his incarceration, and numerous salient aspects of the daily functioning of the prison. Significant portions of the narrative are devoted to the narrator's remembrances and active fantasy life. The narrator escapes from his present situation in the harsh environment of Fontevrault prison by delving into memories of Mettray, the agricultural penal colony in the Touraine region where he was detained during his adolescence. Those remembrances contain much detailed documentary information about Mettray's organization and living conditions. Like the Fontevrault sections, the Mettray portions of *Miracle de la rose* depict the narrator's relationships with his fellow inmates, including their power struggles and their sexual encounters. Beyond those flashbacks, the narrator devotes much mental energy to elaborate and often erotic fantasies, which, like the text's Mettray segments, are interspersed throughout the novel.

Throughout his period of detention at Fontevrault, the narrator is captivated and inspired by a fellow inmate named Harcamone. Condemned to death for the murder of a prison guard, Harcamone—in whom the narrator finds his "Rose"—serves as one of the many pretexts for the composition of the narrative. From the beginning of the text, Harcamone, who was also once at Mettray, is the object of the narrator's admiration and glorification because of his crimes and his fate. That glorification reaches its apex in the novel's final section, which contains an elaborate imaginary sequence in which the narrator pictures Harcamone's last days in Fontevrault before his execution. Over the course of that fantasy, the condemned prisoner performs a series of imaginary and, in the narrator's eyes, miraculous near escapes. The final sequence of events in the fantasy takes place on the night of the execution. As Harcamone awaits his death, the narrator imagines various authority figures (a chaplain, a judge, a lawyer, and an executioner) on a fantastic voyage into the body of the condemned man. There they find and violate a "Mystic Rose" located where they expected to find his heart. The "profanation" of that imaginary "Rose" coincides with the timing of Harcamone's execution and is the last major event depicted in the text. The novel ends as the narrator mourns the death of Harcamone and the loss of other deceased prisoners he has known.

As this summary suggests, *Miracle de la rose* is a dense and complex text. Indeed, part of the narrative's complexity is attributable to the peculiar mixture of documentary detail about prison life and lengthy passages of lyrical prose in which the narrator "sings" the praises of various aspects of his past and present.[3] The narrative is rendered more obscure by the fact that it is unclear where the narrator is situated both temporally and spatially relative to the events he describes.[4] Further complicating critical interpretation is the strong influence of Proust's *A la recherche du temps perdu*, itself a complex text, which Genet clearly sought to imitate in *Miracle*. From the

narrator's nostalgic desire to recapture the essence of his childhood to the inclusion of a *baiser refusé* (73; 101), the Proustian
influence is palpable and, at times, unmistakable.[5] Adding to
the complexity of the narrative are numerous shifts—some of
which are not clearly demarcated—between the past at Mettray
and the present in Fontevrault. Moreover, the narrator not only
departs from the present in Fontevrault through remembrances
but also recounts a number of overtly imaginary sequences, including the final, crucial scenes of the novel in which the title is,
at least in part, explained.[6] As the presence of those imaginary
sequences indicates, *Miracle de la rose* is marked by a constant
tug-of-war between fictionality and poeticity on the one hand
and referentiality and documentary realism on the other hand.
Indeed, the novel encourages autobiographical interpretation of
the prison experiences that are depicted and, at the same time,
refuses that very same type of analysis.

Miracle de la rose is certainly not Genet's only work in which
prison and prisoners play a central role. Among his prose texts,
Genet's first novel, *Notre-Dame-des-fleurs* (*Our Lady of the
Flowers*), bears the most salient structural and thematic similarities to *Miracle*. Indeed, "Genet," the narrator of *Notre-
Dame*, like his counterpart in *Miracle*, claims to be a veteran
prisoner and provides a variety of details about life behind
bars and the execrable conditions of sanitation he must confront daily.[7] As in *Miracle*, the narrator's present incarceration
serves as the "reality" from which the narrator-protagonist departs into sexual fantasies involving a host of marginal figures
from a criminal underworld. However, unlike *Miracle*, while the
narrator situates himself in prison as he writes and fantasizes,
the prison milieu—its living conditions, its power dynamics,
its rituals—is not a principal concern of *Notre-Dame*. Rather,
the mental gymnastics one prisoner performs to distract himself from his current incarceration dominate the narrative. As
Sartre observed, *Notre-Dame* is "the epic of masturbation"

(448; 498). Commenting on the limited scope of the work, he continues: "There is only one subject: the pollutions of a prisoner in the darkness of his cell; only one hero: the masturbator; only one place: his 'evil-smelling hole, beneath the coarse wool covers'" (448–49; 498–99). Unlike the novels examined in this study, *Notre-Dame* lacks a strong documentary thrust in relation to life behind bars, despite its heavy reliance upon carceral imagery for artistic and erotic effect.[8]

From both thematic and formal standpoints, the work in Genet's corpus that most closely resembles *Miracle de la rose* is the only film ever directed by the author, *Un chant d'amour* (*A Song of Love*, 1950). That silent, black-and-white film wavers—like *Miracle*—between fantasy and "reality." The action unfolds entirely in and around a prison, with the exception of the fantasy sequences, which take place in the open countryside. Like *Miracle*, Genet's film creates a sense of a dichotomous relationship between the bucolic, oniric countryside and the harsh, bleak reality of the prison. In both works, the countryside is depicted as a place for mental retreat, where a reprieve from the brutality of the prison of the present can be found. Moreover, *Un chant d'amour* provides detailed depictions of inmate interactions and sketches an outline of how power relations function in the prison (specifically, through the portrayal of the warden's physical and sexual abuse of the inmates). However, it is important to note that the representation of daily prison life is not a primary concern of the film. In spite of the precision with which it shows the inmates' erotic play, particularly the scenes in which the inmates spy on each other and use straws to blow cigarette smoke through holes in the walls, the film lacks documentary pretension. As he does with *Notre-Dame-des-fleurs*, Genet here uses the prison primarily as a vehicle through which homoerotic fantasies can be depicted. Details of the prisoners' collective habits are included not in order to give the viewer a sense of how real-life inmates spend time behind bars, but are simply incorporated for sensual and artistic effect. Nico Papatakis, the producer of the film and owner of the nightclub in which the film was shot, commented on the writer-turned-filmmaker's creativity: "Genet had fantastic ideas, poetic and gratuitous, such as the exchange of cigarette smoke through a straw. Such a hole in a prison wall is impossible realistically, but the image works" (qtd. in E. White 365).[9]

Miracle de la rose, like the works by Genet mentioned above, relies heavily on carceral imagery and the prison serves as a locale for sexual activity and erotic fantasy. However, *Miracle* differs from both *Notre-Dame-des-fleurs* and *Un chant d'amour* in that it provides much information about life in penal institutions along with textual markers indicating to readers that that information should be interpreted as documentary. The documentary leanings of *Miracle* are in part explained by the novel's genesis: it initially existed as two separate, short texts, one called "Les Enfants du malheur" ("The Children of Misfortune," which was later destroyed), and another titled "Miracle de la rose" (E. White 234). Commenting on the differences between the two works, Edmund White states: "The one about Mettray is realistic, detailed, sociological, and the other is abstract (we know almost nothing about the prisoner, Harcamone) lyric, exalted, more a poem than a novel. In soldering the two together Genet exaggerated the aspects of continuity and suggested that many events at Mettray had foreshadowed those at Fontevrault" (234). The stylistic disparity between the two original texts explains, to some extent, why *Miracle* wavers between lyrical fantasies and documentary precision. Moreover, we should note that in the final version of *Miracle* both the Mettray sections *and* the story about Harcamone have referential and autobiographical tendencies.

The documentary pretensions of *Miracle de la rose* become apparent in the novel's opening pages. The text begins with the following deeply personal revelation: "Of all the state prisons in France, Fontevrault is the most disquieting. It was Fontevrault that gave me the strongest impression of anguish and affliction" (5; 9). The novel's intimate first sentences take on a testimonial and autobiographical quality when, just a few pages later, some sparse dialogue between the narrator (who has just been transferred to Fontevrault) and a prison guard reveals that the narrator goes by the name "Jean Genet." To be sure, the author's insertion of his own name into a literary text is a technique that is difficult to ignore. Indeed, Philippe Lejeune argues that it fundamentally changes how information in a novel is read: "From the 'truth' of the primary name (that is, the identity shared between the character-narrator and the author . . .), the reader has a tendency to deduce, if not the truth of the facts (as is the case with any testimony, the reader can have doubts), at least the fact that the author furnishes them as true" (*Moi aussi* 47).[10] To use Lejeune's terminology, "the referential strength" (47) of the author's proper name changes how "facts" are interpreted. The use of the author's name in the text brings the reader, if not closer to believing what is depicted in the narrative, then at least closer to accepting that the information is intended to be read as credible and representative of actuality—referentially valid, in other words.

The inclusion of his own name in his text is but one of many tactics Genet uses to bolster the referentiality of *Miracle de la rose*. Indeed, he relies on a number of conventions and narrative strategies normally found in traditional autobiographical texts. Commenting on Genet's literary endeavors in general, White remarks: "Genet borrows the prestige of the confessional autobiography" (xviii). True to White's observation, in addition to the fact that the narrator-protagonist and the author have the same name, the various alleged pretexts for the composition of *Miracle* also follow conventions of autobiographical discourse. In an essay titled "The Style of Autobiography," Jean Starobinski writes that "one would hardly have sufficient motive to write an autobiography had not some radical change occurred in his life—conversion, entry into a new life, the operation of

Grace." Starobinski continues: "It is the internal transformation of the individual—and the exemplary character of this transformation—that furnishes a subject for a narrative discourse in which 'I' is both subject and object" (78). The narrator of *Miracle* proffers a few reasons to explain why and how he will compose his story, and many of those reasons indeed suggest deeply personal transformative events. Those changes involve a transformation from a disillusioned adult into an individual who is more in touch with the poetic powers of his childhood. As a thirty-year-old criminal who has already done much prison time, "Genet" complains about seeing the Fontevrault *maison centrale* in too utilitarian a light. Upon entry into a paddy wagon (the "Black Maria") on the way to Fontevrault, he claims he perceives the world with alienating precision: "I noticed that the Black Maria was divested of its charm, that air of haughty misfortune which, the first few times I had taken it, had made it a vehicle of exile, a conveyance fraught with grandeur, slowly fleeing, as it carried me off, between the ranks of a people bowed with respect. It is no longer a vehicle of royal misfortune. I have had a clear vision of it, of a thing which, beyond happiness or unhappiness, is splendid. It was there, upon entering the prison-wagon, that I felt I had become a true, disenchanted visionary" (7; 12). The new, stark vision, which enables the narrator to perceive clearly the harsh conditions and scrofulous inhabitants of the prison, stands in marked contrast to the manner in which he saw prison life prior to his detention in Fontevrault. "This world, which is new to me," he states, "is dreary, without hope, without excitement. Now that the prison is stripped of its sacred ornaments, I see it naked, and its nakedness is cruel" (30; 43). His place in that alienating universe is not a privileged one: "I am therefore dead. . . . I now act and think only in terms of prison. My activity is limited by its framework. I am only a punished man" (31; 44–45).

The narrator's stated intentions for the writing of his text are related to his alienation as an adult prisoner: "the aim of this book is only to relate the experience of freeing myself from a state of painful torpor" (27; 39). His desire to liberate himself from lethargy and hopelessness is intertwined with his desire to regain the poetic powers of his childhood. "My childhood was dead and with it died the poetic powers that had dwelt in me," the narrator states. "I no longer hoped that prison would remain the fabulous world it had long been. One day, I suddenly realized from certain signs, that it was losing its charms" (24; 35). The brutality and starkness of the present necessitate the narrator's psychological meanderings: for "Genet," memory and fantasy serve as an escape from a world that is too cruel, and too real, to bear. "I want to try to relive my moments at Mettray," he notes. "The atmosphere of the prison quickly impelled me to go back—in going back to Mettray—to my habits of the past" (32; 45). The newly discovered realistic present therefore serves as the point of departure for the narrator's Proustian journeys into his adolescence at the Mettray reformatory. And much like Marcel, the narrator of Proust's *A la recherche du temps perdu*, he finds that memory is triggered by elements that exist in the present. In the case of "Genet," those elements are his fellow inmates at Fontevrault who were also detained with him at Mettray: "Through Harcamone, Divers and Bulkaen I shall again relive Mettray, which was my childhood. I shall revive the abolished reformatory, the children's hell that has been destroyed [le bagne d'enfants détruit]" (13; 20).[11] The text, which appears to have been composed by "Genet" while in Fontevrault, will be an account of his attempt to regain his poetic powers, and even re-expose himself to the "former powers of the Prison" (33; 47). When he is able to access his memories, his love of Mettray begins to influence and infuse his perception of the present: "At the beginning of this book, I spoke of a kind of disenchantment with prison. . . . I must have loved my Colony for its influence to halo me even now. I mean—and as far back as I can remember—that it is a *precise stretch of time*, but that it irradiates, that this *present past* diffuses a dark vapour, composed chiefly, I think, of our suffering, which is my halo and to which I turn, in whose downiness I often forget the present" (109–10; 149–50). True to the tradition of confessional autobiography, the process of self-rediscovery is linked to the process of writing. The narrator remarks: "For I tear my words from the depths of my being, from a region to which irony has no access, and these words, which are charged with all the buried desires I carry within me and which express them on paper as I write, will re-create the loathsome and cherished world from which I tried to free myself" (33; 47).[12]

The narrator's quest for poeticity and personal transformation reaches its apex through his fantastic exploration of the state of being of the condemned man, Harcamone, during the final days of his life. For not only is the narrator in search of poetic power, but he is also on a quest for the sacred. The prison becomes a holy space for "Genet" due to the presence of Harcamone, the object of his glorification, his "God" (141; 192). His devotion to Harcamone and his imaginary exploration of the condemned man's state of being is consequently cast as his personal search for sainthood. "Genet" writes that Harcamone's presence radiates throughout the whole prison: "I cannot believe that the Prison is not a mystic community, for the death cell, in which a light burns night and day, is the chapel to which we direct our silent prayers" (91; 124). The narrator states that while other prisoners—Divers and Bulkaen, who were also at Mettray—help provide him with access to his childhood at the colony and serve as a "pretext" for his narrative, Harcamone serves as the book's "sublime and final cause [la fin sublime]" (39; 56). That element of the sacred distinguishes *Miracle de la rose* from the remembrances contained in Proust's *A la recherche du temps perdu*. Indeed, Richard Coe, whose 1968 *Vision of Jean Genet* remains one of the most complete studies of Genet's oeuvre, writes that Genet superimposes "a third plane of experience over and above the Proustian levels of past and present. This is the plane of the sacred" (74).[13] The narrator's worship of Harcamone represents an extreme form of the adulation thrust upon the condemned that is frequently depicted in prison narratives and films. Much like the rest of the portrayal of prison life in *Miracle*, that adulation is imbued with lyricism, corporal intimacy, and elements of the sacred and the fantastic.

The confessional autobiographical facets of *Miracle de la rose* contribute to the referential, testimonial, and documentary nature of Genet's project.[14] The novel's referentiality is further bolstered by the irrefutable consistency of some of—but not by any means all of—the details in the text with aspects of the author's life. For instance, the intertextuality between *Miracle* and other works by Genet indicates that the narrator has a life outside *Miracle*. His references to Pilorge (376, 255; 279, 188) and Weidmann (53; 74), two real-life criminal-heroes also mentioned by the narrator of *Notre-Dame-des-fleurs*, point to the narrative's basis in actuality.[15] Furthermore, the narrator of *Miracle* claims to have written a poem, "Le Condamné à mort" (104; 142), which is indeed the title of a poem by Genet dedicated to the aforementioned Pilorge. And in terms of raw autobiographical detail, it is well known that Genet spent the bulk of his adolescence at Mettray, the now-defunct agricultural prison colony for minors, as did the narrator. Furthermore, as we will see in this chapter's final section, the novel includes much accurate information about the colony as well as Fontevrault prison. The narrator even mentions journalists (such as Alexis Danan [105; 143]) who wrote about the treatment of the children held at Mettray. Add to that information verifiable and accurate details about the Nazi invasion of France (such as a deserted Parisian landscape immediately after the southward exodus of the population [7; 11]) and small but important hints that the narrator does not wish to reveal too much information about his crimes for fear of self-incrimination ("the robbery at the Museum of P." [162; 221]), and *Miracle* appears to be a referential and verifiable text.

Paradoxically, however, it is the verifiability of information in Genet's text that points to its fictionality and exposes the hollow nature of its referential pact. While some of the information in the novel corresponds accurately to the author's life, other portions are fictitious. Inconsistencies between the lives of the narrator and the author have not gone heretofore undetected, and Genet has left his readers dissecting such discrepancies for more than half a century. Sartre, for instance, points out that the narrator's claim that "I always carried out my burglaries alone" (162; 220) is false, by simply—almost contemptuously—pointing to Genet's autobiography in a footnote ("Incorrect. Cf. *Journal du Voleur*").[16] That inconsistency is hardly the most glaring one found in *Miracle*, given the fact that Jean Genet—unlike his narrator-protagonist "Jean Genet"—never served a sentence in Fontevrault prison, as Edmund White, Genet's most thorough biographer, attests: "Genet was never a prisoner at Fontevrault. There is no notation of it in his precisely documented prison record."[17] White surmises that Genet gathered information for his novel through research, not by doing time: "No doubt he visited the prison, part of which was open to tourists, in order to correct his descriptions of it" (250).

White notes that that significant discrepancy is hardly unique and states that Genet was known to "rework" the truth about his life in his fiction: "one must never forget that Genet was writing fiction, not autobiography, and his account must be corroborated by outside sources. . . . Genet consistently blurred the personal facts in his novels, plays and film scripts" (xviii). Not only must critics corroborate information in Genet's accounts, but they should also engage in close textual analysis of his works to locate signposts of fictionality. For the narrator in *Miracle de la rose* even gives his readers hints about his own propensity toward invention and telling lies. In a general remark about the nature of prisoner interactions and storytelling behind bars, he notes, "convicts lie. Prisons are full of lying mouths" (43; 60). Sartre writes that that statement applies above all to Genet himself: "He wants to make money from his writings, but on condition that the money be obtained by fraud: the purchaser will derive no advantage from his acquisition, it is unusable; Genet lies no more than does an academician, but he lies otherwise and his lies are not edifying" (485; 538). In a similar line of thought, Sartre also comments on the empty referentiality of Genet's work: "Genet gives us *nothing*: when we shut the book, we shall know no more than we ever did before about prison or ruffians or the human heart. Everything is false" (519; 575). In another telling moment, the narrator describes his text as "treacherous" (*traître*): "[This book] is as treacherous as the mirror systems that reflect the image of you which you did not compose" (141; 192). The narrator's use of the image produced by an unreliable mirror to describe his book is fitting, as it corresponds to Genet's crafting of an artificial autobiography and, by extension, a falsely documentary depiction of the carceral universe.

Both White's and Sartre's cautionary words underline the referential expectations established by Genet's fiction. Indeed, to claim that Genet lies in his fiction, as so many have done, and to call for corroboration of the "facts" in his novels is to underline the fact that he provides markers indicating that his work should be read as an autobiography. Coe prefaced his *Vision of Jean Genet* with the following observation: "this Jean Genet—the Jean Genet of *Our Lady of the Flowers* and of *Miracle of the Rose* not to mention the *Thief's Journal*—while he may have roots in the real Jean Genet's emotions and experience, is essentially imaginary. . . . Nothing that Jean-Genet-the-Writer says about this character is necessarily false; but neither is it necessarily true. Jean Cocteau, who was one of Genet's earliest champions, once uttered a famous paradox: *Il faut mentir pour être vrai*" (vii).[18] The narrator furnishes so much detail about his life that it is impossible to determine exactly how much of it refers to actual events in the life of the author. What is important to note for our purposes, however, is that the narrative bears the markers of a referential, verifiable text. So strong is the referential thrust of Genet's novel that it is understandable that it has been read as an autobiography. John Updike, for example, wrote in his 1967 review of the first edition of the American translation that it is "more accurate to consider *Miracle* not as a novel but as a mixture of essay and pensée, memoir and letter, confession and self-revelation" (qtd. in Webb 112). The fictional *Miracle* has even influenced public perception of Fontevrault prison. In his book *Encore 264 jours à tirer: Pénitencier de Fontevrault* (264 Days to Go: A Fontevrault Penitent), Bertrand Ménard cites Genet's incipit ("Of all the state prisons in France, Fontevrault is the most disquieting") and then writes: "Through these words . . . Jean Genet contributes to the powerful image of the Fontevrault central prison of detention as a place that cannot leave one feeling indifferent: a house of correction in a royal abbey, a veritable carceral town in the middle of a vast monastic ensemble" (14). Ménard's observation serves as a Wildean example of life imitating art. Although *Miracle* is a fictional text and its author was never incarcerated in Fontevrault, Genet's narrative about a make-believe prison sentence still influences perception of the real-life prison.

Narration: An Eyewitness Approach

"Genet" is a self-conscious narrator. Throughout the narrative he reveals that he is aware of both the type of story he is telling and how he acquired the information he conveys to his readers. Moreover, he comments repeatedly on the selective nature of his memory as well as on his process of remembering, which can at times be difficult and unproductive.[19] The narrator consequently appears to be forthright with his readers about the veracity of information included in his story. The self-conscious narration of "Genet," therefore, reinforces the narrative's eyewitness and documentary qualities. The narrator appears to take on the role of a witness and even claims to keep documents from his past which he shares with his readers. As we will see, however, although the general characteristics of Genet as a narrator appear to contribute to and reinforce the text's testimonial and autobiographical discourse, close analysis of *Miracle de la rose* reveals that documentary authenticity ultimately remains elusive.

As if testifying to a lived experience, the narrator tells his story from a non-omniscient point of view. He repeatedly emphasizes that he records only what he has witnessed, and warns readers when he is describing something that he did not himself see. In such cases, he informs his readership that he complements his own knowledge with either invented details or hearsay. That absence of omniscience is artfully cultivated by Genet, for the limited knowledge displayed by "Genet" has a direct relationship to the narrative's referential pact. For if readers are led to believe that the narrator tells them explicitly when information is invented or comes from other sources, then they are encouraged to interpret as referential the remainder of what "Genet" has told them. An example of such a warning comes when the narrator is pondering the fate of Harcamone, who has been sentenced to death for the murder of a prison guard. He says: "I cannot tell exactly how the idea of death occurred to him. I can only invent it. But I know him so well that I am likely to be right" (49; 69). The narrator exposes more gaps in his knowledge when trying to complete the actual telling of Harcamone's slaying of the guard, as he did not witness the killing: "I have no way of knowing how Harcamone happened to be present when the guard passed by, but he was said to have rushed up behind and grabbed him by the shoulder, as if he had wanted to kiss him from behind" (53; 73–74).

The telling of Harcamone's crime is not the only example of the narrator's underlining of his own lack of omniscience. Another such instance is found in the narrator's piecemeal account of the deaths of two of his fellow inmates, Bulkaen and Botchako, during a failed escape attempt. "Genet" depicts himself as forthright regarding his limited knowledge. "And the following is what I was told," he quips, informing his readers, unambiguously, that the story he is telling is based on secondhand information (223; 301). The narrator then recounts the information he has learned with as little subjective interference as possible (there is only one "I think"—"je crois" in the original). For the bulk of the telling of Bulkaen's and Botchako's deaths, the narrator, as if to emphasize that the information he is imparting is not his own, abandons the long, difficult, and often lyrical phrases that are a distinguishing mark of his style. His sentences suddenly become short and informative, highlighting the raw action of the scene: "Bulkaen had to climb faster. The guards arrived. Botchako grabbed the hanging rope and also started climbing" (223; 301). The story goes on and the narrator continues to claim to be dependent upon the eyewitness reports of other prisoners so that he himself may testify: "Later, I got other, more brutal information. . . . I followed Bulkaen's scarlet adventure as a passionate expert, as a witness who remembers an earlier one that was a kind of dress rehearsal for this one . . . it was the crowd of inmates who informed me of the beauty of the adventure" (224–25; 303). The narrator, always seemingly determined to relate Bulkaen's and Botchako's swan song accurately, even highlights the storytelling tendencies of one prison guard who, in his own way, tailored part of the narrative: "despite the rule that forbade him to talk about such things, and in such a tone, the guard, who knew of my friendship with Bulkaen, as did all the guards, related, for he had been present, what had happened that night. He laid stress on the rain, which had bothered him, so that I would realize how it had treated [Bulkaen]" (224; 303). The story changes, we are told, simply because the guard knows that the narrator was the lover of the dead prisoner. The narrator's exposure of the skewed nature of the guard's telling bolsters the confessional and referential aspects of the narrative, as it is consistent with the narrator's attempt to document events as they unfold before him.

As we have seen from Dorrit Cohn's analysis of signposts of fictionality, too much omniscience on the part of a first-person narrator can be an indicator of invention.[20] Genet's near categorical avoidance of such omniscience is consistent with his construction of a narrative that imitates the conventions of the confessional autobiography. However, the tension between fiction and documentation in *Miracle de la rose* becomes apparent in one of the narrator's many stories about his fellow inmates. In a story about Sister Zoé, a nun at Mettray, who is killed by an inmate (Daniel), the narrator demonstrates too much knowledge and credits neither his fertile imagination nor hearsay in telling that tale. *Miracle* therefore contains a signpost of fictionality similar to those apparent in *Les hommes dans la prison*, when Serge's narrator slips unexplainedly from first-person narration into the third-person omniscient mode. In telling the story of the murder of the nun, the narrator uses a third-person omniscient voice to describe the thoughts of the actors in the drama without explaining how he has come to that knowledge.

The passage, found near the end of the novel, begins with the narrator's description of Daniel performing his duty as morning bugler for the colony. While he was on the job one day, Daniel happened to catch a glimpse of Sister Zoé, who had earlier disciplined the young bugler by slapping his fingers with a convent key. The morning Daniel saw the nun, she was on her way from the infirmary to the chapel to attend mass. Upon seeing her, Daniel—who had vowed revenge because of the key incident—is seized with rage and knocks her into a pond, where she freezes to death. The narrator describes in detail her experience in the water: "Utterly astounded, she toppled into the water. Her skirts kept her afloat for a moment so that she looked like a huge, ridiculous water-lily, but they very quickly absorbed water and pulled her down. She was mute with fear and shame. The contact of the water with her legs, thighs and stomach, the novelty of the element she was no longer used to, paralyzed the virgin. She dared not make a movement or utter a cry. She sank" (232; 312–13). The narrator has unexplained access to the nun's mental state and feelings. She is "mute with fear and shame," and he somehow knows how the water feels upon her legs, thighs, and stomach. Such information would obviously be unknowable had the event occurred as described, for the nun died during the incident. The passage appears therefore to be marked by outright fabrication, although it is not characterized as such by the narrator (unlike his creative meanderings throughout the remainder of the narrative).

The narrator's sudden omniscience is but one of many signs of tension between fiction and nonfiction in *Miracle de la rose*. Other signposts of fictionality appear when the narrator attempts to document elaborate details about his experiences at Mettray and Fontevrault. For example, "Genet" gives a false documentary veneer to a speech given by an official at Mettray (whom he refers to derisively as "Dudule") by interpolating italicized text into the narrative.[21] The speech, as well as follow-up remarks by a bishop from Tours (also italicized), serves as a means for the narrator to insert the official discourse and policies of the Mettray administrators into *Miracle*.[22] From a formal standpoint the speech appears authentic, given the fact that it is italicized and readers are directly exposed to the official's monologue. However, closer examination reveals that the speech is partially, if not wholly, invented by the narrator. Although the Mettray official speaks in his own voice, the narrator states, just before the beginning of the speech, "I want to try to remember the tone of Dudule's welcome speech" (207).[23] Rather than providing a summary of the speech, he includes an artificial version thereof, one that he struggles to reconstruct through memory. The fake speech is therefore as tainted by the narrator's bias as a summary could be, but more deceptively so. As Sartre commented on the pandemic artificiality in Genet's literary corpus in his brief introduction to *A Thief's Journal*, "behind the first-degree myths—The Thief, Murder, the Beggar, the Homosexual—we discover the reflective myths: the Poet, the Saint, the Double, Art. Nothing but myths, then; a Genet with a Genet stuffing" (6). Like the "Genet" presented by the author, in the case of the Mettray official's speech we find neither the speech itself nor a summary of it but rather a counterfeited version, a fake, a fiction.

Another example of such a counterfeit is found in one of the Fontevrault segments of the story, when the narrator claims to interpolate the text of what is supposedly a letter he received from his lover Bulkaen early in their romance. The narrator introduces the letter by stating, "Here is the second, which I managed to preserve" (64; 89). Use of the term "preserve" emphasizes the alleged authenticity of the document to which readers are privy. Closer examination of the narrator's treatment of his lover's missive reveals, however, that although the discourse surrounding the inclusion of the letter points to referentiality, the authenticity of the letter is questionable. At first the narrator claims to be presenting the actual letter to his readers, and the formatting of the letter in the text—it is italicized and separated from the main body of the narrative—appears to bolster the narrator's contention.[24] The main objective of the missive—addressed "Dear Jean" in classic epistolary fashion—appears to be the smoothing over of a potential misunderstanding between the two friends. Bulkaen begins the letter by praising the letter-writing skill of "Jean" and ends the message by reassuring him that he (Bulkaen) is honest and frank and has no doubts about the authenticity of Jean's friendship. After three short paragraphs, two of which end with ellipses, the letter ends abruptly with no signature or closing formula. While the formal aspects of the letter imply documentation, the commentary following the epistolary text makes it clear that the missive is substantially edited. The narrator comments on Bulkaen's use of parentheses and quotation marks, although there are none in the letter. The narrator also mentions other details in the letter about Bulkaen's activities outside prison as well as his sign-off—"the word 'kiss' with which the note ended" (65; 90)—which are also conspicuously absent. The text that is allegedly the actual letter written by Bulkaen is therefore presented through the filter of the narrator. The ellipses in the letter's first two paragraphs also point to editing on the part of the narrator. Although the missive is initially presented as an authentic document from the narrator's incarceration, closer analysis reveals that Genet keeps his readers at a distance from that alleged piece of reality.

Dramatic reenactments of speeches, letters, and murders are not the only signposts of fictionality in *Miracle de la rose*. Indeed, temporal and spatial ambiguity around the composition of the narrative as a whole also point toward fabrication. The narrator mentions that he composed at least part of his narrative in Fontevrault.[25] As we have seen, independent research has revealed that Genet was never a prisoner at Fontevrault. But one does not need outside confirmation of that fact to suspect something is amiss in the placement of the narrator in that central prison of detention. On the final page of the story, the notation "La Santé. Prison des Tourelles, 1943" informs the reader where and when the narrative was supposedly written or finished. The spatial specification is the only mention of a possibility that the narrative was composed outside Fontevrault, in spite of the fact that the narrator never evokes his exit from that prison. Indeed, in the final paragraph of the text he is apparently still in Fontevrault and states that "if" he gets out he will someday be able to sift through memories and old newspapers about his late companions, Harcamone and Bulkaen (279; 376). The 1943 date poses a problem as well. Early in the story the narrator explains where he worked in the prison: "After assigning me to a dormitory, Number 5, they assigned me to the workshop where camouflage nets were being made for the German army which was then occupying France" (11; 18). "Then" signifies that at the time of the writing the Germans were no longer occupying France, which they were in fact doing in 1943. That detail seems to reveal that at least part of the narrative was composed after the Nazi defeat, which is a distinct possibility, given the fact that it was published in 1946.[26] The temporal inconsistency highlights, if not the fictionality of the narrative, at least the hollow nature of its referentiality. Further putting into question the novel's alleged date of completion is a photograph showing the cover of a notebook in which Genet wrote *Miracle*. Written on the cover, an image of which is included in Jeremy Reed's *Jean Genet: Born to Lose*, is the following: "Miracle de la rose, IIe partie [Part II], 1943–44" (Reed 66). A 1944 completion date is far more plausible given the indications in the novel about the circumstances surrounding the end of the Nazi occupation of France. However, Genet chose the fictitious (or, at best, inaccurate) 1943 date for the published version of his novel.[27]

Mettray and Fontevrault, according to "Genet"

As is the case with the other prison novels examined in this study, *Miracle de la rose* contains a curious mixture of fiction and nonfiction, of signposts of fictionality and documentary realism. Genet bolsters the documentary aspects of his novel not only by imitating confessional autobiographical conventions but also by including much information about the penal institutions he portrays in his narrative. The novel's Mettray sections depict—in many cases, accurately—power relations among inmates as well as their linguistic tendencies, the horrific living conditions they endure, the bureaucratic processes that rule their routines, and their status in the institution's rigid organizational apparatus. And even though he was never a prisoner in Fontevrault, Genet manages to insert similar details regarding that central prison of detention into *Miracle*. Indeed, the information the narrator provides about Fontevrault heightens the documentary effect of the novel in much the same way as the information he furnishes about Mettray. Much like Victor Serge, Genet emphasizes the unpleasant, the unsanitary, the cruel, and the unusual aspects of the carceral environment. However, as we will see, Genet does not reject that universe as a manifestation of a vicious society whose destruction would be a welcome event, as does Serge. Quite the contrary, Genet embraces his prisons and all that is untoward about incarceration as a means of accentuating his role as a social outcast, a position he took on throughout his career as a writer and political activist. The testimonial and documentary aspects of the text bolster Genet's narrative authority, rendering his position as an outcast all the more potent and his embrace of prison all the more scandalous.

Mettray officially opened on 22 January 1840, and the institution survived—with varying degrees of success, failure, praise and controversy—for nearly a century.[28] The colony was a product of the period of great prison reform in France during the first half of the nineteenth century. That era of philanthropic reform was distinguished by a desire not only to monitor and punish prisoners but also to reinsert them into society after having transformed them into responsible citizens and disciplined, productive workers. This was especially true in the case of Mettray, whose founders sought to rehabilitate the troubled youth that came under their purview (Gaillac 80). The inspiration for Mettray came from a source across French borders. Mettray's founder, Frédéric Demetz, was inspired in large part by a German institution called the Rauhe Haus, whose pedagogical methods were based in agriculture, horticulture, and domestic labor. The population of young prisoners at Mettray, like that of its German predecessor, was separated into "families." "Colonists" were required to learn agricultural and domestic skills as part of their rehabilitation. Located in the Touraine region on land donated by Viscount Brétignières de Courteilles, Mettray had no walls, gates, or armed guards to keep the inmates within the confines of the institution's grounds (Gaillac 23, 81). That open architecture corresponded to a slogan promoted by its founders: "Show trust in order to inspire it" (Gaillac 85).

Mettray received much praise in the years after its opening and was a source of pride in France, for the endeavor was seen as an expression of republican values.[29] Alphonse de Lamartine, in his role as president of the provisional government of the Second Republic, stated in a speech praising Demetz that the French *patrie* (fatherland) had a very favorable view of the founder's devotion to his cause and that to fear for its future would be an "outrage to the Republic" (Gaillac 23). Mettray and other institutions like it were seen as a possible antidote to the corrupting influences of urbanization and industrialization.[30] Philanthropist Charles Lucas, the most influential penal reformer of the era, even saw the colonies as a means of strengthening the French nation as a whole by contributing to a strong agricultural labor force. The idealism that motivated the creation of the colonies was distilled in an aphorism describing Lucas's point of view: "Save the colonist through the earth and the earth through the colonist" (Gaillac 71–72).

Mettray and other agricultural colonies like it were not without their critics, however, who labeled the institutions not only too expensive but also fundamentally impracticable because of the inmates' resistance to disciplinary methods and their basic aversion to the agricultural environments.[31] Many colonies failed in the second half of the nineteenth century, and those that survived beyond the turn of the century were criticized all the more forcefully in the 1920s and 1930s for failing to fulfill the ambitious and noble missions of their founders. Critics used the term *bagnes d'enfants* (penal colonies for children) to describe and deride the institutions, evoking the notorious and feared tropical penal colonies, which, at that time, were used for forced labor and deportation of hardened recidivists. Alexis Danan, a prominent journalist and a leader of newspaper campaigns for the abolition of the agricultural colonies, compiled a substantial amount of information on Mettray. Danan cited the deaths of children and widespread graft as evidence of the colony's failure, findings that led the government to investigate Mettray. State reports on conditions in the colony were far from flattering and cited serious problems such as drunken, brutal, and incompetent guards. Because of those investigations, the ministries of justice and public health removed all the children for whom they were responsible from Mettray and closed the colony permanently in 1939 (Gaillac 285, 289–90, 320).

Miracle de la rose was published during an era in which the reading public was more likely to be familiar with the cruelties of the agricultural colonies than with their founders' benign and idealistic goals.[32] I would even argue that Genet counts upon the colonies' reputation as hellish places, for his nostalgia for Mettray—which his narrator refers to provocatively as a *bagne d'enfants*—accentuates the position of the narrator-author figure as a pariah. Indeed, the very telling of the narrator's experience in Mettray and Fontevrault is based upon a supposed fundamental separation between himself and his imagined readership. That distance is largely predicated upon what the narrator perceives as a sociocultural rift between criminals, outcasts, and prisoners on the one hand and his imagined bourgeois readers on the other hand. The narrator embraces his role as a denizen of an underworld in which crime is glorified and the victims of capital punishment, like Harcamone, are sanctified. At the same time, the narrator rejects and mocks institutions and concepts that he perceives as central to the bourgeois value system, such as patriotism and religion.[33]

In *Saint Genet*, Sartre repeatedly refers to Genet as the "Other" of mainstream society and writes that, as a social outcast, Genet was imbued with an understanding of bourgeois values at an early age. "Work, family, country, honesty, property. such is his conception of the Good," writes Sartre. "It is graven forever upon his heart. Later on, despite the fact that he steals, begs, lies, prostitutes himself, it will not change. The local priest says that his is a religious nature" (6; 14). In the case of *Miracle de la rose*, his understanding of the value system of the world outside the prison walls is essential to his role as the outcast social critic. As Sartre notes, "the world must remain sacred so that his acts all retain an aspect of the sacrilegious" (165; 189). Although the bourgeois readers for whom the story is composed are not part of the narrator's criminal universe, they make frequent appearances in the narrative (as "you"); and when they are not overtly invoked, their presence is implicit in the narrative's discourse. As we will see, Genet uses that imagined readership—which, at bottom, is a fictional construction—to enhance the documentary effect of *Miracle*. The narrator defines inmate jargon, explains the nature of the prisoners' activities, and delineates basic details about daily life in prison for the benefit of his readers, who, as law-abiding citizens, are allegedly ignorant of the functioning of the prison.

For all the artfulness, lyricism, and complexity of *Miracle de la rose*, Genet provides a straightforward code for interpreting the ideological implications of his novel in a brief text titled "L'enfant criminel" (The Criminal Child, 1949). An essay on young criminals and their treatment in the justice system,

"L'enfant criminel" was originally written to be read aloud by Genet on French radio following a question-and-answer session (an "interrogation" conducted by Genet himself) with a judge, a prison warden, and a government psychiatrist. Genet, the outcast par excellence, was not only snubbed by his would-be guests but was even refused access to the airwaves. That his grandiose plans for the radio failed is no great surprise, given the controversial manner in which he treats his subject. Indeed, Genet does not prove to be a responsible advocate for the betterment of children's lives, as one might expect in the years following Mettray's scandal-provoked closure. Quite the contrary, he praises the cruelties endured by, and even cultivated by, the children in the colonies.

The stated goal of his radio address was very similar to what Genet accomplishes in *Miracle de la rose*: "I had wanted to make the voice of the criminal heard. And not his complaint, but his song of glory" ("L'enfant criminel" 379). Much as he does in *Miracle*, Genet establishes a distance between himself and his listeners, whom he sees as bourgeois consumers of art. That distance is crafted through an embrace of evil which he defines as social rebellion, or "the will, the audacity to pursue a destiny contrary to all rules" (383). Genet states that only evil can truly elicit his enthusiasm as a writer, and he asserts that he speaks to his audience as both a poet and an enemy (which he sees as being one and the same). His readers are, as they are in *Miracle*, cast in the role of "good" ("braves" [382]) and "honest people" ("honnêtes gens" [388]). Those "good" people are put on the defensive by Genet, as he compares processes in their juvenile justice system to the crimes of Hitler.[34] In spite of (or perhaps more accurately *because* of) such comparisons, however, Genet embraces conditions in the colonies, and he claims to view child criminals not as victims of society in need of rehabilitation but rather as courageous rebels inspired by romantic sentiments. For him, the children actually desire harsh punishments, because stringent discipline reminds them of their success as criminals and rebels. Genet, the poet-enemy, therefore criticizes efforts to save the children, especially the feeble attempts to mollify their experience in the colonies by using ridiculous euphemisms to describe the institutions and their staff (e.g., employing the term *surveillant* (watcher) instead of *gardien* (guard) [384]). True to his inverted vision of both crime and punishment, Genet laments the closure of Mettray, writing, "Mettray, during my youth, was among the most prestigious names: after succumbing to the blows of a generous idiot, Mettray has disappeared" (382).

Genet's discourse about the treatment of juvenile criminality in a bourgeois context in "L'enfant criminel" finds strong parallels in *Miracle de la rose*. Similar to the observations Genet makes in "L'enfant criminel," the narrator of *Miracle* decries as "idiotic vandals" the journalists who sought closure of the colony (163; 222).[35] Furthermore, despite his repeated use of the term *bagne d'enfants* (which evokes negative press reports and horrific treatment of young prisoners), the narrator insists upon Mettray's sumptuousness and writes that it was located in "the fairest spot of fairest Touraine" (13; 20). "Genet" idealizes his Proustian quest for the lost world of his childhood even if that world may appear to his bourgeois readers to be utterly unworthy of mourning. For example, even the memory of ordinary citizens setting traps in the countryside for escaped colonists provokes, "within my affliction, a greater affliction, fills me with frightful gloom at the thought that this childhood world is dead" (14; 21). And in spite of descriptions of the guards as "vile brutes" who were forced to live in poverty, the narrator states that they were "necessary to the beauty of my sunken life" (95; 130). Basic physical and sanitary facilities at Mettray were also lacking, a characteristic that renders the colony all the more endearing to the narrator. "Genet," for example, documents how the colonists had to improvise in the outhouse. "At Mettray, we went to the toilet as follows," he says, describing routines for a readership that he imagines as uninitiated to inmates' habits at Mettray: "the shithouse was in the yard, behind each family dormitory. At noon and at 6 p.m., on our way back from the shops, we would march in line, led by the elder brother, and stop in front of the four urinals. We would leave the line in fours to take a leak or pretend to. At the left were the latrines, which were four or five steps high so that the crap can was on a level with the ground. Each boy stepped from the line and went to one or the other, depending on the need he felt. He would let his belt hang from the door to show that the place was occupied. There was never any paper. For three years I wiped myself with my forefinger, and the wall whitewashed my finger" (163; 222). If that final intimate detail about the narrator's routine is not enough to shock the imagined readership, the narrator then embraces what he experienced: "I love the Colony for having given me such moments" (163; 222).

The narrator of *Miracle* adds an element of the sacred to his nostalgic remembrances of Mettray, taking aim at the religious beliefs of his imagined bourgeois readership. Citing Genesis and the apocryphal book of Enoch, the narrator states that he had considered calling his book *The Children of the Angels*, as he was captivated by stories in which children were given a divine origin. "When I came across these texts," he writes, "it seemed to me there was no better way of painting or depicting the secret realm of the colonists. With a rush of dizziness I seize upon the idea that we are all the youthful descendants, learnèd by birth, of Angels and women" (141; 193). "Genet" imagines the world of Mettray in a way that is quite different from the way the institution was documented by French government officials and journalists. He sees it as a mythical space, isolated from the rest of the world by the colonists' gestures, language, and habits: "We were a land that had been spared by a very ancient cataclysm, a kind of Atlantis which preserved a language that had been taught by the gods themselves" (55–56; 77).

Despite the strong presence of nostalgia, poeticity, and the sacred, *Miracle de la rose* provides a number of details about the daily functioning of Mettray, many of which are documentary in nature. The narrative includes much information concerning the physical structure and organization of the institution, such as the lack of walls around the grounds (110; 151), the separation of the inmate population into families (90; 124), the colony's strong religious influence (107; 146), the participation of the colonists in naval training exercises (55; 76), and dormitories filled with hammocks instead of beds (107; 147).[36] The narrator explains in detail the hierarchies among the prisoners and the distribution of power in the families. He notes that "each family, all of whose members occupied one of the ten cottages on the Big Square, which was covered with lawn and planted with chestnut trees, was called Family A, B, C, D, E, F, G, H, J, or L. Each of the cottages housed about thirty children who were ordered about by a colonist huskier and more vicious than the others. He was picked by the head of the family and was called the 'elder brother.' The elder brother was supervised by the head of the family, who was usually some retired civil servant, a non-commissioned officer, an ex-trooper" (90; 124). Such minute details—especially the narrator's mention of letters of the alphabet to designate families—bolster the documentary effect of the narrative and, by extension, strengthen the authority of the narrator.

"Genet" further demonstrates his knowledge of Mettray as an institution by inserting information about the history of the colony into *Miracle* through a variety of strategies. The founders of Mettray, for instance, are mentioned in the narrator's recollection of the colony's cemetery (the existence of which is itself an accurate detail [Gaillac 81]): "at the end of the cemetery, in two chapels, were the vaults of the founders, Monsieur Demetz and Baron de Courteille, who rested 'among the children they loved so dearly'" (182; 247).[37] The narrator also informs his readers of the founders' intentions through the inclusion of re-enactments of the speeches by "Dudule" (the high-ranking official at Mettray) and the bishop from Tours that he claims to have heard as a youth. In his speech, given to celebrate the bishop's visit to the colony, the Mettray official evokes the founding mission of the colony. Those details in the fictionalized speech closely resemble the goals expressed by nineteenth-century reformers. "We know that your excellency has more than once turned his thoughts—with most paternal kindness—to this institution of re-education and religious and moral regeneration to which we are dedicated," states "Dudule" (152; 208). The official refers to the colonists as "repentant sinners" (153; 208) who honor and respect the presence of the bishop, whom they welcomed in a calm and orderly manner.[38] In his response, the bishop echoes the sentiments, beliefs, and goals of penal reformers like Lucas and Demetz, stating that Mettray's main enterprise is to rehabilitate "wayward children" (153; 209). He also mentions the corrupting influence of urban environments, from which Mettray was meant to isolate the young children: "It is a very deep comfort to me, coming from cities where perverse unrest tries to make men forget God, to enter this oasis of religious calm" (153; 209).

Genet's inclusion of those religious and highly moralistic goals in *Miracle* renders all the more subversive his depiction of the colonists' flouting of Mettray's rules, especially their clandestine sexual activities and nighttime mischief.[39] Genet informs his readers about how inmates lived within the organization, transforming it from an idealistic model of discipline into a perfect space for the children to create their own universe. Mettray, as Genet depicts it, is an environment that does anything but make children conform to the wholesome mold sought by the institutions' founders. Genet does not show any "corrective" effects of his narrator-protagonist's term of detention. Indeed, he accentuates the fact that even the children's most banal leisure activities are in the pursuit of vanity or pleasure, which the narrator deems "practical." "All our activity had practical aims," the narrator notes: "concocting a brilliant polish for our sabots, hunting in the yard for a flint that would fit in a cigarette-lighter" (173; 235). Readers are informed that the inmates expend a great deal of energy secretly collecting objects (their "treasure") to enhance their social status and rank in the society of captives: "During his stay at Mettray, every colonist contrived to amass a treasure. It was made up of what had been obtained by confiscation, fraud, theft, inheritance and transaction" (124; 170).

In "L'enfant criminel," Genet writes that the children themselves add a layer of brutality to the already difficult institutional conditions at the colonies. That brutality is clearly visible in *Miracle de la rose*. For instance, when Divers, who was at Mettray with the narrator, subdues another inmate, Riton, with relentless punches and kicks, the narrator remarks that such behavior is nothing unusual: "No sooner did Riton drop to the ground than Divers went at him again with his feet and fists, in keeping with the inexorable method of Mettray" (126; 172).[40] Beyond mere beatings, power relations among the inmates are complex, and the narrator's sensitivity to the hierarchies and groups among the inmates makes itself apparent in his portrayal of the colonists' rituals. "Genet" claims that he used his knowledge of the inmate hierarchies to his advantage. In one anecdote, "Genet" remembers that soon after his arrival at Mettray, he threw a bowl of soup at the head of his "family" (63–64; 88). That gesture, states the narrator, might have earned him more respect from one group of the colonists. As Gene Plunka remarks in *The Rites of Passage of Jean Genet*, "Each child is physically tested upon arriving by the toughs and big shots at the colony, and his actions immediately determine his status" (79).[41] Not only do they establish sets of cliques, but the colonists follow certain social customs, such as the avoidance of shaking hands, which the narrator interprets and tries to explain to his readers: "It was not customary at Mettray for colonists to shake hands openly. I think that this is to be regarded as a secret agreement on their part to reject whatever recalls civilian life and might make them miss it" (82–83; 113).

At both Mettray and Fontevrault, "Genet" and his fellow inmates aspire toward a clear division between the civil society on the outside and the criminal underworld of the prison. Indeed, while locked in Fontevrault, the narrator laments the fact that the prisons are becoming diluted by populations of "innocents" who find themselves incarcerated simply because of the black-market conditions created by World War II. Their presence makes the prison lose its "hard glitter," and they dilute the image of the pimps, making them seem more like "solid citizens" ("les macs s'embourgeoisent" [112; 153]). "When the prisons were filled with honest people who had been driven from the woods by hunger," he says, "they lost their fine, lordly bearing, but the crashers [les casseurs] remained a haughty aristocracy. The great evil of this war has been its dissolving the hardness of our prisons. The war has locked up so many innocent people that the prisons are merely places of lamentation" (26–27; 38). Such detail about Fontevrault is characteristic of the depiction of that central prison of detention, as it not only accentuates the distance between mainstream society and "Genet" but also claims to provide documentary information about the prison as it existed during the war. As we will see, Genet bolsters the referential implications of his portrayal of Fontevrault by providing other key details about the prison's history and conditions.

The edifice and tourist destination known today as the Centre Culturel de Fontevrault was, from the early twelfth century to the French Revolution, a royal abbey and then served, from the early nineteenth century to 1963, as a penal prison.[42] Converted by Napoleonic decree into a prison barely a quarter century after the seizure of church property during the Revolutionary era, Fontevrault was for a time the second-largest prison in France, holding adult men and women inmates as well as children. In an effort to reduce promiscuity and moral corruption among inmates, the former monastery became a prison for adult male criminals only around the middle of the nineteenth century; children were transferred to special institutions such as Mettray and Saint-Hilaire, and adult female prisoners were transferred to Rennes. As they did with other *maisons centrales* of its era, Fontevrault's planners sought to create an institution distinct from the dark and unhealthy holding cells of the ancien régime. Its architect envisioned a space conducive to security, hygiene, and religious education. Because work was seen as integral to prisoner rehabilitation, Fontevrault had a number of workshops within its walls for a variety of ends, from ironwork to weaving. The workshops also produced clothes and shoes for the army and even for the prison's own guards. Fontevrault was designed to hold between a thousand and twelve hundred prisoners, and its population wavered between about a thousand and eighteen hundred inmates throughout its history. In 1943, when "Genet" claimed to be incarcerated in Fontevrault with two thousand other inmates (63; 86), the prison actually held twelve hundred prisoners.[43] In spite of enduring years of pillaging by locals for raw materials immediately after the Revolution, not to mention its radical transformation into an industrial prison, Fontevrault retained evidence of its royal origins in the form of recumbent statues (*gisants*) representing Henry II Plantagenet, Richard I the Lion-Heart, Eleanor of Aquitaine, and Isabelle d'Angoulême, all of whom are buried at the site (Chédaille 3–5, 25–26).

As if to emphasize the authenticity of his account, Genet inserts accurate historical detail about Fontevrault very early in the narrative. Upon his entry into the *maison centrale* the narrator encounters a surly guard who expresses his power by mocking Genet's surname, stating, "What if I feel like saying Plantagenet? Do you mind?" (9; 15). The narrator, who initially does not understand the joke, offers no response, a show of ignorance that the guard does not seem to appreciate: "The guard gave me a dirty look. Perhaps he despised me for not knowing that the Plantagenets were buried in Fontevrault" (9–10; 15). Historical references go beyond the mentioning of the Plantagenet dynasty. Genet also draws parallels between the unisex prison milieu and the population of the old monastery at Fontevrault: "There are things one could say about destinies, but note the strangeness of that of monasteries and abbeys: jails and preferably state prisons! Fontevrault, Clairvaux, Poissy! . . . It was God's will that these places shelter communities of only one sex" (62; 86). The forced labor, the "homespun" (*bure*) the prisoners are forced to wear (62; 86), and the rule of mandatory silence represent further parallels between the prison populations and the monastic existence of Fontevrault abbey's former religious denizens.[44] Genet fully consummates the link between the origins of Fontevrault and its current state as a prison through the narrator's aspirations toward sainthood and his worship of his "God," Harcamone.[45] The link between the prison and the sacred, as we have seen, allows Genet to accentuate the separation between his fictional alter ego and his audience.

As is the case with the Mettray portions of *Miracle*, the distance crafted by the narrator between himself and his imagined readers serves a practical purpose related to the construction of a documentary prison narrative. Genet's readers are constructed such that they are ignorant of the rites and rituals of prison society and are unfamiliar with even its most basic facts and phenomena. The narrator often describes and elucidates, therefore, common and everyday details of prison life in Fontevrault. For example, while describing clothes the prisoners are forced to wear, he notes that "The underpants were white and the letters A.P., which stand for *administration pénitentiaire*, were stamped on them in thick ink. The undershirt was made of homespun . . . and had a small pocket on the right side. The coarse linen shirt was collarless. The sleeves had no cuffs. Nor buttons either. There were rust spots on the shirt which I feared were shit-stains. It was stamped A.P. We changed shirts every two weeks" (12; 19). Genet also elaborates on the physical aspects of his surroundings. For example, when the narrator tells the story of his punishment for loitering too often around Harcamone's cell, he interrupts his flow of ideas simply to provide a few documentary details: "I walked by the murderer's cell too often, and one day I was caught. Here are a few details: The carpentry shop and the shops where the camouflage nets and iron beds are made are in a court in the north part of the former abbey. They are one storey buildings. The dormitories are on the first and second floors of the left wing, which is supported by the wall of the former chapter-house. The infirmary is on the ground floor" (24; 35). While such details could be eliminated from the passage without hamstringing the reader's comprehension of the narrative (rendering them, in a certain sense, useless), they reinforce the cultural distinctions between the intra-and extramural societies and enhance the narrative's documentary effect.

Although "Genet" does not reach the same level of sociological precision as Victor Serge's narrator, *Miracle de la rose* furnishes a great deal of factual information about the functioning of the penal administration as well as carceral conditions and relations. As is the case with the portrayal of Mettray, in spite of the veneer of the sacred that Genet places over his depiction of Fontevrault, many of the details about life in the *maison centrale* are realistic and accurate. Indeed, much of the information the narrator provides is common to the operation of real prisons and to the behavior of prisoners. Those details include the measuring of each prisoner upon entry (169; 230); a routine dictated by a precise schedule; punishment by restriction of meals, solitary confinement, and forced marching in the disciplinary cell (37; 52); the use of prisoners as laborers in a variety of workshops (11; 18); graffiti on the walls of the cells (31; 42); tattooing (144; 196); the existence of specific types of prison jargon (59; 82);[46] the use of special cells illuminated day and night for the condemned (91; 124); and prisoners' obsession with time (51; 71). The narrator even reports being forced to salute the guards (11; 17), which inmates at Fontevrault were in fact required to do.[47] Again, the inclusion of such details often means very little to the progression of the narrative; they are woven into the novel to heighten the illusion of referentiality and documentation.

Outcast Author—Alienated Audience

The distance articulated between the incarcerated narrator and his imagined readers finds a parallel in the relationship cultivated by Jean Genet—the author—between himself and his audience. Indeed, by rendering the generic status of his text ambiguous, Genet cultivates a rift between himself and the real literary public similar to the one he crafts between his narrator and his caricature of bourgeois society in "L'enfant criminel" and *Miracle de la rose*. As Barrett J. Mandel writes in his essay on autobiography, "A reader who at first mistakes fiction for autobiography or vice versa feels cheated. One wants to know whether the book is one or the other: it makes a difference in terms of how the book is to be read" (53). Genet avoids ensuring the correct generic reception of *Miracle*, thereby leaving ample opportunity for readers to feel "cheated" and at a distance from the truth. In spite of its strong documentary effect and testimonial impulse, the text, as we have seen, is filled with fiction about the narrator-author and his prison experiences. Even the author's imaginary religious, moralistic, law-abiding and patriotic audience is a fictional construction. Although it bears many of the markers of testimonial and autobiographical literature, *Miracle* is hardly a forthright account of time the author spent while incarcerated.

To be sure, Genet, like most other prison writers, depicts the horrors of life behind bars. But unlike the vast majority of writers who have documented their hellish experiences with incarceration, from Fyodor Dostoyevsky to Rubin "Hurricane" Carter, Genet chooses to adopt that cruel and violent carceral universe as his own sacred realm. *Miracle de la rose* is not a text that constitutes a quest for social justice, as do the works of Victor Serge, Victor Hugo, and the writings of any number of other novelists, philanthropists, and public figures who have testified to the atrocities they witnessed in prison with the specific goal of ridding the world of them. Rather, Genet is a prisoner-turned-writer who embraces the role of pariah bestowed upon him by society in order to flout the values—religious, patriotic, moral—of that very same society. Genet's primary target is not what is manifestly base in that social order (slovenly prison guards, unsanitary prisons) but rather what is considered sacred or untouchable (God, the state). In his adherence to his position as an outcast, "Genet," the character and public persona, ultimately highlights the failure of the state's punitive mechanisms to reform prisoners. Although he was incarcerated for his crimes, the penal system failed to render that notorious narrator-author either penitent or "corrected."

Touted by some as a "female Genet," Albertine Sarrazin tells the story of a quasi-autobiographical avatar in her 1965 novel

La cavale (*The Runaway*).[48] Like her fellow outcast and predecessor, she melds autobiography and fiction to depict the vicissitudes of prison life. However, while Genet renders sacred the
prison and exults in his status as a prisoner and pariah, Sarrazin
paints a realistic portrait the carceral environment, emphasizing the debilitating aspects of incarceration and its deleterious
effects on her narrator-protagonist, Anick Damien.

[THREE] A RECIDIVIST'S TALE

On 3 December 1962, the woman who later became known to the public as Albertine Sarrazin wrote in her journal that the library at Versailles prison was at long last giving her "decent books" (*Passe* 184). Interestingly enough, her first experience as a reader since the library's sudden evolution in taste involved "the '61 Goncourt winner by Jean Cau," a prison novel titled *La pitié de Dieu* (*Mercy of God*) based on Sartrian existential philosophy. A complex and tangled narrative, Cau's novel depicts the experience of four longtime prisoners and their abusive treatment of a new arrival, whom they eventually drive to suicide. Once a secretary of Jean-Paul Sartre, Cau bases the prisoners' situation on the "Hell" endured by the three main characters in his mentor's play *Huis clos* (*No Exit*). Sarrazin makes her only other comment on the novel the following day, suggesting that she finished the three-hundred-page book in a twenty-four-hour period. Her reaction to the text is cryptic, which is understandable considering the fact that the then-unknown and unpublished Sarrazin was writing her journal only to be read by herself and perhaps later by her husband, Julien Sarrazin. The young prisoner hints that *La pitié de Dieu* fails to fill a specific void she perceives in literature: "4 lifers in a dream cell. But the problem still isn't addressed. . . . A truth *must* be written. Will it be me? Ah, if they only gave me the time!!" (*Passe* 184).

Given its pronounced autobiographical slant and the vast amount of detail about the carceral universe it provides, *La cavale*—the novel Sarrazin worked on during that particular sentence in Versailles prison—was in all likelihood her attempt at a "truth."[1] Although both her novel and Cau's text deal exclusively with life behind bars, *La cavale* and *La pitié de Dieu* diverge widely in their treatment and depiction of that life. Sarrazin's text contains much realistic and accurate information about conditions and relations in women's prisons; moreover, its documentary value is enhanced because it is based largely on the author's own extensive experience with incarceration. Cau's text, in contrast, is better described as a rehashing of Sartre's treatment of the human condition than as a realistic depiction of prison life. As we will see, *La cavale*, the focal point of this chapter, was an ambitious attempt at delineating the characteristics of life in women's prisons. Focusing on the plight of narrator-protagonist Anick Damien, the novel stages a variety of circumstances that underscore the difficulties faced by female prisoners, illustrating how the prison and legal system gradually pacify and debilitate even the most independently minded, defiant, and rebellious inmates.

Sarrazin wrote prolifically while in prison. As it exists today, *La cavale* is more than five hundred pages long, and the original version is said to have been about a third longer.[2] Not only did Sarrazin produce *La cavale* during her various stints in prison, but a personal journal was her constant companion in her cell, and she composed vast quantities of letters to her husband both openly and clandestinely. So accustomed was Sarrazin to writing in an enclosed and restricted environment that when she had finally served her last sentence and could write in a comfortable place she could call home, she had Julien construct a "cell" in their house so she could work in familiar conditions.[3] After her release from Versailles prison, Sarrazin continued to rework *La cavale* and began her second novel, *L'astragale* (*Astragal*), which is a fictionalized telling of her real-life escape from prison and her life on the lam. She completed a portion of *L'astragale* during a subsequent prison sentence in 1964. Her third novel, *La traversière*, written after her final prison sentence came to an end, constituted her greatest challenge as a writer.[4] Feeling the pressure brought on by the remarkable and immediate success of her first two novels, Sarrazin had hoped to write a text in the third person that, unlike her first two works, was not based entirely upon her personal experience. To the dismay of the young author, that first version of *La traversière* was rejected by her publisher, Jean-Jacques Pauvert. Josane Duranteau, Sarrazin's biographer and fervent admirer, writes: "The young woman, who had just recently been overjoyed by so much glory, weathered a discouraging and anxiety-provoking blow for the future: had she lost the trust of her publisher? Did he think her literary talent had been exhausted? In prison, she had written for a single judge and critic: herself. What a feeling of helplessness the blank pages brought on, since it was now necessary to please others than herself" (197). Sarrazin eventually found creative productivity and solace in the familiar territory of first-person narration in the final version of *La traversière*. And, as in her first two works, she relies heavily on her personal experience for that text's story line.

Sarrazin's meteoric rise from solitary confinement to literary stardom is never more apparent than in her correspondence from late 1964 to the middle of 1967, which is collected in a single volume titled *Lettres de la vie littéraire* (Letters from Literary Life).[5] Addressed primarily to her publisher, her husband, and Christiane Gogois-Myquel (a prison psychiatrist whom Sarrazin refers to as her "one-sixteenth of a Mom," and to

whom she dedicates *La cavale*), those letters document Sarrazin's transformation from a recovering ex-prisoner and aspiring
writer into a full-blown media phenomenon. The early letters
reveal a Sarrazin consumed with the machinations of rework-
ing her books into publishable form. After the publication of *La
cavale* and *L'astragale*, the young writer suddenly finds herself
embroiled in the daily reality of interacting with the media and
dealing with the unfamiliar circumstances brought on by her
newfound fame. Sarrazin's transformation is crystallized in a
remarkable letter she sent to the French minister of the interior
in September 1965 in which she asks for a suspension of her
"interdiction de séjour," a court injunction imposed when she
was released from prison that forbade her from visiting Paris.
The court order threatened to prevent her from working with
her publisher on the final version of her texts, not to mention
the promotion of her books. She writes:

> *Mr. Minister,*
>
> Please allow me to appeal to your kindness: you, more
> than anyone, are certainly able to assess fully the motive
> behind my request.
>
> As a result of serious errors in my youth, I endured
> many long years of imprisonment; I put those years to good
> use, I worked very hard to rehabilitate myself, I took exams
> (the baccalaureate, with honors), I wrote two books. . . .
>
> My editors have asked me to come to Paris to attend
> the signing session organized by their press services for the
> launching of my two books and to finalize several other
> projects.
>
> And yet, I am restrained by an *interdiction de séjour*,
> which is valid until October 1968.
>
> I am making an appeal to your kindness to suspend that
> ban for a few weeks to allow me to travel to and remain in
> Paris. (*Vie littéraire* 97–98)

Included in her letter is also a request for Julien's court-ordered interdiction to be lifted. As the letter immediately following the above missive indicates, Sarrazin's request regarding her own court order was successful. Her husband, on the other hand, was unable to make the trip. Indeed, Sarrazin's first letter from Paris is to her "beloved little hero," informing him that her stay in the French capital would last longer than expected.

It was during that period that the French news media embraced Sarrazin. The young author had interviews in mainstream magazines and with news outlets on both radio and television. Her media-friendly face and her gift for appearing accessible in public contexts contributed to her fame. Her publishers were obviously well aware of the magnetic attraction created by her persona, as pictures of her face dominate the covers of the Poche editions of *L'astragale*, *La cavale*, *La traversière*, and her *Lettres et poèmes* (1967). Poche, moreover, plays on the Western mythology of the prison writer by including photographic reproductions of her handwritten scrawl—ostensibly jotted down behind bars—on the back cover of *La cavale*. Sarrazin's success even went beyond print media: she was recorded on vinyl reading her brief text "Voyage en Tunisie," and a film based on *L'astragale* (directed by Guy Casaril) hit the silver screen in 1968. Sarrazin—the prisoner turned writer turned media darling—was launched.

A Recidivist's Trilogy

The "Trilogie de *La cavale*" places Sarrazin's protagonist in the various situations and contexts that can arise from crime, imprisonment, recidivism, prison escapes, and rehabilitation. In *L'astragale* we see a younger Anick escape from prison and lead an existence in the underground that involves prostitution and theft. *L'astragale* provides an interesting perspective on the lives and interactions of former inmates. Whereas *La cavale* minimizes—even dismisses—the importance of solidarity among prisoners, *L'astragale* shows that ex-prisoners are able to form a special bond due to their common experiences. In one of her first interactions with Julien, Anick notes that "long before he said anything, I had recognized Julien. There are certain signs imperceptible to people who haven't done time: a way of talking without moving the lips while the eyes, to throw you off, express indifference or the opposite thing; the cigarette held in the crook of the palm, the waiting for night to act or just to talk, after the uneasy silence of the day" (23; 22). Anick's insights into the behavioral patterns of prisoners help her establish a strong attachment to Julien, who serves as her protector for a good portion of the time she spends running from the law. Anick's plight as an escaped convict enables Sarrazin to play on the notion that life on the outside can be as much of a prison as life on the inside. The protagonist's movements are restricted; she is paranoid and hyperaware of what transpires around her in otherwise normal everyday situations; and she is forced to learn how to live in a new and unfamiliar environment, just as inmates must adapt to life in prison. Even though she is far removed from the carceral milieu, Anick remains trapped by old habits and modes of thought developed during her prison sentences. When in the hospital to have surgery on a bone broken during her prison escape, for example, she finds herself slipping into behavioral patterns she acquired in prison. She notes that her response to a nurse's command to get undressed is a bit too automatic: "Prison still surrounded me: I found it in my reflexes, the jumpiness, the stealth and the submissiveness of my reactions. You can't wash away overnight several years of clockwork routine and constant dissembling of self" (46; 41). The novel ends with Anick's recapture, but her return to prison is not depicted.

In *La traversière*, Sarrazin's protagonist gains her first impressions of life on the outside as a reformed criminal. Indeed,

in that novel the author explores the difficult process of reintegration into mainstream society. The outside world seems
unfamiliar and challenging, and she—like the protagonist of
L'astragale—feels that her release is tantamount to a rebirth.
The simplest of gestures and tasks remind her of the culture
shock with which she must cope. For example, on her first evening out (during which she admits to have drunk far too much
alcohol in celebration), she evokes the lack of control prisoners have over their own schedules: upon seeing what time it is,
she notes that she had long ago forgotten the gesture of moving her eyes towards her watch (43). Furthermore, the narrator-protagonist comments that she even feels alien in cities that
should feel familiar, because of the time she spent in those cities'
prisons. She offers the perspective only a recidivist can have on
city space: "For me, many cities represent nothing more than
the imprisonments that I've endured and, although I know the
insides of some of their buildings by heart, I feel like I'm in foreign territory" (53–54). In spite of her feelings of alienation,
Sarrazin's fictional alter ego does make an honest attempt at social reintegration and rehabilitation in La traversière. In accordance with the rules of the prison administration, she finds a job
(stocking shelves in a retail store), but notes that her past thefts
had brought in a great deal more money than her honest labor.
She continues to find herself tempted by crime, and is even arrested at one point for petty theft from her workplace, a transgression that earns her a six-month sentence in prison (which
is later reduced to two months by appeal). The book ends with
the young woman embarked on her career as a writer.

   La cavale represents Sarrazin's attempt to examine the plight
of her alter ego as she slowly meanders through the French
judicial system, imprisoned all the while. Although the novel
was the first Sarrazin wrote, its events transpire between those
portrayed in L'astragale and La traversière. The story begins
just after Anick Damien has been arrested and transported to

prison. It then depicts the narrator-protagonist's experience in three different prisons, none of which are named: the first is a dormitory-style jail in which the narrator must share living and working space with several other women; the second is a departmental jail where Anick must patiently await her sentencing for months in yet another communal cell (although, for a time, she has the space entirely to herself); finally, the third prison is an individual-cell institution, "the real thing" (338; 358), where the protagonist spends a great deal of time working and reflecting in solitude.

La cavale portrays a total of about twenty months of Anick's struggle with the prison and legal system.[6] Not long after she is locked up, the protagonist, who is restless and fiercely independent, resolves to revolt against the system and escape from prison. Anick's primary motivation to escape is to live in freedom with Zizi, her lover and partner in crime, who has also been incarcerated (the couple was arrested for burglary). As Anick and Zizi pass through the various stages of interrogations, appeals, and sentencings, their paths frequently cross, both in court and while being transported to and from court appearances and prisons. For a time they are held in the same prison, although in sections that are segregated by sex. As a result of their frequent meetings and their proximity, the two are able to communicate regularly by smuggling notes to each other through a variety of secretive and creative means.

An older and more seasoned prisoner than Anick, Zizi reluctantly entertains his lover's escape fantasy, and they both attempt to concoct a variety of scenarios that would result in their instantaneous freedom. Alas, they have little success. Indeed, in spite of their frequent clandestine communications and their intimate knowledge of the prisons in which they are detained, the couple makes no progress in building even the initial groundwork of an escape attempt. By the end of the novel, after nearly two years in prison, Anick finds that her resolve to escape has been gradually worn down by the fatigue, routine, torpor, and hopelessness of incarceration. The novel comes to a close as she dries her own tears in solitude in her cell, with little to look forward to other than the passage of time and, perhaps, the gifts she might receive after having spent yet another New Year's Day behind bars.

Although the two main characters of *La cavale* regularly attempt to undermine the authority and the rules and regulations of the prison, Sarrazin's novel is, at first glance, a strikingly apolitical text. The rebellious behavior of the inmates in their day-to-day lives—smuggling letters to each other, trying to make keys to open cell doors, and so on—does not constitute the same type of political mobilization that is depicted, for instance, in Serge's *Les hommes dans la prison*. Indeed, rather than focusing on broad sociopolitical issues, the novel concentrates on the banalities of everyday prison life. That is not to say, however, that *La cavale* presents its readers with a vision of an innocuous prison experience: it is through the very depiction of daily life in jail that Sarrazin presents a critique of the treatment of prisoners and of the appalling conditions in which they must endure their sentences. Furthermore, although Anick seems to weather the difficulties of incarceration fairly well for most of the novel, it is not until the end of the story that readers grasp the extent to which the prison has subdued Sarrazin's protagonist. Indeed, rather than rehabilitate its inmates and prepare them to return to mainstream society on the outside, the prison system, as Sarrazin depicts it, gradually transforms inmates, even the rebellious and feisty Anick, into passive and anonymous creatures.

Text and Paratext

Like the other novels examined in this study, *La cavale* straddles the line between fiction and autobiography. The contract between text and reader is blurred due to a variety of textual and paratextual markers. On the one hand, those markers encourage autobiographical interpretation of *La cavale*, leaving the reader with the impression that the experience depicted therein is based in actuality. That apparent basis renders the text more compelling from a dramatic standpoint and also strengthens the author's critique of the prison system. Central to critical and public interest in Sarrazin's text is the fact that author seems to have lived through the prolonged, difficult, and, in the end, debilitating experiences portrayed in her novel. On the other hand, the fictional elements of the story—its basic plotline and the author's free use of invented material—facilitate the description of carceral space, living conditions, and bureaucratic processes. At first glance, the plot of *La cavale* seems to be more elaborate than the story lines of both *Les hommes dans la prison* and *Miracle de la rose*. The subject matter of Sarrazin's novel involves the various escape plans concocted by Zizi and Anick as they slowly move through the judicial system's various stages of sentencing. Furthermore, much narrative energy is spent describing their love story, which is the primary motive behind Anick's desire to flee prison. However, in the final analysis, the plot of *La cavale* is secondary to its depiction of prison life, especially since the couple's escape plans lead them exactly nowhere at the end of the book's five hundred pages. Indeed, the story line of *La cavale* exists in the service of precise portrayal of the spaces in which the protagonist is held and the rules that govern her existence in prison. Readers also get a sense of the painfully slow legal process the protagonist faces before she is even sentenced, an event that occurs more than a year after her arrest (and more than four hundred pages of text).

Paratextual markers are particularly interesting in the case of *La cavale*, especially when compared to information found in the author's correspondence, biographies, and personal diaries. The text is Sarrazin's first completed and most highly acclaimed novel (it was awarded the Quatre-Jurys prize).[7] According to the date found on the last page of the novel, it was written between April 1961 and June 1962, but from information in the author's correspondence it is clear that Sarrazin continued to rework her text well beyond 1962. Those dates, it seems, were almost chosen at random. In a 22 September 1965 letter to Jean-Pierre Castelnau, the representative of the Jean-Jacques Pauvert publishing house, Sarrazin writes: "I no longer remember what we agreed on, and I didn't make note of it anywhere. But since you seem to be in the same position, let's re-invent: I propose: April '61–June '62" (*Vie littéraire* 90). The dates of composition are not, therefore, as forthright as they seem. As we will see, the remainder of the text's paratextual information appears, at first glance, as clear as the alleged dates of the novel's composition. However, close examination of that information reveals nuances that should be taken into consideration when interpreting and classifying Sarrazin's text.

Much of the paratextual information in various editions of *La cavale* encourages interpreting it as a work of fiction. The Poche edition of *La cavale* bears the subtitle *Roman* (novel), and the text is included in the "*Romans*" section of Pauvert's 1967 volume of her *Romans, lettres et poèmes*. Furthermore, the fact that the author and narrator-protagonist have different names (Albertine Sarrazin and Anick Damien) encourages a nonreferential interpretation of the text. Indeed, lack of nominal identity between author and narrator establishes a distance between the two entities, promoting a fictional interpretation of the text rather than an autobiographical reading. The contract between text and reader in *La cavale* differs, therefore, from the contract established by a text in which the protagonist and the author have the same name (e.g., *Miracle de la rose*). For its part, *La cavale* seems to invite a nonreferential reading, an interpretation that appears to be bolstered by the text's structure: the text itself is separated into three parts, taking on the structure of the realist novel.

However, in spite of what seem to be clear paratextual and structural markers that encourage nonreferential interpretations of *La cavale*, such readings are contrary to the author's preferred interpretation of her text. Indeed, Sarrazin herself appeared to be in favor of an autobiographical reading of the prison drama. In her biography of Sarrazin—part of which is addressed to the deceased writer—Duranteau writes: "In contrast with most novelists that I know—you did not yourself claim any distance between your spokesperson and yourself. 'I am Anick,' you said calmly" (11). Sarrazin's publishers seem to have been aware of the interpretative quandary posed by the author's intentions and the lack of nominal identity between Albertine and Anick. Therefore, in order to compensate for that difference in names, the Poche edition of *La cavale* includes a brief description of the novel, underlining an explicit link between narrator and author: "Anick the narrator is the author personified and this episode takes place during a crucial period of her life when she will marry Julien Sarrazin. . . . For Anick-Albertine, their marriage will be the starting point of a period marked by resignation and rebellion" (5). That prefatory note also informs the reader that the novel's character "Zizi" is actually Julien, a fact substantiated by Sarrazin's extensive use of that nickname for her husband in her correspondence.

Evidence in Sarrazin's extensive collection of letters further supports autobiographical interpretations of the novel's main character, Anick Damien. Indeed, information in the author's correspondence indicates that placing the name "Albertine Sarrazin" on the cover of her works was as much of a decision as finding a satisfactory title and plausible dates of composition. In a mid-1965 letter to her "one-sixteenth of a Mom," Gogois-Myquel, the young novelist makes note of the dramatic changes that have occurred in her life since her troubled youth and mentions the decision to change her professional name: "But all that is dead and in the past, I only wanted to tell you a bit more about the defunct Anne-Marie . . . who will soon come back to life under the name of Albertine Sarrazin: yes, after many exchanges of correspondence, Mr. J. J. Pauvert and I arrived at that name for the cover. Doesn't it make a better impression and doesn't it sing more than Anick? I will keep the latter name for my private life" (*Vie littéraire* 76). The series of names used by the young woman reflect the turbulence she endured throughout the early part of her life. Her birth name was Albertine Damien, which was changed to "Anne-Marie R." upon her adoption in 1939 (the complete surname of her adoptive parents, the "R." family, remains a mystery, as it is not revealed in Sarrazin's published texts or in works on her life and literary corpus). "Anick" is a nickname—acquired at the Bon Pasteur reform school—used by those close to her, even after her rise to stardom. And she herself adopted that nickname, very rarely using "Albertine" in her correspondence. After the "R." family revoked their adoption when "Anick" began to have trouble with the law, she reclaimed her birth surname, Damien. She changed names yet again when she married Julien Sarrazin, taking on the latter's name. The name "Albertine Sarrazin" is thus a composite of sorts, one that the author used largely for professional purposes.

In the light of the information included in the publisher's note, the author's declared intentions, and evidence that the protagonist's experience is based on that of the author, Poche's and Pauvert's explicit classification of the work as a novel appears to be contradictory. Further complicating matters, the distance established between the author and her protagonist through the use of different names is incongruous with the overt attempts in the novel's paratextual information—particularly the use of the designation "Anick-Albertine"—to bridge that same distance. Thus, in spite of what appear to be clear signs that the reader should interpret *La cavale* as a novel, the work is marked by substantial generic tension.

Sarrazin, like the other authors examined in this study, benefits from the tension created by the fictional and the referential tendencies of her narrative. She is able to retell events based on her life experience such that they have a greater impact on the reader than would a mere day-to-day account of her actual time spent behind bars. Elissa Gelfand correctly notes that Sarrazin "speak[s] through her first-person narrators, all of whom live what Sarrazin lives, but in a reorganized way" ("Confined" 48). *La cavale* contains a richer and more thematically balanced depiction of daily life in prison than the version of carceral reality found in Sarrazin's numerous prison journals. In the latter, Sarrazin elaborates on specific elements of her daily life in jail—her struggles with her writing, her obsession with her weight, and her recurring health problems (especially her difficulties with her teeth). Yet, in spite of the presence of some detail about her daily routine, her nonfiction writing provides no extensive meditation on or description of conditions and relations in prison.[8] A substantial portion of her journals is also written specifically for Julien and constitutes no more than an extended love letter to him.[9] As we have seen in her cryptic and incomplete analysis of Cau's *La pitié de Dieu*, her goal in composing the journal was to write, not to be read. *La cavale*, the "reorganized" telling of her prison experience and life story, furnishes Sarrazin with a forum to address the question of daily life behind bars and to document how her protagonist survives her lengthy sentence.

Fiction writing thus allows Sarrazin to construct a version of the carceral universe that gives her readers a broader, more coherent understanding of the details of prison life than does her nonfiction writing. At the same time, while the novel form allows her greater creative freedom, the referential implications of her text enhance the documentary effect and the ideological impact of her depiction of prison. Indeed, emphasis on the work's basis in actuality allows the author to suggest that the debilitating experience portrayed in her work is not a mere figment of her imagination.

In the case of Sarrazin's three novels, critics—much like Genetian critics—have wavered between autobiographical and fictional interpretations. As Warren Motte points out, "Her major texts resist generic classification—are they novels? autobiography? autofiction?" (103). One example of an autobiographical reading of *La cavale* is found in Margaret Crosland's *Women of Iron and Velvet*: "here is a woman writer who invented nothing, she merely wrote down what happened to her" (177). This statement is not entirely accurate, however, and Crosland acknowledges later on in her analysis that certain episodes in Sarrazin's novels are fictional and do not correspond to events that transpired in real life. In the work's second section, for example, the narrator-protagonist marries her lover, Zizi, who also happens to be incarcerated. Although based in reality, that marriage is fictionalized in *La cavale*, as Julien was living on the outside when the two were married. Crosland refers to Sarrazin's fictionalization of her wedding as an "improvement" on reality.[10] A strict autobiographical interpretation of Sarrazin's book would, therefore, be incorrect.

A precise reading of *La cavale* must take into account the distance established between narrator and author by the use of different names. Critics should also factor into their interpretations the work's subtitle, *Roman*. At the same time, readings of Sarrazin's text must also account for its basis in actuality. Indeed, some paratextual and extratextual information encourages an autobiographical reading of *La cavale*, and it is clear that Sarrazin's life story enriched many aspects of Anick's experience. Anick Damien, like Albertine, was born in September and was later adopted (79; 82–83). The protagonist, again like the author, spent much time in prison, wrote creative works while incarcerated (472; 497), and longed to be with her lover,

Julien-Zizi, while in jail. Beyond basic autobiographical parallels, there are also markers in the text that encourage referential interpretation of La cavale, such as references to the Algerian War, to real-life prisons (Fresnes and La Petite Roquette), and to real historical figures, like Caryl Chessman, an American whom many claim was unjustly executed in 1960.[11]

Prison, according to Sarrazin

Sarrazin's vast correspondence and numerous personal journals provide an intimate glimpse into how much work, rework, and discipline were involved in the writing of La cavale. Sarrazin makes repeated references to the process of writing, editing, and reading involved in producing a final version of her novel. Some of her references are integrated seamlessly within her daily routine in jail: "Dentist, re-reading of La Cavale, alone, in summer pants, my legs in the sun shining through the window" (Journal de prison 275). Other references indicate that writing was not simply a matter of personal pleasure and recreation, as one day's sole journal entry shows: "Get up, girl. . . . La Cavale, shoo, enough vacation" (272).

Although she frequently mentions the act of writing, Sarrazin does not use her journals to elaborate on her intentions or on the types of alterations she makes to her text. Contrary to what one might expect, a hint as to her initial authorial intentions for La cavale is found not in her personal journal or correspondence but rather in her third autobiographical novel, La traversière. In that book, Sarrazin's narrator-protagonist writes that her first novel was originally conceived as a documentary text on prison life, with a visual twist. As the story goes, one of her co-detainees was planning on acquiring from her brother a miniature camera that would enable her to take clandestine pictures of "the lousiest prison in France" (21). The pictures would complement articles Sarrazin would write, documenting the abhorrent living conditions in the institution. The ultimate goal would be to send the articles and photos to news outlets and "stir up public opinion to get us out" (21). Alas, the camera never materialized, and Sarrazin was left with her articles, which later became chapters, which, in turn, gradually grew into her first novel. To be sure, we should evaluate this story of the novel's genesis with caution, for it is included in one of Sarrazin's autobiographical novels and, therefore, may be fictionalized. Still, it is worthy of note that the story echoes the young author's stated desire to compose a "truth," which, as we have seen, she mentions in her prison journal after having read Cau's *La pitié de Dieu.*

Whatever the author's initial intentions may have been, the final version of *La cavale* contains a highly detailed portrayal of the daily life of female inmates. The sole novel by Sarrazin that addresses in depth the question of incarceration, *La cavale* furnishes a vast amount of detail about practices, processes, rules, and conditions in the prison. We should recall the inverse relationship between plot and description in documentary narratives, articulated by Evelyn Cobley in *Representing War*. She writes that documentary accounts lend themselves "to extended analyses of description and narration rather than of plot" (12). There are indeed few major events that occur in *La cavale.* Moreover, the novel's basic story line, which centers on the narrator's hope to escape from prison, necessitates precise descriptions of physical space. The slow progression of the narrative reflects the tedious judicial processes that will ultimately keep Anick and Zizi locked up for what seems like a lengthy and indefinite period, as the narrator never specifies their eventual release dates.

The central message of *La cavale* does not become clear until the novel's final scene, for only then does the reader grasp that Anick's hopes to escape the prison have been illusory. For the bulk of the story, Anick—who is cast as a particularly strong and independent inmate—maintains a defiant stance toward her captors and her situation. She repeatedly attempts to deflect their efforts to subdue her and to thwart her ambitions to escape. The story ends, however, with Anick in prison, alone and unhappy, awaiting a seemingly distant date of liberation. Nearly two years of living in prison have profoundly changed the narrator-protagonist: indeed, a central goal of *La cavale* is to illustrate how incarceration gradually debilitates inmates. An element essential to achieving that goal is the exposure of the execrable conditions in which the prisoners are forced to live. Unlike a number of other prison narratives—*Les hommes dans la prison*, for example—the horrible state of prison conditions is not linked to broader sociopolitical issues. Prison is simply a "lousy" place to be, as Sarrazin's alter ego in *La traversière* states, and *La cavale* paints a detailed portrait of conditions and relations behind bars.

Readers of *La cavale*—like those of the other texts examined in this study—are imagined to be unaware of even the most basic characteristics of life in prison. Their alleged ignorance, often implicit in the narrative's discourse, necessitates descriptions of minutiae about the prison environment and general information about the treatment of criminals in the legal system. The relationship between an informed narrator and her less-informed imagined readers is established in the novel's opening scene, when the newly arrested narrator-protagonist is forced to undergo a systematic search through her belongings as well as a corporal search. She must therefore ready herself for a vaginal exam, a regulation procedure for new prisoners. Anick informs her imagined (female) readers what they should do if they find themselves in her situation: "If you are due [si vous êtes promise] for incarceration one of these days, be sure you are always bare-assed or else have a suitcase full of underwear close at hand" (9; 11). This opening scene confirms that the narrative will not simply recount the most intimate aspects of

incarceration but will also explicate those details to an uninitiated imagined readership.

The narrator's sophisticated understanding of the prison system goes far beyond the process of entry into the jail and is
highlighted throughout the narrative. After enduring the physical examination and search, the narrator is exposed to the basic
decrepitude of the dormitory-style prison (the first of the three
in which she will be detained). She is shocked by the state of
the communal cell and asks herself, "But where in the world
are the jails of my youth?" (11; 13). That observation indicates
to the reader, early in the story, that the protagonist is an experienced recidivist, a status that bestows her with authority as a
narrator and witness to the conditions in the prison. Once her
authority is conveyed, the narrator familiarizes herself with her
surroundings, orienting the reader as well. She notes: "I try to
get my bearings: the dormitory is a rooftop dovecote, because
I climbed forever just now, and the tops of the trees come nowhere near the windows. There are real windows—set high
up and barred, certainly, but they don't block all the outdoor
scents of the season like transoms in country jails. The wall is
stained and blistered: have to watch out for the paint, there
are black spots above the beds where heads have leaned back
against it at night as the girls read or sew" (13; 15). The level
of detail in that passage—like that found in Serge's and Genet's novels—is indicative of one of the primary ambitions of *La
cavale*: a precise description of the filthy and decrepit spaces in
which prisoners are detained. The goals of the three authors
are markedly different, however. Whereas Serge uses the prison
to condemn capitalism, and Genet embraces incarceration to
enhance his status as an outcast, Sarrazin simply depicts the
carceral realm to underline how it debilitates ordinary inmates
rather than fulfill its supposed function to rehabilitate and correct chronic recidivists.

As she takes in her new surroundings, Anick makes note

of the filth in and basic disorder of the working and living space. The detail provided in her spatial descriptions bolsters the narrative's documentary realism. For example, taking note of the prisoners' ordinary possessions, she states: "On the window sills, in rows, are onions, empty Nescafé tins, bottles of Dop shampoo with the last bubbles clinging inside; between the windows and dangling down the walls, between the closets and brushing against our heads, are garlands of plaited cotton with blackish clothespins holding up very dirty rags, slightly less dirty napkins; and among the least dirty of the dirty, are the occasional panties that the esthetes hang up to dry every night" (17; 19). The early descriptions of the dormitory-style prison are representative of what is to come, not only with respect to the level of detail provided but also in terms of the horrid physical state of the jail itself. Indeed, it becomes clear over the course of Anick's time spent in the dormitory-style jail that nearly every aspect of the institution is marked by neglect and inadequacy: brooms are strawless, bedsheets are marred by multiple holes, the beds themselves are narrow and uncomfortable, and room temperatures are irregular and unpredictable. Perhaps the worst feature of the organization of the dormitory-style prison is that the toilets are so close to the sleeping quarters that their odors permeate the sleeping area. The narrator even describes the toilets themselves in detail: "Oh, nothing complicated with a handle and a flush tank, no indeed. Once one's intimate desires have been fulfilled, it's enough to step on the pedals in front of the platform: a panel slides back and everything tumbles down into the cesspool. The strong odor of ammonia takes the place of smelling salts when you feel faint" (14–15; 17). Like Genet, Sarrazin spares no detail in describing prison life, dwelling at times on the most base and banal aspects of the experience. And as the narrator-protagonist moves through the three different prisons in which she is held, she encounters levels of filth and discomfort similar to what she experiences upon her entry.

The lack of basic sanitation reflects the prison administration's failure to ensure the cleanliness and health of its inmates. At one point, for instance, Anick must suffer through the arrival of a new prisoner who has been thrown into the communal space without having been properly cleaned or inspected and who, it turns out, is covered in lice (242; 255). The state of medical care is so bad in the dormitory-style jail that Anick laments not having been placed in a central prison of detention, a much more austere type of prison used for long-term and life sentences.[12] At least in the *maison centrale*, she notes, she would have been able to go to the dentist: "Oh, blessed Central Prisons! Central Prisons with your major and minor attentions, where every jaw regardless of whether it's covered by social security or not, from the moment it arrives, is systematically examined, measured, treated, manipulated" (36; 38).

The jail is so poorly run that even pregnant inmates receive no special treatment. As Anick remarks, "Solange is pregnant; naturally, she doesn't receive the little extra rations, the special foods, and the books on painless childbirth that are distributed in the model prisons" (106; 110). The basic discomforts of the carceral environment, however, prove to be of greater concern to Anick than the injustice inherent in the treatment of the pregnant inmate. For while the narrator and her co-detainees have compassion for the "neglected" unborn baby, their feelings of goodwill are limited. The narrator notes with some measure of selfish relief that Solange will be released in her seventh month: "Solange's nauseas, Solange's other ailments, Solange's smell were all beginning to really get on our nerves" (106; 110). Such a reaction is characteristic of Sarrazin's protagonist: her petty concerns take precedence over more abstract, ideological critiques of the prison system. A self-centered survivalist, Anick is most of all concerned with how the prison affects her and her lover, Zizi. Her egocentric nature is especially visible in the solution she devises for her salvation: an escape. Rather than focusing on the plight of the prisoners as a whole, as do many other prison narratives, Anick, as we will see, is focused on preservation of her "Self," her "*Moi*" (14; 16).

As Sarrazin depicts it, the prison is "Like a fat shrew fixed in her habits, [it] yawns, howls, eats, and sacks out every day at the same hours" (82; 86). Indeed, at the various jails depicted in *La cavale*, routines force the inmates into what seems like an endless cycle of eating, sleeping, washing, gossiping, working, trafficking, and, generally, killing time. In many ways, the women in Sarrazin's novel behave in a manner that is consistent with the descriptions of inmate subcultures found in a number of other fictional and nonfictional texts. They spend their free time tattooing each other, telling stories, writing letters, and consuming whatever they can afford to buy from the prison canteen. And Anick, to be sure, dwells on what prisoners consume: from cigarettes, to Nescafé, to the bad quality food the administration provides. She even mentions specific meals they are given on certain nights: "The menu: tuna fish with mayonnaise, chicken, peas, cakes" (21; 24). Not surprisingly, the food is, for the most part, inedible. Fish they are served one night is raw (53; 55), and the roast beef is "like a pale shoe sole" (47; 49).

The bad quality of the food does not keep them from eating, however, and the inmates become obsessed with the weight gain caused by their sedentary lifestyles. At one point, Anick declares openly and loudly her disgust with her own eating habits, exclaiming, "NO MORE CHOW." Then, the narrator, asserting her role as an authoritative witness, informs her readers: "Please note that this is a phrase that is heard periodically. After each month's weigh-in on the scales, no one eats. If you're rich, you set up your line of defense on a supply of crackers, and, if you are penniless, as I have become, it's just dry bread. But, inasmuch as concern for your figure is rather frivolous in such penitential precincts, you begin in a week to pass up the privilege of going hungry" (51; 53). The narrator's ironic remarks are representative of Sarrazin's approach to depicting and critiquing the prison. Anick puts into question the purpose of her incarceration by making light of its ostensible goals: penitence and rehabilitation. She highlights the disparity between her experience and the stated official ideals behind the notion of internment of criminals. By making food and weight loss her protagonist's primary concerns, Sarrazin mocks the myth of the prison in which the criminal is able to meditate on the nature of crime and justice and focus on his or her guilt. Instead, Anick is preoccupied with mundane matters such as how to fry her bread in margarine.

The fixation of the narrator-protagonist on the most banal aspects of her existence, most of which relate directly to her personal comfort and well-being, is particularly well illustrated by her obsession with cigarettes and coffee. She even goes to the point of telling her readers what brand of cigarettes she smokes and exactly how she prepares her coffee. In one telling instance, she describes her elaborate efforts to prepare hot water using her makeshift "grill": "This apparatus is composed of an empty coffee tin whose upper part has been perforated and whose lower part is filled with oil; a piece of cork wrapped in tinfoil with a plaited rag through it serves as a wick. A second box is placed, slightly off center in order to admit air, on the top of the first: this is my pan" (284; 299). Descriptions of such creativity are classic elements of prison narratives and films. Saddled with far too much empty time, inmates are often able to construct a host of inventions with their meager worldly possessions.

Alongside minutiae about leisurely activities such as eating, drinking, smoking, and sleeping, Sarrazin provides descriptions of work performed by the inmates. In the dormitory-style prison, for example, the narrator describes how the prisoners make "string bags" (*filets* in the French). The work is typical of prison labor in that it involves a simple yet repetitive task: "String bags are to this place what tags are to La

Roquette: badly paid busywork, real exploitation of the proles. Prison being the only factory that I've ever set foot in, I want to hear more about it. . . . In one corner there are huge cartons filled with spools of thread, white, red, blue, green, and string shopping bags not yet pulled together, tied up in groups of ten" (20; 22). That description of prison labor is typical of Sarrazin's treatment of the prison. The narrator's mention of La Roquette (short for La Petite Roquette prison, a real-life prison for women and juvenile delinquents) heightens the referential aspects of the narrative. The same can be said of her description of the work performed by the inmates, as the use of prison labor has a lengthy history in the Western world.[13] However, we should note that although Anick mentions the "exploitation" of the lower classes, her critique of prison labor is superficial. Instead of explaining precisely how the prisoners are exploited, the narrative emphasizes her nonconformist and rebellious nature. Indeed, rather than link the inmates' work to broader socioeconomic forces in a more sophisticated way (as does Serge's narrator, e.g.), Anick makes a characteristic play on words, linking it to her legal maneuvering and her escape plans: "Yes, I'll be glad to do them [the bags]. But I have something else to do first. As far as crocheting is concerned, I have to unravel the net in which I'm caught and crochet a cord that will get me out of here" (20; 22).

Anick frequently describes how the inmates attempt to circumvent the administration's rules. Illicit communication, for example, is central to the prisoners' daily lives. The narrator informs her imagined readership precisely how the inmates communicate with prisoners who are locked up in different areas of the prison: "I should point out that there is no contact with the girls in the other workroom except by thread telegram or Aliette-type telephone or by tapping the wall" (55; 58). The terminology she uses is explained at various points in the novel. Wall tapping is the form of communication that needs the least explanation to the uninitiated imagined reader, and it is a practice common among prisoners.[14] The other two types of communication evoked by Anick are, however, a bit more abstruse and are explained in great detail. Use of the "Aliette-type telephone," a tactic also described in *Les hommes dans la prison*, involves communicating through toilets that are located in different bathrooms but linked by the same rudimentary plumbing. Appalled by the process, Anick muses on what her codetainee, Aliette, must do while in the bathroom: "I wonder whether it's really necessary, in order to hear clearly, for Aliette to shove her face right into the hole or whether it may not be enough for her to stand there with uplifted head, like a certain Virgin. No matter: in my opinion people's business should not be shouted from the rooftops, still less in the john" (39–40; 42). The description is simultaneously informative and humorous. Moreover, the narrator's disgust with the enterprise is typical of her attempts to distinguish and distance herself from her fellow inmates. Anick remains focused on her own difficulties and has little sympathy for the plight of her co-detainees.

Readers are also initiated into the process involved in sending a "thread telegram" early in the text, at the same time as the narrator. To be sure, the narrator's description is a clear example of the documentary ambitions of *La cavale*. Anick learns of the process as she climbs onto her bed (which is located just below a window) in the dormitory-style prison for the first time. There, unexpectedly, she is joined by another inmate who proceeds to engage in an elaborate process of retrieving a letter from the story downstairs. Anick states: "Once she's settled herself, she begins to whistle *The Little Ship*, takes a spool of crocheting thread out of her belt, and begins to pay the thread out the window as soon as she hears the chorus of the song whistled back to her from below. It is explained to me that, in order to keep in touch with the pals downstairs, everyone takes turn sending messages this way. If I like, they'll find a pen pal for me" (14; 16). Clandestine exchanges between Zizi and Anick are also portrayed in great detail. In one instance, the couple exchanges a secret message rolled up inside a piece of gum while kissing during a hurried rendezvous (328; 346). They also smuggle notes to each other through various other methods, such as inside tubes of mustard, inside garbage, and so on.

The secret exchange of messages is hardly the only form of illicit trading that transpires in the prisons depicted by Sarrazin. Indeed, trafficking—of pills, tobacco, food, paper, and stamps—is one of the inmates' most preferred means of undermining the institutions' strict regulations. Anick, for instance, mentions that drugs provided by the administration can be used for trading—if, that is, inmates are able to avoid swallowing them while under the watchful eyes of the guards. She describes the complicated maneuvering required to keep from ingesting the drugs: "Sedatives have to be swallowed in the nurse's presence, which drives me to all kinds of digital acrobatics to palm them while I keep her concentrated on the glug-glug of my glass of water. There are days when I lose my touch and my clumsiness forces me to really put them in my mouth; nevertheless I never go so far as to swallow them, but when they're so chewed up and half melted, they lose all their trading value. In stir even sleep can be traded in" (37–38; 40). Far from objecting to being drugged by the prison administration, the narrator-protagonist concentrates on the black-market value of the sedatives. As is typical of *La cavale*, the description emphasizes the narrator's intimate knowledge of the inner workings of the prison system rather than the curtailing of inmates' liberty.

It is not only the prisoners' freedom that is restricted; their privacy is also limited. Anick is forced to interact with her co-detainees in each of the three prisons in which she is held. This is especially true in the dormitory-style jail, which is distinguished by its common sleeping quarters and work space. The narrator-protagonist therefore must cope not only with the limits imposed upon her by the prison administration but also with a group of wary and potentially hostile co-detainees. Such an environment is highly coded: the slightest movement, the smallest gesture, or the most simple, everyday object can be laden with a great deal of significance. As Anick notes, "In the beginning the girls keep a closer watch on you than the matrons do" (13; 15). With this in mind, she has two main concerns upon entry into the sleeping quarters on the first night of her confinement: to avoid appearing like either a rookie or an informer ("a stool pigeon" [13; 16]). The savvy protagonist knows that being perceived as either could make her stay in the jail unnecessarily difficult. Therefore, in order to appear like a veteran prisoner, she carefully measures her first movements and informs the reader of how she must behave: "The first thing to do is to show them I'm hip by making my sack up exactly right. A first-timer even if she's a chambermaid on the outside, won't come off so well as an old hand whose bed is always made for her outside" (12; 14).

Whereas Serge was able to envision the prison community as a group of men united behind a common political cause, such solidarity is an impossible dream in Sarrazin's prisons. Solidarity proved to be a source of strength and, ultimately, salvation for Serge's protagonist, whereas Anick perceives little besides tension, betrayal, gossip, and politicking in the inmate population. The hostility and wariness that Anick encounters early in her prison experience are, in many ways, representative of the difficulties she will confront throughout her imprisonment. Toward the end of the novel, the process has worn her down. Tired of her environment and mistrustful of the people around her, she states: "Prison is a perpetual, a frightful disharmony; between heart and words; between the broad morning smile for the newborn day and the dull routine, with its dirt and its burdens; between the trust that constantly is on the point of being offered and the deceits, the indifference, the callousness of others. I've had enough of it, I want to sing" (463–64; 488). Periods during which the prisoners are friendly are exceptional. Describing a day in which there seems to be a generalized truce among the prisoners because of a birthday celebration, Anick refers to it as "a day without shouts, without incidents, without quarrels, a let-me-see-you-smile-and-don't-make-me-kick-your-ass-day" (119; 125). Furthermore, the inmates' standard mode of behavior involves, not bonding, but rather dishonesty: "You trade, you whisper, you lie. It is an atmosphere of perpetual plotting, of secrets that everyone knows and discusses, without interrupting the incessant murmured vow not to tell, sworn on the heads of children, husbands, or dogs. Not to mention the fact that inevitably there are two or three stoolies, to make the proper contact between the said secrets and the penal administration or even the judiciary" (38; 40). To protect herself from the toxic atmosphere in the prison, Anick repeatedly distinguishes and distances herself from her cellmates. For instance, she comments on one inmate, Simone, who immediately upon being incarcerated engages in what the narrator terms "gluttony": "With her peasant logic and her vegetable stupidity, like all women winos, she arrived with the famous slogan: 'They put me here, it's up to them to keep me alive'" (227; 239). When Anick finds an inmate with whom she is able to establish a common bond, a real friendship is difficult to maintain because of sudden and frequent transfers. Commenting on the precipitate departure of one of her cellmates, Anick notes that, "whether by choice or by force, you always leave jail in a hurry" (108; 112). She rarely becomes attached to other inmates, and when she does forge bonds with them, her attachment is short-lived and easily forgotten once she and her friends are separated. Indeed, rather than establishing the groundwork for friendship, the protagonist often makes alliances with other prisoners to get advice for or assistance with her escape plan.[15]

As is clear from Anick and Zizi's attempts to escape, inmates in *La cavale* regularly attempt to undermine authority, rules, and regulations. Their behavior, however, is not explicitly linked to wider sociopolitical issues or ideological movements. Indeed, beyond its critique of society's failure to rehabilitate its inmates, the novel does not attempt to contemplate or assess whatever social or economic processes may lie beneath that failure (capitalism, e.g., or systematic neglect of those on the margins of society). One scene during which the death penalty is evoked illustrates quite clearly that the main concern of *La cavale* is an intense focus on daily life in prison rather than overarching ideological critiques.

The topic arises during a discussion among the inmates. Initially, their conversation focuses on the execution of a man who had denied his guilt until the very end. One of Anick's co-detainees claims that the state had no real proof against him, yet it proceeded nonetheless to cut off his head. Perceived as an intellectual by the other inmates (because of her glasses and her way of speaking), Anick is dragged into the conversation. She contributes little to the discussion, stating only that, given the choice, she would prefer the death penalty to life in prison (25; 27). Although her true feelings about the death penalty are more complex, Anick avoids sharing them with her fellow inmates. She does, however, share them with the reader through descriptions of the thoughts that race through her mind during the brief discussion. She describes the death penalty in those private thoughts as "ridiculous," explaining, somewhat cryptically, that if people deny a crime for a long enough time, they "eventually exonerate" and "dissociate" themselves from it (25; 27). She even remembers, with a measure of sadness, Caryl Chessman, an American whom many claim was unjustly executed in 1960.

Those thoughts, however, are not revealed to her cellmates. Indeed, in spite of her peculiar stance against the death penalty and the sadness she expresses for Chessman, the topic is not of great importance to Anick. She simply hopes the conversation will end. During a brief pause in the discussion, she thinks to herself: "The moment of silence that follows makes me hope that the subject has been exhausted" (26; 28). She even believes that talking about the death penalty is futile, noting that her personal misery is more important than such an abstract issue. She remarks (again, not in dialogue): "Why talk about the death penalty when you're condemned to go on living, living without a respite, shackled to life like a punishment, a festering sore?" (26; 28). In the end, the inmates are unable to find common ground on the death penalty, and the discussion even provokes a spat between Anick and the inmate who had dragged her into the conversation. Interestingly, not only do the prisoners fail to reach a consensus against the death penalty, but the topic of the guillotine is literally effaced from the novel by a very ordinary event: the sudden entry of an Algerian woman, who is seen as a menace, into the dormitory. Once the foreigner enters the prison, the conversation about the death penalty ends, as the petty racism of the inmates permanently diverts their attention. Anick wryly notes: "All this makes the guillotined man a totally dead issue" (30; 32).

The conversation provides nothing of substance to debate about the death penalty, which had not yet been abolished in France when *La cavale* was first published.[16] Sarrazin makes no effort to craft the prisoners in her novel such that they are united against capital punishment. Whereas both Serge and Genet construct fictional texts that promote points of view that run against dominant sociopolitical currents, Sarrazin does not use her fiction to embroil herself in such controversy. The scene also reveals a great deal about Sarrazin's depiction of incarceration in *La cavale*: the author prefers to illustrate her critique of the prison through a portrayal of everyday life rather than through sweeping, ideologically based pronouncements against specific of methods of punishment, capital or otherwise. Indeed, the manner in which the discussion about the death penalty ends highlights the fact that incarceration in group jails creates tension among diverse groups of inmates. That tension, rather than the abstract sociopolitical issue, is given precedence.

From Defiance to Resignation

In an interview with her biographer Josane Duranteau, Sarrazin explains her deeply personal motivations behind writing about prison: "I have the duty to write, not to destroy certain myths—myths that are ineradicable anyway—about the environments I describe, but to compensate for all that I lived through that was wasted, painful, or dirty" (*Sarrazin* 157). There are echoes of those comments in *La cavale*: Anick endures years wasted in decrepit and filthy environs away from her beloved Zizi. Indeed, the novel's final message emphasizes that the discomforts and enforced lethargy inherent in a lengthy prison term eventually wear down even the most defiant inmates.

At the beginning of the novel and throughout most of the story, prison represents nothing more than a temporary interruption in the life of the strong and independently minded protagonist. It is a mere interlude, the difficulties of which can be deflected through irony and fantasies of escape. At the end of the novel, however, prison is no longer just an inconvenient intermission. Rather, confinement represents the foreseeable future for the narrator-protagonist: the story comes to a close not at the end of Anick's prison sentence but when she finally realizes that she will not escape from jail and will simply await the end of her term. In the novel's final scene, the protagonist finds herself alone in her cell, drying her tears with a regulation prison blanket. That final scene stands in contrast to the opening scenes of the novel, in which Anick reacts to her new confinement with irony and combativeness.

La cavale, as we have seen, follows the classic paradigm of prison narratives, introducing readers to the carceral realm by depicting the traumatic process of entry in the opening scene. Like both *Les hommes dans la prison* and *Miracle de la rose*, the novel portrays an entry ritual that attempts to diminish or curtail the self of the incoming prisoner.[17] Anick is stripped, searched, humiliated, separated from her possessions, and immediately made aware of her status as a disempowered individual. So rigidly defined are power relations in the prison that she cannot even wash herself upon arrival: "I ask the matron about the chances of cleaning up soon, which got me an outraged: You certainly aren't thinking of washing tonight?" (11; 13). Already the "matron" imposes her will upon the powerless narrator-protagonist. In spite of the efforts to dehumanize her, Anick is determined from the beginning of her sentence to maintain possession of her "Self," her ego. As her thoughts drift to her personal life on the outside, she remarks: "I left all that in the property room tonight. I know you never leave your Self for long, never long enough, in the property room, and you get it back without the superintendent's permission" (14; 16).

Recuperation and protection of her "Self" remain preoccupations of the narrator-protagonist throughout her experience behind bars. She notes: "I want only to remain entirely within myself and to keep this Me far away from here, somewhere where nothing and no one can make it other than what I want it to be" (201; 211–12). Anick claims that the distance she maintains between herself and her environment has always allowed her to forget with ease her time "in stir" (382; 403), an ease she attributes to the fact that she has resisted one of incarceration's main ostensible goals: penitence. "At least as far as I'm concerned," she explains, "I never 'realized' my prisons; I never saw them as anything but intervals, as pretexts for doing things that had no relation to them and to the purpose that had been assigned them; in these penitential precincts I've made jokes, if I have suffered it has never been in my conscience" (382–83; 403–4). Not only does she have a clear conscience, but she states that the "concept of expiation" lacks validity for her. She even claims that she will resist and defy the system's attempts to make her understand that very concept (383; 404).

Based upon her behavior at various points in the novel, Anick apparently does have a clear conscience, as she demonstrates no remorse about her crimes. In one of her court appearances, for example, she refers to the victims of her burglary as "Messrs. My Balls" (404; 426) and can barely stay awake during the proceedings. She asks: "And what sentence in all this cold heap of red tape can be true enough to make the sluice-gates of our eyes open?" (404; 426). The narrative provides little substantive detail about her various court appearances and her legal case in general, reflecting the narrator's lack of interest in those matters. In one of her moments in court she simply endures, without describing in detail, the "orchestra," the "circus," and the "judicial acrobatics" that transpire all around her (402; 425). Her main concern during those moments is her own physical discomfort. "I need to pee," she tells the reader, ignoring the legal processes that will determine her future. "Oh, to sit down!" she whines to herself, as the court reporter documents the proceedings to which readers are not privy (403; 425).

Irreverent humor, as Anick's courtroom commentary indicates, is a staple of her description of her twenty-month experience in prison. That humor serves as a tool for self-preservation throughout the novel. Indeed, the protagonist's protective shell of irony is revealed in the first scene when Anick criticizes the absurd rules of the institution, rules that prevent her from taking her belongings into the dormitory with her. When her fur coat is confiscated and put into storage, for example, she notes: "The fur remains in the property room: it may run the risk of feeding the moths for a few seasons, true enough; but no prison authority is willing to be responsible for the possibility of its being swapped and going up in cigarette smoke" (9; 11). Anick's flippant attitude contrasts vividly with the reverence adopted by Genet's narrator when, upon entering Fontevrault prison, he becomes aware of the presence of his soon-to-be-martyred "God," Harcamone. The sense of dread and persecution felt by Serge's narrator is also absent. For Anick, the arrest appears to be simply part of her routine, and she tries to dismiss the difficulties and humiliation inherent in entering into prison. As the first sentence of the novel indicates, she will protect herself, in part, through sarcastic humor. Describing her outfit, which includes the aforementioned fur, she notes: "I am really done up for my entrance into prison tonight: possum and slacks" (9; 11).

The narrator's struggle to maintain her sense of independence in prison is constant. An element of that struggle is an aversion to conformity. Anick focuses on the subtle details that distinguish her from the prisoners who have already been subdued by the administration. Regarding the special denim dress she may be required to wear, she comments that "once I've begun to wear it, I'll even begin to feel a certain affection for it little by little. But careful: prison is in that dress, you must not love it. Thus far, simply through the power of my possessions, I had managed to erect and maintain an impenetrable barrier between myself and the clan of the brown dresses. And soon enough, along with the outfit of the finally sentenced prisoner, I'll take on that character" (361; 382). Anick even vows that if she is made to wear the outfit of the "sentenced prisoner" she will continue to resist "beneath the denim" (362; 382) and further develop her plans to escape.

Anick's desire to keep her "Self" intact and to preserve her independence is symbolized, above all, by her *cavale*. That *cavale*—the original French title means "escape" but also designates a type of mare—remains her most reliable companion in her various carceral settings, proving to be a comforting fantasy during difficult times. The "runaway mare" serves as an imaginary barometer that measures the protagonist's state of mind and the progress of her escape plans. When a letter and diagram Anick has tried to smuggle out of the prison gets confiscated, for instance, she states: "Yes, indeed, my runaway mare is fatally wounded; but she'll recover, tomorrow or next year, she'll come back to life in one way or another" (189; 199). At another moment, when she is feeling a bit more indifferent about being in prison for the full length of her eventual sentence, Anick remarks: "This runaway mare was born tired, she keeps missing her footing and slipping" (181; 190). At still another moment, on one of the rare occasions when she enjoys an evening with her cellmates, she notes: "Sometimes the atmosphere of the dormitory is magically changed . . . the runaway mare goes back to the stable, and everything is suddenly very cool and crazy" (93; 97).

The title of the novel is also an ironic reference to the protagonist herself, as she is the "Runaway," *la cavale*, who does not succeed in getting out of prison. Indeed, if we interpret the novel solely based on the narrator-protagonist's success as a "runaway," the final message of *La cavale* is most certainly a pessimistic one, illustrating how the defiant protagonist has been subdued by the prison and the sluggish legal system. Early in the novel she is feisty and independent, frequently describing with irony even the most degrading aspects of her incarceration. In the final chapters of *La cavale*, however, her defiant attitude toward her possible escape changes, and she gradually comes to accept the notion that the prison will prevent her from rebelling. Echoing the lament made by the narrator of *Les hommes dans la prison* about the indestructibility of the prison, Anick states: "Our punishments and our lives will pass, but the denim dress will never pass. The prisoner does not wear out his clothes: it is the clothes that wear out their prisoner" (432; 455).

To be sure, Anick does not wait until the end of the novel to describe how life in prison slowly saps her mental and physical energies. While still being held in the dormitory-style prison, she notes that "days and months of living in low gear drain you of the capacity to think and act at the same time" (92; 96). After her transfer from the dormitory-style prison to the second departmental jail, she claims that incarceration is even beginning to soften her mind: "A kind of tepid dopiness is taking hold of my mind, I'm barely simmering and I feel myself getting soft, like some dull dish cooking on the stove that refuses to get done" (198; 208). The implication of her mental decline is a broad one, for if such regression can affect Anick, who is depicted as an intellectual among her peers, it is likely that other, less intellectual and less defiant inmates will experience the same sort of decline.

In characteristic fashion, the narrator jokes that such "dopiness" is attributable to the fact that life in modern prisons is simply too easy. At one point she states: "How can I manufacture repentance and good resolutions under such conditions? Modern prisons soften instead of punishing; where whips should have been employed, there are comforts" (458; 482). She claims that she would have preferred the legendary prisons of the past: "I think I would have liked the jails of other times, prisoners arrayed against keepers, wooden shoes and rough hoods, severity and shit; all the things to which it was impossible to grow accustomed, to submit, unless you had been born in jail. Nowadays the can makes a hard life impossible . . . ('say, Anick, how about a little more butter?')" (458; 482). Although the comforts of prison serve as a source of irony for the protagonist in some moments, in other, less flippant moods she reveals that she actually grows to enjoy the lethargy of incarceration: "I like this idleness, this deliberate slowness that disintegrates and protracts every action. The day becomes divided into little rituals: washing and dressing, making coffee on the burner, listening from my bed to the hour of broadcast music; lunch, bed again until exercise time" (350; 369–70).

Anick makes the frank admission about the extent to which she enjoys incarceration in the third and final prison in which she is held. It is a moment anticipated earlier in the novel, when she is transferred from the more chaotic dormitory-style jail to the sparsely populated departmental prison. She takes note of the calm environment of that second jail: "This one is not such a bad deal, it has no more than the normal amount of stupidity and dirty dealing; the contents, animate and otherwise, are the same as those of any other. But I'm afraid. Afraid of this cleanliness, this silence that masks outcries, the bright stones that sweat a kind of anguish, constant vague threat; the banality of the days batters me, penetrates me, blocks my pores; neither dangerous nor of any consequence, the routine rocks me and lulls me" (181; 190). That moment of apprehension foreshadows the pacification of the narrator-protagonist that is realized at the end of the novel.

A key moment in her transformation from a defiant prisoner determined to escape into an inmate resigned to waiting out the end of her term occurs when Anick is, at long last, sentenced. Her change in legal status exacerbates her alienation from the prison as well as from herself as a prisoner. The inmates from whom she used to distinguish herself now serve as a mirror image. She remarks that "they make me angry because they're greedy, because they're ugly, because their shabby outfits remind me that I'm wearing the same thing and that I too must be ugly" (416; 439). Not only does she physically resemble her co-detainees, but sentencing further complicates her incarceration, as it involves compulsory work. Taking note of the departure of Lerouge, who worked as the "trusty" in the prison (an assistant to the matron), Anick remarks: "The prison authorities changed me into Lerouge after she had been whisked off to Central Prison" (427; 450). That "transformation" into

Lerouge reflects the leveling effect brought on by incarceration. The "Self" that Anick fought to protect finds itself endangered because prison rids its inmates of individuality, molding them into anonymous "jailbirds." She remarks: "But, when best and worst had been fused into the common product, the jailbird, which has nothing of the superlative about it; when the pigs have resigned themselves to the weekly shower and the clean ones have equally resigned themselves to the absence of deodorants from the canteen list; when the educated have made some attempt to talk like all the others and the illiterate have learned to read old magazines by means of their illustrations" (418; 441–42). Now part of the "common product," Anick appears to be on the cusp of failure in her goal of remaining on the margins of the society of captives.

Initially, Anick vows to fight the order for compulsory work, but she knows that she will relent. Indeed, she no longer has the energy to endure the punishment that would ensue from such a refusal: months in solitary confinement (431; 454). Her resistance to the work order is short-lived, and she recognizes that her defiance is merely symbolic. The comforts and privileges from which she will benefit will outweigh the satisfaction garnered from resistance. She learns how to justify her behavior: "Visit, letter, official or sneaked: for all that I can give in, even though I know that I ought to refuse; but with these reasons, I may perhaps elude complete enslavement. I can always tell myself that I yielded in order to get something by it, and not just because I wanted to yield" (436; 459). Yet, even after she acknowledges the futility of her resistance, she continues to hope for an escape. But after one final plot to break out of prison fails (with the help of Zizi, she tries unsuccessfully to make a duplicate key [444; 467]), she gradually begins to accept that she will just have to await her liberation. All of her fantasies of an immediate release will likely prove illusory: "The landslide of clemencies, amnesty, the return of the tools, the escape, all the things that may never come" (473; 499). Indeed, her defiance grows weaker with every failure, and her efforts to resist grow ever more symbolic. Near the end of the novel, after she realizes that her efforts through legal channels to precipitate her release are going nowhere, she states: "I have not yet, however, reached inertia; I will never resign myself to accepting the props sanctified by tradition, to counting the days backward until I reach the end, in the fashion of every conscript private in the world and some of my companions" (474; 499–500). But slowly, gradually, her indifference wins. She begins to take comfort in the "downiness of the life" that she had rejected. Indeed, she sighs, "what difference does it make, it is all right the way it is, I will stay here" (478; 504).

At the very end of the novel, a glimmer of hope is left for Anick: it resides in her escape fantasy, which is inspired by her relationship with Zizi, the "golden thread" in her life (474; 500). Yet, in spite of that flicker of hope, which surfaces when Anick dries her eyes in the book's final scene and tries to get back in her imaginary mare's "saddle," the protagonist is still in prison. Indeed, the "secret break" she envisions is, in the end, nothing but a private illusion, a figment of her imagination (480; 506). The runaway, *la cavale*, has failed to realize her dream.

Anick-Albertine: Criminal-Prisoner-Writer

In the remainder of the trilogy, Sarrazin's protagonist has the same character traits and self-centered motives as in *La cavale*. In both *L'astragale* and *La traversière* she behaves in a manner that highlights her single-mindedness and strong will. Indeed, her independence and strength are exemplified by her defiant act in the opening scene of *L'astragale*, in which she escapes (successfully) from prison by jumping from a thirty-foot-high wall. Elissa Gelfand has noted that *La cavale* "signals a new perspective on women's prison experience" because of its "thoroughly unorthodox protagonist, its defiant narrator" (*Imagination* 217).[18] We should note, however, that a primary lesson of *La cavale* is that the protagonist's defiance has its limits. For while Anick's escape in *L'astragale* is successful, in *La cavale* all of her escape plans fail, and by the end of the novel the protagonist has accepted her role as an inmate, acknowledging that her resistance is relegated to the realm of her imagination.

There is, however, one cause for optimism in *La cavale* that is tangential to the text's primary story line of a failed "runaway." Indeed, during Anick's final meeting with her lawyer, which occurs near the very end of the novel, it is revealed that the narrator-protagonist has dabbled in some creative writing while behind bars. She tells her lawyer that she has "a few little things that I've written here in stir: short stories, poems" (472; 497). Although that is the first time creative productivity of that sort is mentioned in *La cavale*, writing is an important element of Anick's identity, and she makes a number of references to the fact that she writes while in jail. Upon her arrival in prison, for instance, although she suffers from a broken wrist, she is so comfortable in her role as a writer that it does not pose a problem: "I am ambidextrous only with the ball-point Bic and a lefty for everything else" (16; 18).

Anick, to be sure, relies on her pen while in prison. One of her first acts upon arriving into the dormitory-style prison is to sit down and write: "In stir, the Bic is my gun" (20; 23).[19] The fact that the protagonist puts pen to paper so early in her jail sentence, and in such a public manner, highlights that her writing is an important element in how she wishes to project her identity to her co-detainees.[20] A solitary act, writing allows Anick to accentuate the distance between herself and the other prisoners. Her "gun" also furnishes her with a valuable form of currency in the prison: able to write letters for her less literate companions, she does so on a regular basis. Her talent even mollifies the demeanor of unpleasant cellmates, for when they are expecting a favor from her they are more respectful of her space and demands. Writing also furnishes Anick with a distraction from the daily difficulties of prison life. For instance, after breaking a glass, which she will have to replace with money from her own pocket, she notes: "Well, I'll try to take my mind off that by going to work on the conjugal letter" (459; 483). The narrator-protagonist's casual evocation of her literary productivity in jail, which her lawyer finds "extremely interesting" (472; 497), suggests that although Anick is in a state of resignation at the end of *La cavale*, writing represents hope for the future, beyond what seems, for now, like an endless prison sentence.

Writing played a similar key role in the life of Albertine Sarrazin, for upon her release from prison she greeted her husband, Julien, with suitcases filled with pages upon pages of manuscripts and journals, and among those pages was the rough draft of *La cavale*. Throughout her short life—which ended prematurely due to negligence on the part of her surgeons during a kidney operation in 1967—Sarrazin's greatest wish was to see herself in print.[21] Indeed, the trajectory of the protagonist of the autobiographically inspired "Trilogie de *La cavale*" follows the same path that Sarrazin followed in her life, from criminal to prisoner and, finally, to successful writer. While *L'astragale* is perhaps her most widely read work today, *La cavale* constitutes a much more ambitious project and, within the context of her trilogy, is the centerpiece of her literary production. Further enhancing the value of *La cavale* is the tension cultivated between referentiality and fictionality, which transforms Sarrazin the writer into a witness. And, as a reflection of Sarrazin's own prison experience, *La cavale* constitutes the author's "truth" about incarceration she wished to contribute to the literary tradition.

As we will see in the following chapter, François Bon's note-worthy contribution to the French tradition of carceral writing, *Prison*, contains a compelling and innovative mixture of both documentary and fictional material. Like Serge, Genet, and Sarrazin before him, Bon provides fascinating and politically charged commentary on the treatment of prisoners in the French criminal justice system. A depiction of the inner workings of a youth detention center in late-twentieth-century France, *Prison* portrays young men and boys as they shuttle repeatedly between prison and hostile environments in modern French cities and suburbs.

[FOUR]   CORRECTED INMATES, CORRECTED TEXTS

On Tuesday, 10 December 1996, the following article appeared in Bordeaux's daily newspaper, *Sud Ouest*.

FOR A TRIVIAL MOTIVE

"Carcass," a 21–year-old homeless man, admitted stabbing his companion in misfortune. He did not want to kill him, he wanted to push him away.

Tall, lean, and 21 years of age, Frédéric Miremont is nicknamed "Carcass" by his homeless friends. It is he who, Sunday afternoon, spontaneously presented himself to the Bordeaux police station on the advice of his friends to say that he was the perpetrator of the deadly stabbing in the squat on the rue des Douves. . . .

Everything took place in the middle of the night from Saturday to Sunday, in front of and then inside the building at 28 rue des Douves, between André-Meunier Square and the Capucins market. That building has been used by about 20 squatters for about the past ten days. . . .

The tragedy took place in the middle of the night. Between only two men: "Carcass" (Frédéric Miremont is known essentially by that name) and a 39-year-old homeless man originally from Metz who shares the same first name and whose last name is Hurlin.

It seems to have all begun with a quarrel over "territory." "Carcass" was one of the first people to squat in the building on the rue des Douves. After his discovery of the site, however, "Carcass" took a trip to Oléron Island and, while he was gone, Frédéric Hurlin apparently wanted to take advantage of his absence. "Carcass" returned and did not like the fact that Frédéric Hurlin had come to squat there.

The scene allegedly unfolded in the following manner. What began as a lively exchange of words transformed into an exchange of blows, with Frédéric Hurlin losing his glasses in the fight. "Carcass" allegedly attempted to flee the scene and was on his way back to the room that he had claimed in the squat. Frédéric Hurlin then caught up to him. It is apparently at that moment when matters definitively took a turn for the worse. Fearing severe retaliation, "Carcass" retrieved a knife from his bag and, at the very moment when his pursuer was coming through the door, he used it. Only to push him away. Alas, the long knife blade hit Frédéric Hurlin in the middle of his abdomen. The wounded man collapsed. In a panic, "Carcass" fled the scene.

Despite the speed of the emergency services and the medical care that was given to him, Frédéric Hurlin died at three in the morning at the hospital. . . .

The party involved and the victim were already known by the police. The former for acts of violence, and the latter had just served a prison sentence. The weapon was found, and yesterday, at the end of the day, an autopsy was performed to establish the exact causes of death.[1]

The first chapter of François Bon's *Prison* bears the same title as the above *Sud Ouest* article, "For a Trivial Motive." It opens with a prison guard alerting the text's anonymous narrator to the murder of a recently released inmate: "And did you hear that Brulin was stabbed? . . . It was in the paper this morning. In a squat, a guy named Tignasse, whom we know too" (7). Stunned, the narrator—who had just directed one in a series of writing workshops in the youth detention center—seeks out the article reporting the death of his former workshop partici-pant. "The newspaper *Sud-Ouest*. . . . I bought it at the train station and found the article right away . . . two imprecise col umns (the ages were wrong and apparently they thought it was enough to say about each person that they were *companions in misfortune*)" (8). After having read that inaccurate and dismis-sive article, the narrator, determined to get a better sense of the site where the murder occurred, embarks on a detective-style journey through the city of Bordeaux. He visits the "squat" at 28 rue des Douves and then walks by the medical institute where the autopsy was performed. He complements the story of his wanderings with ruminations on his interaction with Bru-lin in the workshop. Distinguished by his broken glasses, his worn-out clothes, and his peculiar way of standing too close when talking, Brulin never fit in with the other prisoners. He was even placed in isolation toward the end of his sentence to put an end to the repeated beatings he received from his fel-low inmates (23). Brulin appears beset by bad luck wherever he goes, and the narrator's exasperation with the young man's fate is palpable. The narrator even runs through scenarios in which the ex-inmate, who came from the northeast of France, is not murdered: "And if, with one more week, he had had the strength to take the night train—even if it meant sleeping un-der the seats or locking himself in the restroom to not have to pay—and head up north instead of trying his luck in the squat; round and round it goes in my head" (26). In the end, the nar-rator's remembrances serve as a tribute to a young man who, on the surface and in the media's eyes, would appear to be just

another member and victim of a violent population of vaga-
bond youth in the city of Bordeaux and its suburbs. Expressing
his sense of loss, the anonymous narrator laments that he now
must add "a name to the very long list, the one that every one
of us keeps, of those who are absent from the world" (29).

While he is only mentioned in passing after the text's first
chapter, Jean-Claude Brulin—that is to say, his real-life counterpart Frédéric Hurlin—was the driving force of the composition of *Prison*. In explaining why he chose such a simple, universal title for his book, Bon remarks, "I think that I, too, was
in a prison—the prison in which I was placed physically and
mentally by the death of Jean-Claude Hurlin [*sic*]. I never called
that book by another name, nor did I ever attempt to come up
with another title."[2] And just as Brulin's murder has its basis
in a real-life event, the context surrounding the fictionalized
killing (the writing workshop, the youth detention center, the
urban setting) is also firmly based in actuality. In this chapter I
examine how François Bon accentuates that basis in actuality
in *Prison* and, at the same time, uses his creative license to depict the carceral realm. Through an analysis of the formal aspects of Bon's work—its hybrid structure, its creative blurring
of the line between fiction and nonfiction—I show how the author furnishes a humanizing and realistic portrait, albeit a fictionalized one, of incarcerated young men. It is not by chance
that the author begins his book with a critique of a newspaper
article, as Bon's text serves to counterbalance the superficial
treatment the "companions in misfortune" received therein.
Bon presents a more complete picture of the experience of his
workshop participants as they pass through the revolving door
between the prison and a chaotic urban environment. Like Victor Hugo and Victor Serge, Bon seeks to portray what inmates
endure, linking their condition to broader social issues. For his
part, Bon highlights a connection between criminal behavior
and a striking lack of stability in the lives of the transient young

men. That lack of stability is the result of a number of factors, such as drug use, homelessness, recent immigration, poverty, fractured families, and an inadequate social safety net. As we will see, the author uses a number of techniques that are normally particular to fiction writing to complete his portrayal of juvenile offenders in late-twentieth-century France. These techniques include multiple changes in narrative stance, the seamless weaving together of imaginary and nonfictional material, and the conflation of several real-life individuals into one fictional character.

A compelling mixture of documentary and imaginary details, *Prison* is a fictionalized account of Bon's experience directing a writing workshop in a youth detention center in Gradignan, a Bordeaux suburb. Between October 1996 and April 1997, Bon conducted twenty-one separate writing sessions with a total of sixty-two inmates. Prior to their arrest, many of the detainees were homeless or resided in low-income housing. A number of the participants were either immigrants or born in France to immigrant parents. As workshop director, Bon proposed diverse themes, touching on social issues such as homelessness and urban living as well as more intimate topics like dreams and personal suffering. One strategy he used in the workshop was to introduce the inmates to literary texts—like Apollinaire's "Zone" and Khalil Gibran's *The Prophet*—from which they were expected to find the beginnings of a narrative thread. The choice of themes and texts implies a recognition of and engagement with a specific set of marginalizing social and economic factors as the author sought to elicit testimonies from the inmates about the vicissitudes of urban and suburban life.

Bon compiled the entire corpus of prisoners' texts in an unpublished manuscript titled "Parfois je me demande" (Sometimes I Wonder), a copy of which he shared with me after a lengthy interview.[3] Their writings—which come to approximately two hundred typed pages in length—are organized neatly into thematic and chronological sections. The title of the collection is a direct quote from an inmate's untitled text that is structured in unrhymed verse. Fittingly, the experience depicted therein is in many ways representative of the plight of a number of the young men at the detention center. The inmate writes:

> After my nights in staircases and entryways,
> now my youth is ruined because of prison
> I was only 16, and at the end of my sentence, I was twenty-two
> sometimes I wonder
> if prison is life. ("Parfois" 25)

This text contains a few of the themes that recur throughout the collection: homelessness and squatting, youthful transgressions, and time lost in prison. The above quote is all the more representative of the ensemble of prisoners' writings, given the fact that it is composed in the first person, as are the overwhelming majority of the texts in the compilation. Moreover, the somber tone of his reflection, "sometimes I wonder / if prison is life," raises a central concern of the juvenile offenders: how prison relates to their past activities and how it impinges on their future.

Bon was originally scheduled to conduct the prison writing workshop for the entire academic year of 1996–97, but he ceased working there a few months early. His premature exit was directly related to the appearance in the workshop of Hurlin's murderer, Frédéric Miremont, who had been incarcerated in the youth detention center as a result of the slaying. In a letter to Miremont's attorney, Bon comments on the effect Miremont's arrival had on the workshop: "We continued the workshop, but in spite of my warnings, the socio-educative service of the youth detention center enrolled in my cultural workshop a youth who was linked to the death, a fact that was clear to both them and me. I took it upon myself for two sessions to limit myself to an anonymous and purely technical interaction with him. I never exchanged a single private word with that inmate" (24 May 1998). During the third session, Miremont produced a text that revealed suicidal impulses, alarming Bon to the point that he decided he could no longer continue his efforts in the workshop: "I received from that inmate a text that had no link whatsoever to the subject I had proposed, a text whose seriousness put me on the alert" (24 May 1998).[4] Bon sent a copy of the text and a recommendation for psychological treatment to one of the prison's administrators. With that letter, he also sent his resignation. Bon's departure is mirrored in *Prison*, as the anonymous workshop director is confronted with the same problem. Upon reading a text by Miremont's fictionalized alter ego (Tignasse) expressing suicidal thoughts, the director comments, "I decided to no longer come back because none of this had anything to do with me and it was just too much" (21).

Generic Ambiguity — Narrative Hybridity

Each of *Prison*'s six chapters concentrates on discrete episodes and events. The book's episodic nature lends itself to significant variation from chapter to chapter in both form and content. Each chapter also contains different combinations of narrative voices: some are overtly the product of the author's imagination, whereas others originated or appear to have originated in the prison's writing workshop. Indeed, Bon uses a variety of strategies to showcase real texts produced by the inmates in the youth detention center. Throughout his portrayal of the workshop environment and of the activities of the young men in the city and the prison, he inserts excerpts of varying length from the inmates' texts, sometimes even including their spelling and grammar mistakes. In some instances the prisoners' texts are included as such, while in others they are seamlessly woven into the book's many stories. Some prisoners' texts appear exactly as they do in "Parfois je me demande," while others have been altered by the author. Furthermore, some portions of *Prison* that appear to have been produced by inmates in the writing workshop were actually composed by Bon himself. The result is a literary work that is peculiarly hybrid in form and content: the text alternates among the observations of the workshop director, excerpts from the slang-filled texts of the prisoners (some of which are fictionalized), and commentary by third-person omniscient narrators.

The subject matter of *Prison* centers on incarceration and writing in prison. In spite of that consistency, it is necessary to provide a brief overview of the book's six chapters because of significant thematic and structural variation therein. The first chapter, as we have seen, depicts the aftermath of Brulin's murder. The second chapter, titled "At the Edge of Cities," tells the story of a joyride in a stolen car, recounted three times from the perspective of three different inmates, all of whom are arrested and record their escapade in texts produced in the writing workshop.

The third chapter, "The Mistake, Fifty-three Times," serves, in Bon's words, as an "inventory" of the inmates' texts.[5] It provides a lengthy and complex sampling of their writings, many of which are quoted verbatim from the source material produced in Bon's workshop. The prisoners' texts are either presented in the form of direct quotes or retold by the workshop director with remarkable loyalty to the original versions. This chapter includes much detail about the inmates' crimes and conflicts with the police, their living situations (in shelters, in low-income housing projects, and on the street), their aimless travels around Europe (most often without train tickets), and, in some cases, their experiences as immigrants in France. This chapter also gives the reader an idea of the conditions in the writing workshop itself (the director's methods, the behavior of the inmates, etc.). Most of the prisoners are introduced with the words "The one who" ("Celui qui"). A typical description of an inmate reads as follows: "The one who writes: 'linked to the pain that is deep inside me.' *For my part, I get these episodes of madness linked to the pain that is deep inside me, but it is very hard for me to talk about it because I don't control it.* And the following week he will stay silent over his blank sheet of paper, and will end up writing three lines that he will not want to show me, and he will fold his paper carefully into his back pocket" (57). The portrayal of this inmate is representative of the descriptions in Bon's "inventory": it contains a brief introduction, followed by a direct quote (the italicized portion), which in turn is followed by an observation made by the workshop director.

In the fourth chapter, titled "The Idea of the Road," Bon juxtaposes two of his anonymous narrators' experiences: first, his interactions in a prison writing workshop (outside of the Bordeaux region) with a talkative inmate who goes by the name "Ciao"; and second, his trip by car to Bordeaux with a silent, unnamed hitchhiker. This chapter deals less with incarceration than the other five do: it is a meditation on the theme of traveling and on the transient nature of the lives of some young people in modern French society. In contrast, the fifth chapter, "The Solitude of the Wanderers," focuses entirely on the Gradignan writing workshop, covering both its textual production and its methodology. This chapter depicts a dramatic reading of inmates' texts in the prison. The reading is performed by the workshop director—accompanied by a colleague on bass guitar—in front of a group of young detainees. The context provides Bon with yet another opportunity to showcase the prisoners' writing and emphasize the referential qualities of

Prison. As is the case with the third chapter, readers are exposed to a variety of the prisoners' meditations on their experience in prison and on the margins of the city. The sixth and final chapter tells the story of one inmate's experiences while isolated in his jail cell.

Basic structural choices made by the author, such as the italicization of the prisoners' texts or the placement of their prose in quotation marks, render the mixture of narrative voices in *Prison* easily apparent. Much less apparent, even deliberately obscured, is the mixture of fictional and nonfictional elements. To be sure, there is nothing exceptional about the use of real-life events as fodder for artistic or literary production. What is worthy of note, however, is the author's free use of both fictional and nonfictional material in a text whose generic status is remarkably unclear. The difficulty in assigning a single, unambiguous generic category to Bon's text arises from a variety of textual and paratextual factors. As we will see, fictional and nonfictional elements of *Prison* are not only intertwined but are presented such that fiction can take on the guise of factual information, and vice versa. The result of the artful combination of fact and fiction is an ambiguous—and sometimes duplicitous—contract between text and reader. Fictional information is used to fill in the details of stories that are based in, and presented as, fact; and authentic factual data is used to enhance the documentary effect of fictional stories. Somewhere in the middle of this confusion, the reader attempts—with some difficulty—to determine how to read *Prison*: as a work of fiction, as a work of nonfiction, or as some cross between the two.

Analysis of the alterations Bon makes to his source material underlines specific facets of his sociopolitical perspective and artistic intentions. Like the other works examined in this study, Bon's text attempts to leave open the possibility for both referential and nonreferential interpretations, and fictional material serves as a complementary device to well-established documentary underpinnings. While emphasizing his work's basis in actuality, Bon takes advantage of the text's ambiguous genre to provide his readers with a more humanized portrait of the inner-city "youth" (*jeunes*) who often receive harsh treatment in the news media in contemporary France.[6] For example, using fictional narratives, the author explores the aftermath of Brulin's murder by showing its dramatic and deleterious effects on the murderer himself, the murderer's family, and even on Brulin's ghost. Furthermore, comparisons between *Prison* and "Parfois je me demande" allow us to analyze Bon's creative process and understand how he uses fiction to underline specific aspects of the inmates' lifestyles when outside of the prison (the transient nature of their movements, their complicated family lives, and how their daily activities and living conditions can easily lead to crime and imprisonment). Finally, we should note that, in *Prison*, Bon presents his readers with a cohesive, thematically balanced version of the experiences of the young detainees while behind bars. Bon stated that he never asked his workshop participants to write about their confinement, preferring to focus on their experience not as inmates but, rather, as "citizens."[7] Consequently, none of the texts in "Parfois je me demande" describe daily life in a prison cell in detail. Without weaving fictional material into his narrative, Bon would not have been able to explore the experience of incarceration, which he does in the book's final chapter through the voice of an anonymous, fictional detainee.

Whereas Bon's recycling of the texts composed in his writing workshop is, for the most part, faithful to and representative of what inmates actually produced, there are subtle yet important disparities between their texts and his portrayal of the young inmates in *Prison*. The changes Bon makes in transforming his source material into a publishable work are diverse in nature. On the one hand, some changes are clearly made for cosmetic purposes: for example, he edits stories to eliminate repetition or to maintain thematic equilibrium. On the other hand, some alterations are more ideological in nature: they reflect, challenge, or in some cases reinforce common perceptions of juvenile offenders. Some significant modifications render the inmates more palatable to Bon's imagined reading public, who—like the imagined readers of Serge, Genet, and Sarrazin—appear to be uninitiated to basic aspects of life in prison and life on society's margins.

Beyond understanding the nuances of Bon's transformation of his own experience into text, it is also important to ascertain as precisely as possible the terms of the contract between text and reader. Bon chose to render the generic status of his text ambiguous: *Prison* purports to be neither entirely fictional nor entirely nonfictional. That is not the result of chance. By carefully straddling the line between fiction and nonfiction, the author is able to manipulate his source material without a breach of contract between text and reader. He therefore has the freedom to transform and build upon his source material creatively without the threat of his work stirring up public controversy, as have other documentary and quasi-autobiographical works in cinema and literature. Michael Moore's 1988 documentary film *Roger and Me*, for example, was criticized and discredited because the filmmaker manipulated chronology to strengthen his critique of the American auto industry.[8] More recently, James Frey was roundly panned for fictionalizing his life's events in his autofictional text, *A Million Little Pieces* (2003), which was published and promoted as a memoir. Readers expressed outrage at what they perceived as Frey's violation of his text's autobiographical pact, as the author fabricated a number of significant details in his book to sensationalize his life story.[9] Bon's choice of an ambiguous contract between text and reader shows greater authorial integrity and artistic responsibility, as it allows for a strong documentary effect and, at the same time, creative flexibility. The author's sociopolitical message is therefore doubly strengthened, first by careful manipulation of source material and second by maintaining the pretension and, in some cases, the illusion of documentation.

In spite of the importance of fictional material in his work, when discussing *Prison*, Bon refers to it simply as a "livre" (book) and denies vigorously that it is a novel. "I had no motivation to write a novel," asserted Bon.[10] But avoiding the term "novel" is not tantamount to denying fictionalization. Indeed, if there is any doubt regarding the degree to which fiction and actuality are intertwined in the text, Bon's accidental conflation of the names of the real-life murder victim and his fictional counterpart—"Jean-Claude Hurlin," quoted above—is quite telling. Moreover, although Bon asserted in an interview that "There is nothing, absolutely nothing fictional in *Prison*, everything is based in reality," he did reluctantly admit, in the same interview, that there are elements in the text that are fictional. Despite the presence of fictional material in the work and its carefully crafted generic ambiguity, readers have nonetheless interpreted *Prison* as nonfiction. Indeed, so strong is the documentary effect of Bon's text that Christian Molinier, in his critique of the work, refers to the first chapter's narrator as "the author."[11] That designation is incorrect, as Bon maintains the anonymity of his narrator, a factor contributing to the book's calculated generic ambiguity.

The attempt to classify *Prison* as fiction or nonfiction is further complicated by its paratext, which accentuates the work's documentary slant and, at the same time, signifies the use of fictional material. The text's subtitle is the notoriously slippery term *récit*, which can be translated into English as "story," "account," or "narrative." Depending on its usage and context, the term can designate—and has designated—both fictional and nonfictional narratives.[12] The murky intended meaning of the subtitle is further obfuscated by the remaining paratextual information. At first glance, the publication information found in the opening pages of Bon's volume would seem to indicate that *Prison* is a nonreferential work of fiction. The book's "Notice" reads: "The events, places and people in this book are fictional and therefore do not seek to reflect or to pass judgment on actual events involving similar people or places. The works quoted are anonymous" (6). Given the indisputable resemblance between the *Sud Ouest* article and the events described in *Prison*'s first chapter, this rejection of documentation of or commentary on real-life events seems more than a bit hollow. Moreover, the following note of thanks is found immediately beneath the disclaimer: "Thanks go to the DRAC Aquitaine, the Aquitaine Library Cooperative, to the socio-educative service of the Gradignan Youth Detention Center, and to Kasper T. Toeplitz" (6).[13] Strangely enough, Toeplitz makes an appearance as the bass player in the book's fifth chapter (83), thereby further tarnishing the credibility of the "Notice." The disclaimer, moreover, contradicts Bon's declaration about the nonfictional nature of his text ("everything is based in reality"). The book's content and the author's commentary seem to be more compatible with a note at the back of the book, immediately following the end of the main body of text, which reads: "I would like to pay tribute here to all those—Laurent, David, Christian, Djamel, Damien, Frédéric, Sefia and the others—who helped turn collective writing into a realization of the greatest equality, a responsible equality within the loose fabric of the city and all its constituents" (122). The "I" is François Bon, and the individuals listed all took part in his writing workshop, and their texts—by-lines included—are found in "Parfois je me demande." Some of their names are even found in the main body of *Prison*. While the "Notice" deliberately attempts to steer the reader away from a referential interpretation of *Prison*, the note at the end of the text encourages that very type of reading.

In the final analysis, the indeterminacy of the term *récit* makes it an appropriate generic designation for the book, reflecting the singular mixture of nonfictional and fictional material in *Prison*. By choosing such a fluid term to define his narrative, Bon is able to transcend generic constraint while remaining focused on literary production, *écriture* (writing). He remarks: "The literary process is independent of genre: there is *écriture*—the word *récit* is simply the bare minimum of a definition, even if that genre has its own tradition in France."[14] Bon's emphasis on writing and the act of writing is revealing, as it is consistent with his workshop project in the youth detention center. *Prison* would not have the same documentary and sociological implications without the dominant presence of the voices of prisoners therein.

Degrees of Fictionality

Close comparative analysis of "Parfois je me demande" and *Prison* reveals that the six chapters of Bon's final work are fictionalized to different degrees. The third and fifth chapters, for example, are dominated by the presence of texts produced in the writing workshop: the central purposes of those chapters is to showcase the prisoners' texts and underline the referential grounding of *Prison*. Although there are minor variations between Bon's source material and the excerpts provided in the book, his recycling of texts in those two chapters is remarkably loyal to "Parfois je me demande." The third and fifth chapters are therefore the least fictionalized of all the chapters. In contrast, the first, second, and sixth chapters are the most hybrid sections of the text and, for that reason, are the most pertinent to our study of Bon's fictionalization of his experience. As we will see, analysis of the form and content of those three chapters opens a window onto both Bon's creative process and the sociopolitical motivations behind his project as a whole.[15]

The first chapter concentrates on the immediate shock caused by Brulin's death, the narrator's investigative journey through the city of Bordeaux, and the arrival of the murderer ("Tignasse") in the writing workshop. A comparison of the details found in the novel and in the *Sud Ouest* newspaper article reveals that the story recounted in the first chapter of *Prison* is remarkably representative of what happened to Frédéric Hurlin after his release from the youth detention center. Precise references to the actual newspaper article—its title, use of the newspaper's authentic name, and accurate quotes from its text and subtitle—serve as prime examples of the author's attempt to heighten the documentary effect of his book. Descriptions of the city of Bordeaux are also precise and accurate and include central and easily verifiable landmarks such as the Place de la Victoire and the Capucins market (8). The narrator even mentions specific bus routes (8) and the wording of street signs (10).

The mechanics of the writing workshop are introduced to the reader in the first chapter, and Bon gives a sample of the types of texts produced therein. One text in particular, which is italicized to accentuate its authenticity, evokes the violence endemic to the inmates' lives. It tells the story of a stabbing that echoes the struggle between Brulin and Tignasse. The following is an excerpt:

> And why I'm in prison it's because I needed money for the business I wanted to open and during a deal with a buddy things went badly and we started fighting and he tripped and pulled me towards him and the knife that I had fell from my pocket and he picked it up . . . before we started fighting he threatened me and my family so when I saw that he took my knife it was me or him but today it's me who finds himself in prison and if it had been me who had died it's him who you would have found here instead because he threatened me and he swore that it was me or him. (15)

In the original French, the excerpt in *Prison* reads:

Et pourquoi je suis en prison s'est que il me fallait de l'argent
pour le commerce que je voulait ouvrire et l'or d'un Bisnesse
avec un copain sa sais mal passer et on a n'est venue au main
et il a trébucher et il ma tirer ver lui est le couteau que je por-
tée et tombée de ma poche et il la ramassé . . . envant quont
n'en vient au main il m'avais menacer moi et ma famille al-
ors quant je les vue quil sestait enparus de mon couteaux
saitaient moi ou lui mes aujourd'hui ses moi qui se retrouve
en Prison est si saurait était moi qui serait mort ses lui que
vous aurait trouver à ma place car il mavait menacer et il
avait jurer que sétait moi ou lui. (15)

The excerpt's semblance of authenticity is accentuated by its
many spelling and grammatical errors. The text is indeed a
quotation from "Parfois je me demande" (80). However, Bon
appears to have manipulated this text by exaggerating its grammatical and spelling errors. A sample of the original prisoner's
text, whose grammar and spelling are noticeably more correct,
reads as follows:

> Et pourquoi je suis en prison, c'est qu'il me fallait de l'argent
> pour le commerce que je voulais ouvrir. Et lors d'un biz-
> ness avec un copain ça c'est mal passé et on en est venu aux
> mains et on a trébuché et il m'a tiré vers lui et le couteau que
> je portais est tombé de ma poche et il l'a ramassé et sur la
> peur je l'ai retourné plusieurs fois sur lui mais avant qu'on
> en vienne aux mains il m'avait menacé moi et ma famille.
> ("Parfois" 80)[16]

Bon's alterations are neither artistically nor ideologically innocent. Rather, they serve not only to heighten the text's semblance of authenticity but also to accentuate the alterity of the
prisoners as a group.

Alongside those detailed, documentary descriptions of Bordelais urban space, quotations from *Sud Ouest*, and excerpts from what are presented as authentic prisoners' writings, Bon interpolates four overtly fictional monologues to complete his telling of the slaying and its impact on the writing workshop. The narrators of the speeches are Brulin's ghost, Tignasse (the murderer, who has two monologues), and a young woman whom the narrator imagines as Tignasse's sister. The four monologues are the only instances in the entire book in which the distinction between the imaginary and the real is both overt and unambiguous: the fictional narrative voices are clearly demarcated from the remainder of the text. The narrator introduces Tignasse's first monologue with the phrase "he who will be facing me from this point on never wrote or spoke thus" (12), and the murderer's next speech is described as "Tignasse's second imagined monologue" (19).[17] The remaining two monologues are introduced as fiction in equally unambiguous terms, as one is pronounced by Brulin's ghost, and the anonymous narrator presents the fourth with the remark, "the words one imagines are necessarily false" (26). As is the case with the fantasies of the narrator in *Miracle de la rose*, the imagined monologues of *Prison*, within the grammar of the narrative, are presented as fictional departures from the reality of the remainder of the story.

Like the strong documentary effect created by certain key details in the book's first chapter, fictional material is of fundamental importance to Bon's retelling of Brulin's murder. The fictional monologues attributed to Tignasse are particularly interesting, as they complement and reinforce the information the narrator is able to garner in the prison workshop and during his walk through the city. The monologues provide a glimpse of the fictionalized murderer's troubled and conflicted emotional state after the killing as well as his side of the murder story—elements to which Bon's readers would not have had access were it not for the author's use of fictional material. The first monologue begins with an expression of remorse from Tignasse, who bemoans the terrible burden brought on by his error (13). Bon uses the remainder of the monologue to describe, from Tignasse's perspective, how the latter stumbled upon Brulin in the squat and how Brulin failed to obey the unwritten codes of the use of space in the squat. The second monologue provides further elaboration on the event, detailing the murderer's emotional fragility both during and after his encounter with Brulin. Tignasse speaks of his nightmares in prison and of his fear of being attacked by Brulin's friends. This second fictional monologue is much less remorseful in tone, as Tignasse tries to justify his behavior by mentioning his petty annoyances with Brulin, whose characteristics—particularly how he stood too close when talking and always wanted to mooch cigarettes and food—are based on Bon's observations of the actual victim while he was in the workshop. Tignasse even further claims that Brulin started the fight and mentions that he just wanted to "push him away" (20), a detail Bon borrows from the *Sud Ouest* article. The monologue ends as Tignasse speaks of his feelings of panic after the murder, and of how he decided to turn himself in "with my head drenched in sweat, and my palms clammy with murder" (21).

The repercussions of Tignasse's crime are further elaborated through another fictional monologue, which is attributed to a young girl whom the narrator sees in the train station and imagines as the murderer's sister. This monologue also illustrates the importance of fictional material in the narrative, as Bon uses it to include the perspective of a family member of an inmate, a perspective that is absent from the rest of the work. The monologue provides a detailed, documentary-style description of what families endure when their loved ones are in jail. The young girl is also the only female narrator in the entire work. She begins her monologue by asserting her loyalty to her brother: "Because no matter what he did, he's still my brother. And I will go every week to visit him with a change of clothes in the little white plastic bag" (26). After a description of their conversations, Bon then places particular emphasis on what people must do simply to enter the prison for a visit with an inmate. About one-fourth of the page-and-a-half monologue is devoted to the precise process of entry into the jail, and the description focuses on her movement through the institution's security system. She states:

> I went to visit my brother and again went past the green metal door with the rectangular bars, the more narrow entryway where you have to strip yourself of anything metal, keys and change, to pass through the metal detector, and further up, there is the scale where you put the plastic bag containing the change of clothes, because they weigh it and there is a limit and then the long wood table where they do a search (they don't search through everything, they don't search you), and then finally the series of wood boxes that run the length of the room, where four by four you are face to face. (27)

The highly detailed content of the monologue renders it clear that the use of fictional material serves as a strategy not only to give psychological interiority to an aggrieved loved one but also to show readers an important aspect of the prison environment. As is the case with the other prison novels examined in this study, the amount of detail provided about processes and rules reveals that Bon's imagined readers are uninitiated to the basic elements of prison life and that a primary function of the text is to portray those minutiae.

The fourth fictional monologue in the first chapter is spoken by Brulin's ghost, who moves through the tables near the narrator's seat in the Bordeaux train station (23). Bon uses this monologue to elaborate on his prior knowledge of Brulin and imagine the latter's thoughts as he is ostracized and beaten by his fellow inmates. After the narrator ruminates on what the administration described as "bad treatment by his co-detainees," the ghost of Brulin is introduced. The monologue begins: "They said *bad treatment* but nothing else that would testify to what you endure, from one to the other, the five of them sent me back and forth like the edges of a table would do to a billiard ball, their sweatsuits and their hightops have brand name logos and it seems like it starts just because you aren't dressed like them and that no one has come to see you in the visiting room and you don't have the money to buy anything in the cafeteria" (23–24). The narrative continues and Brulin speaks of how he endured the beatings and then tried to hide his injuries from the administration. The guards, the ghost informs us, eventually moved him to the adult prison to isolate him from the youths in the detention center. The fictional monologue enriches Bon's portrayal of Brulin's psychological interiority and adds an element of pathos to the story. It is inserted when readers are already fully aware of Brulin's senseless murder upon his release. Readers are given even more of an impression of a hard-luck case, as they see the victim attempting to cope with the abuse from his fellow inmates and struggling to keep his broken glasses on while being beaten.

The mixture of fictional and nonfictional elements in the first chapter of *Prison* makes for a compelling narrative about crime, punishment, and the difficulties faced by transient and alienated young people in late-twentieth-century France. It is, however, crucial to note that the clear distinction between fiction and nonfiction made in this chapter creates a problematic and deceptive expectation for the book's remaining five chapters, namely, that unless there is an overt signal to the contrary, the reader should interpret information in the narrative as nonfictional. The remainder of the narrative does not follow the principle established in the first chapter, as there are a number of fictional passages that are not explicitly designated as such.[18] The reader thus may be duped into interpreting stories that originate in Bon's imagination as referential narratives, such as the story about a stolen car and joyride (examined below) that immediately follows the story about the Brulin murder.

The second chapter, "At the Edge of Cities," tells the story of three young men who cross paths by chance and are linked by a single crime: driving together to the beach in a stolen Ford Cosworth. The story is broken up into four sections, each with its own narrator. The first three deal with the experience of the young men before and during their joyride, and the fourth depicts their activity in the writing workshop. Although the first three tales revolve around the common denominator of crime, they focus primarily on the young men's daily lives and their routines in the city and suburbs, describing the events that led to their involvement in the crime. Bon uses their narratives to further develop the major theme introduced in the first chapter: how homelessness and poverty can expose young people to violence and create fertile ground for crime. The authenticity of each of the narratives is emphasized through a variety of strategies. Like the story of Brulin and Tignasse, the narratives are situated in Bordeaux and its suburbs, and Bon again highlights easily identifiable Bordelais neighborhoods and landmarks (e.g., the Saint-Michel neighborhood, the Garonne river, and the pedestrian thoroughfare named rue Sainte-Catherine). Furthermore, portions of the testimonies about life in the city are italicized and placed in quotation marks. Those formatting choices—following the expectations established in the first chapter—lead the reader to believe that those testimonies are excerpted from authentic prisoners' writings.

The fourth segment of the chapter is narrated by the same anonymous workshop director whom readers encountered in the first chapter. In this section, the director describes in detail the youths' entry into the prison: "At the clerk's office they left everything except their clothes. They got their numbers, they were searched then saw the social worker who asked them whom to notify and they were separated" (43). The director then describes how they eventually find their way to his workshop. On that day in the workshop, the participants are told to write about a voyage that left them with a lasting and powerful memory. The director suggests they reflect on the few images from their travels that have remained fixed in their minds. After that description of the activity of the day, the narrator skips to his reaction upon reading the texts: he is dumbfounded by a coincidence found among the various papers handed to him by the inmates: "And, on that Tuesday, the same word Cosworth (I didn't even know it was a car) surfaced in the urban night on three separate pieces of paper" (44).

Given the implied contract between text and reader established by the book's first chapter, it is only natural to assume that the stories of the three prisoners are intended to be read as referential. There are no unambiguous indicators pointing out fictional material like the ones found in the first chapter. Furthermore, the integration of the stories into the context of the prison writing workshop underlines their alleged authenticity. However, comparisons of three narratives and the source material in "Parfois je me demande" show that these stories are indeed fictionalized. Although it appears to be as grounded in actuality as the murder of Brulin, the theft of the Cosworth is the product of Bon's imagination. The author uses the fictional stolen car story to showcase the experience of three different detainees in urban and suburban settings. The Cosworth narratives allow Bon to develop the themes of movement and contingency as they relate to the experience of young men on the margins of modern French society. Without the benefit of examining the writings in "Parfois je me demande," however, the reader has no way of knowing that the stories have been altered and that the entire context of criminality was invented by the author.

Comparisons between *Prison* and "Parfois je me demande" provide a glimpse into Bon's writing process and into the manner in which he mixes both documentary and fictional information in the three joyride stories. The first story is told by an unidentified third-person omniscient narrator and is based primarily on a text titled "Early in the Morning" ("Parfois" 138–41) composed by an inmate named Daniel.[19] In his original text, Daniel recounts how he spent a typical day as a homeless person in the northeastern French city of Mulhouse in 1992, milling around in more or less idle fashion and searching for diversions to pass the time, like going to the FNAC (a video and book store), eating, and talking to his friends. Bon alters Daniel's text by adding a number of details that make it consistent with the remainder of the chapter and the *récit* as a whole. First, the author places the young man in Bordeaux rather than in Mulhouse. The documentary realism of the segment is heightened by references to authentic city landmarks, such as the Place de la Victoire and Mériadeck (the name of a modern part of town and shopping center). Second, Bon invents two crimes and writes them into Daniel's narrative: the theft of a video camera from the FNAC and, more significantly, the automobile theft. After stealing the fictional car, the anonymous thief picks up two hitchhikers and they begin the drive to the beach town of Lacanau "without even knowing each others' first or last names" (35). It is that final invented detail—the introduction of two new characters—that allows Bon to springboard into the other vignettes.

After the theft of the car is described in the first prisoner's narrative, there is a clear section break in the chapter and another story begins in a markedly different style. Whereas the first narrative is told by a single narrator and entirely in the third person, the second is noticeably more of a hybrid text, complete with italicized text, which is intended to be read as actual text from the workshop. Two distinct narrative voices are present in the section: an unidentified third-person narrator and a first-person narrator that is partly fictional and that partly originates from direct quotes from the text of a real inmate named Luc. That workshop participant resided in a low-income housing area on the right bank of Bordeaux's Garonne river in a project called California 1 and 2.[20] Luc's original text, like Daniel's, recounts the routine of a typical day in his life. Bon elaborates upon Luc's short text and complements it with his own fictional writing.

The vignette begins with a description, written by Bon, of the right bank of the river and of its relationship to the rest of the city. The spatial contextualization is established by the third-person narrator, who describes the urban environment in realistic and unflattering terms, especially as one gets near the low-income housing project: "In front of the project there is the river . . . and between the project and the river there is that vague terrain where, when they were kids, they made their forts, where a few wire fences still separate old community garden plots, and where abandoned cars, those that people didn't have the heart to push into the Garonne, are used as landmarks for meetings" (35). The narrator then introduces the unnamed protagonist of the vignette: "He is in the basement of his building with four good friends, its their staircase and they stay down there" (35). It is that "he" who begins narrating (in the first person) the story of life in the project. The young man begins his story by explaining that they are waiting in the staircase to complete a drug deal: "Nothing else to do but wait for it to come to your door. . . . We put the stuff in the mailbox . . . and the exchange happened easily, with small, ready-made packages" (36). Following that description, there is not a narrator shift but rather an author shift: Bon inserts into the story an italicized paragraph, which, although it is uttered by the same narrator, was composed not by Bon, like the previous descriptions, but by the real prisoner, Luc. The passage, excerpted directly from "Parfois je me demande," complements the telling of the drug deal: *"Because in my project, that's how it happens, because there are several pretty long buildings, and at almost every entrance there's someone waiting for clients, and that makes for competition"* (36).

The remainder of the second vignette is a mixture of direct quotes from Luc's authentic text and Bon's own writing. Some—but not all—of the inmate's text is designated as such via quotation marks and italicization. The story meanders from the explanation of the drug deal to a description of the rest of his and his friends' day in the project to a telling of one specific evening in the city. The narrative emphasizes the transient and random nature of the youths' wanderings around and outside the city: the main character goes to a nightclub he has never been to, gets separated from his friend who took him there, and is then forced to hitchhike home with a friend of still another friend. Finally, the narrator and his friend-of-a-friend are picked up by the driver of the stolen Ford Cosworth, who stops only because he cannot figure out how to operate the windshield wipers. The second section ends as the narrator states: "And since the car was a Ford Cosworth, I knew how, and I showed him, and then I complimented him on the car, and we went to Lacanau because it was on the road sign, just to see how the car drove" (40).

The narrative about the third individual involved in the joyride begins after yet another section break. In this story, Bon conflates the writings of more than one prisoner—in this case, texts by workshop participants Claude and Ramzi—into the voice of a single fictional character. While the story is indeed based in the reality of the two texts produced in the workshop, the seamless conflation of the texts of two different prisoners into the voice of a single inmate constitutes a fictionalization on the part the author. Claude's text, "Beer or Sandwich" ("Parfois" 138–39), recounts three events, all of which are found in *Prison*: purchasing some beer, finding (and absconding with) a bag containing forty-two hundred French francs, and using part of that money to eat at McDonald's. Ramzi's text, titled "Building" ("Parfois" 141–43), is more detailed and concerns the young man's daily routine and family life. Ramzi, a nineteen-year-old who lives in Paris, describes a typical day in his life: he wakes up, listens to music, gets dressed, sees his friends, smokes marijuana, talks to his father (who scolds him for not having a job), and goes out at night to drink in pubs. He ends his text by describing his drunken walk through empty Parisian streets and his arrival at home. Once in his room, he listens to music, smokes more marijuana, and goes to bed.

In *Prison*, Bon transforms the Parisian Ramzi into a Bordeaux resident and then weaves Claude's story into Ramzi's lengthier, more detailed narrative. The narrative in Bon's *récit* begins just as Ramzi's does: "Waking up is tough, I get out of bed and I look around me just like every morning at the same time" (40; "Parfois" 141). The story remains consistent up through Ramzi's awkward conversation with his father. However, in the final *récit* the anonymous fictional character—instead of going out in Paris, then returning home to listen to music, smoke, and sleep (as Ramzi does)—goes to hang out at a gas station, which is on the same road that leads to the beach town of Lacanau on the west coast of France. It is at that point that Claude's story about the theft of the bag full of money and the subsequent trip to McDonald's is woven into the narrative (42–43). Bon then invents what occurs after the narrator eats at McDonald's: the young man goes back to the gas station and recognizes someone he knew a long time ago. That man is hanging out with his friends near a car: "He saw me and introduced me to them" (43). The man who performed the introduction leaves, and then the narrator is invited by the two remaining strangers near the car to go to the beach. Near the end of his story, he states: "With the rest of the sack of money, I wanted to go to Lacanau too and we left" (43). Through the involvement of that third and final character in the joyride, Bon emphasizes the random character of the lives of the young men: he is in the car simply because one of the first two hitchhikers, whom he knew a long time ago, introduces him to the car thief and the other hitchhiker. Soon thereafter he finds himself in a prison writing workshop. To tie the three Cosworth narratives together, Bon crafts a comment that he attributes to the fictionalized inmate. The newly detained young man ends his story by saying, "Today, I know that the three of us are here and why we're here" (43).

Although it may be clear why the three characters are in prison (they were in a stolen car), whether they deserve to be there is another matter entirely. Indeed, two of them had nothing to do with the car theft. As Bon constructs the story, they were just in the wrong place at the wrong time and happened to cross the path of someone who actually did commit a crime. Moreover, the manner in which the fictional car theft is told deemphasizes the criminal nature of the act. The car is stolen in the middle of the night by the homeless protagonist of the chapter's first section. Separated from his friends after a night on the town, the narrator is looking for a place to sleep. Unable to find the building in which he normally squats, he ends up walking around in the rain. Then, Bon writes, "He started to look at the cars, just randomly, without anything else in mind, and he found one that was unlocked, and decided to just get inside. Only once he was inside did he think that it would be better if he took it further away, so he could sleep longer" (34). He then starts the car with the help of his pocket knife, and "the old girl started up as if she was very happy that someone was interested in her . . . and because the knob was turned to the red side, she even offered him her warmth after just three blocks" (34). And, just like that, the feminized car seduces the passive and sleepy young man into theft. The crime is broken down into its incremental stages, and the theft appears to be merely a matter of circumstance rather than a result of actively criminal behavior. This is not to say that Bon condones criminal behavior in *Prison*; however, the manner in which he constructs the fictional crime attempts to disabuse his readers of the notion that a car theft is necessarily an act of premeditated evil. It would seem that the fact that the young man is homeless and needs a place to sleep is more important than any other motive. As a determining factor behind any crime, homelessness—rather than, say, the desire to sell the car for drug money—has a greater chance of arousing compassion and sympathetic understanding. Homelessness can result from a variety of circumstances beyond a young person's control, such as a bad family life, inadequate governmental assistance, and so on. The crime thus appears to be more a result of a wider social problem than a question of individual deviance or senseless transgression.

Ultimately, Bon's fictional telling of how the three young men land in jail constitutes an attempt to normalize the experience of the inmates and render them less threatening to the imagined reading public. Based on the evidence included in the narrative, transient lifestyles—not demonic behavior—are at the root of crime and juvenile delinquency. In the sixth chapter of *Prison*, titled "Isolation," Bon uses creative license in a similar way to depict the experience of one anonymous prisoner incarcerated in a private cell in the youth detention center. The anonymous inmate's voice is, according to Bon, based on the impressions the author garnered from his interactions with a specific workshop participant. Bon notes that he created the first-person voice in part by "placing himself in the shoes of Lionel in solitary confinement."[21] Beyond inventing a fictional experience based on the voice of an inmate he knew personally, Bon uses two other fictionalization techniques to create the story of the anonymous "I." First, he extracts material produced in the writing workshop and conflates the experiences of multiple inmates into the personal background of one prisoner. Bon uses at least six different texts, composed by three different prisoners in the writing workshop, to create the voice of the anonymous "I" in the sixth chapter.[22] Second, he uses multiple narrative voices in "Isolation," moving frequently from third-person omniscient to first-person narration. As we have seen in *Les hommes dans la prison* and *Miracle de la rose*, sudden demonstrations of omniscience constitute clear signposts of fictionality.

Typically, prison narratives recount the basic elements of incarceration: entry into the prison, daily living conditions, institutional space, inmate relations, the administration's assertion of power over detainees, and, at times, what prisoners experience upon their release. Although *Prison* may appear to diverge from other prison novels because it lacks a more standard arrest-to-release structure, on a thematic level it shares a great deal with its generic counterparts primarily because of the content of the book's final chapter. In the "Isolation" narrative, the experience of one anonymous prisoner is depicted as being typical of what all inmates endure, thereby bolstering the story's relevancy and social importance. Like the other prison narratives examined in this study, "Isolation" emphasizes description rather than plot. No major events are depicted in the chapter: readers are simply given a sense of the routine of everyday life behind bars through the musings of an anonymous protagonist who is spending a sleepless night alone in his cell.

The use of an anonymous narrator is but one strategy Bon employs to highlight the exemplary nature of the confinement narrative in *Prison*. The author includes a number of broad generalizations about prison life, thereby transforming the narrative into a kind of Everyman-in-prison story similar to the one found in Serge's *Les hommes dans la prison*. In some instances, Bon uses specific sentence structures and grammatical choices to accentuate the fact that those generalizations are representative and typical of the experience in the youth detention center. In one passage, for example, the author uses the pronoun *on* (meaning "one," which I will translate as "you") nine times in a single, short paragraph that describes the routine of solitary confinement. The inmate begins his description by reflecting on why one feels rested after ten days in *le mitard* (the hole), a strange fact since "the hole" serves, in theory, as a severe form of discipline for those who are already incarcerated:

> [Y]ou really can't say why. You don't get outside, the morning comes and the hours of the day stream past in the shadows of the window, it is cold, then it is hot, you hear vague noises, from the other stories, you have an hour to be in the yard that is even more bare than this room, you hear nothing, you don't count the moments of the day, but you only wait for the end of the ten days, everything is silence, you wait, you empty yourself and that's what is restful. And after that, you come back [to the ordinary cell block]. (102)

Beyond punitive solitary confinement, Bon also gives readers a sense of what prisoners do in and out of their cells (they watch television and play basketball in the courtyard), what they eat (bread and couscous) and drink (instant coffee), and which recreational drugs they take (pharmaceuticals). A typical prison cell is described through the protagonist's remembrance of another cell he previously occupied. The description is nearly a page long and includes minutiae such as soap, graffiti, photos, a stool, and a table.[23] The chapter also describes the creative and mischievous side of the prisoners, giving details about how they try to smoke lawn clippings for lack of tobacco and how they try to heat water in their cells with makeshift coffee machines (by plugging forks into the wall outlets for heat, a process that causes repeated disruptions in the prison's electrical system).

As in most prison narratives, readers are given indications about relations among inmates. In *Prison* the detainees are depicted hazing each other through innocent and humorous banter. Although usually harmless, the hazing can rapidly lead to violence. Indeed, Bon makes it clear that although it may seem that the prisoners live comfortably behind bars with a free place to sleep, regular meals, and cable television, violence is endemic to their environment. Inmates practice self-mutilation and even set their own mattresses on fire to protest their incarceration (106). Guards can also be victims of the violence, as inmates have been known to poke their eyes out with forks when the guards look through the judases of the cell doors (104). Such information is typical in prison narratives and films as writers seek to illustrate that the prison is its own subculture with distinct behavioral codes, practices, and unwritten rules.

In addition to such subcultural information, Bon includes a number of details that humanize the Everyman prisoner depicted in "Isolation." In spite of the potential violence in the prison environment, the inmate is able to engage in calm meditation while behind bars. He has time to reflect in peace at a distance from the fast-paced "community of humans" assembled in the city (105). The protagonist also describes how prisoners maintain their psychological independence and keep secrets from the administration. Prisoners find ways to resist their incarceration in spirit, for example, by practicing moderation in eating. The inmate notes: "You couldn't care less about hunger and their tray of food, you leave everything in piles, at least half of it . . . what would it mean to clean your plate? That you accept the prison in your blood and guts" (104). The inmates even know how to circumvent the routine searches conducted by the guards: "Once a month you get your cell tossed. They come get you (even if you're in the writing workshop or wherever), they take you, and in front of you they shake the little of what you have, they overturn the mattress, they look under the clothes shelf, they search you too. We know where you have to keep stuff that is secret, the stuff that they can't reach" (109).

Bon interpolates at least six different stories produced by three inmates from the youth detention center to enrich and humanize his depiction of the prisoner in solitary confinement. He gives readers no indication that he is conflating the voices of those three prisoners to construct the fictional voice of the narrator-protagonist. Readers without access to Bon's unpublished source material are therefore led to believe that all the elements of that life story originate in one inmate's experience. However, as in the story of the stolen car in the second chapter, comparisons between "Parfois je me demande" and *Prison* provide a glimpse into the author's creative process and his alterations of his source material.

The six narratives produced in the workshop serve a variety of purposes in "Isolation." Three that are included almost verbatim from "Parfois je me demande" describe instances of childhood mischief. In one italicized excerpt, based on a tale by an inmate named Lionel, the narrator gets lost in town while surreptitiously following his mother on her way to work and, after his reunion with his family, understands how much pain he caused her (108–9). Two other stories about childhood transgressions were written by an inmate named Tahar and are found in the same paragraph in *Prison*. One describes the repeated theft of candy, and the other tells how the narrator and one of his friends dumped a bucket of dirty water on an unsuspecting passerby (110–11).[24] The transgressions are innocent enough and do not seem intended to describe a life of crime that inevitably led to prison. To be sure, there are any number of texts describing disturbing and criminal behavior in "Parfois je me demande," and Bon elected to include those three narratives describing innocent and childish behavior. While each of the three stories evokes a different type of rebelliousness, the narratives serve mainly to enrich the background of the fictional character in the "Isolation" narrative and render him more sympathetic.

A fourth excerpt from "Parfois je me demande" corresponds to themes found in the preceding chapters of *Prison*. The excerpt is based on a text by Mark C. and describes a trip taken to Spain and the difficulties of traveling by train with no tickets or identity papers (114–15). In that story, the protagonist and his friends manage to reach their destination (on a night train without paying). While in Spain they encounter some problems with the police (they are thrown out of a stairwell in which they squat for the night), then decide to take a trip around the whole country. The narrator-protagonist comments that he did not have his identity papers, so the group decides to go back to Bordeaux to retrieve them.[25] They never are able to hop onto a another train, so the group ends up walking from Irun to Saint-Jean-de-Luz. That narrative extends and elaborates on the theme of the inmates' marginality and how their lack of stability and of real homes contributes to criminal behavior (i.e., riding on trains illegally).

Bon uses a fifth story from "Parfois je me demande" that describes a nightmare. In the original text the inmate describes a dream he had about a murder, a failed cover-up, and a search by the police that uncovers the victim's body. The nightmare is inserted into *Prison* virtually unchanged, except Bon turns it into a recurring bad dream had by the protagonist of the sixth chapter. Although Bon does not change its fundamental details, his transformation of the bad dream into a recurring nightmare gives readers the impression that the narrator is haunted by crime and violence and is unable to find real peace.

As this analysis shows, Bon is, for the most part, loyal to the spirit of the prisoners' writings, and most of his changes amount to editing for style and thematic consistency. One story in the sixth chapter, however, is significantly changed, and the alterations recall Bon's fictionalization of the joyride in the second chapter. The original text, titled "Anarchist and Wild," written by Lionel, concerns the relationship of the inmate with an *éducateur* (teacher) who served as a kind of mentor and helped the young man temporarily pull his life together (58). Lionel describes how, at the age of seventeen, he already had a significant criminal record and no shelters or mentors wanted to work with him. Through the help of a friend, Lionel is able to find a stern but helpful *éducateur* who helps him improve his life: "I started to chat him up to get some money out of him. He stopped me right there and said 'I won't give you money for drugs.'" After the mentor's initial intervention, Lionel writes, the two started to examine Lionel's "problems," and for a time he felt his life was improving: "After that, I really got attached to him. . . . I did things that I didn't even think I was capable of. For a year, I did not use any drugs, except for weed. But I had stopped the pills, the heroin, the cocaine. And at that time I didn't drink. That came later." Unfortunately for Lionel, after his remarkable turnaround he ceased working with the *éducateur*, because the latter had to have surgery and then was hired to work in a homeless shelter. "After that, they gave me another mentor," Lionel writes, "but it didn't work out, and I fell into my old habits. And after that I spent a year fucking around for no reason, I was like a wild anarchist." He ends his text by stating that, in spite of his downward spiral, "I kept contact with that teacher, we still write each other."

Lionel's story is inserted into *Prison* with a few noteworthy changes. Two references to his drug use are eliminated. The first is in the context of the narrator's first interaction with the mentor. In *Prison* it reads: "I started to chat him up to get some money out of him. He stopped me right there and said 'I won't give you money'" (112). In the original, the mentor refuses to give Lionel money "for drugs." The second instance is in reference to the young man's rehabilitation. In *Prison* the inmate remarks: "For a year I didn't recognize myself, I had stopped everything" (112). The inmate's transformation appears to be more dramatic in *Prison* than in "Parfois je me demande," since the reference to continued marijuana use is eliminated. Furthermore, the omission of the indications that he experimented with a variety of hard drugs ("the pills, the heroin, the cocaine") normalizes the inmate, making it easier for the reader to sympathize with the experience of the fictional detainee.

Those changes, however, are minor compared to how Bon tells the story of the events that led to the end of the young man's relationship with his mentor. In "Parfois je me demande" their relationship ends due to a combination of bad luck (the mentor's illness and surgery) and bureaucratic forces (his new job). In *Prison* the relationship ends only because of bureaucratic forces: "And one day that teacher was hired as a director of a homeless shelter" (112). Furthermore, unlike in the original text, there is no reference to attempts to find a new mentor. Thus, the inmate, who appeared to be on the road to a dramatic recovery, seems to be a victim of an inadequate social infrastructure, abandoned by a system that was effective only temporarily. In "Parfois je me demande" the fault does not lie entirely in the support infrastructure, since the mentor's illness played a key role in the ending of the relationship. That modification, combined with the fact that Lionel's recovery from drug addiction is not as clear-cut in real life as it is in *Prison*, shows that Bon manipulates his source material to criticize as inconsistent and neglectful the social services available to needy young people.

The inmate's struggle with an inadequate support system raises a question of capital importance: How are prisoners to reintegrate into the outside world upon their release? In the sixth chapter Bon uses his fictionalized narrator-protagonist to examine, from the perspective of an inmate, the nature of the boundary that exists between the city and the prison. At the end of the chapter the narrator-protagonist meditates on his return to the outside world after serving his sentence. His reflections reveal indifference to his release from prison as well as his resigned awareness that he will probably be incarcerated again in the future. Contrary to what is often depicted in prison narratives (e.g., *Les hommes dans la prison* and *Miracle de la rose*), the inmate does not await his exit impatiently by obsessively counting days, weeks, and months; rather, he states, "One day, waiting in front of the door will happen, a plastic bag in hand. Taking the bus towards the city (the G bus that goes to Gradignan) will happen, the loop that comes here is not one of the frequent ones but you prefer to wait at the bus stop close by, you prefer to get in the bus and sit down and, at the next stop, nobody knows" (120–21). Based on past experience, the narrator knows that he will rapidly blend in with the general population on the bus. He mentions that upon his return to his routine on the outside he will be free to do as he pleases. The inmate notes that he will be stunned by the variety of colors in the outside world and that he will see faces he recognizes from prison. In short, the release back into the city appears to be a routine exercise: "You have crossed from the other side of the world, and you now know how to use and cross over the boundary" (120).

Contemplating the nature of that boundary, the anonymous first-person narrator ends his reflection with the comment, "I will be in the city, and city and space are all the same to me now because what counts is time: it doesn't matter much if I come back here" (121). The chapter and book thus end on a note suggesting that, for the young detainees, no distinct boundary exists between the city and prison. From their perspective, chronic recidivism is not an abstract social problem but rather just one of many factors in their everyday lives. By using the fictional "I" in the sixth chapter, Bon places his readers in a position to understand an individual who has firsthand experience with repeated imprisonments. The porous boundary between the prison and the city takes on a different social significance when it originates in the thoughts of an inmate, even if that inmate is fictional. That prisoner's indifference serves as a point of access to sociopolitical issues that are explored throughout *Prison*. It evokes, in particular, the ineffectiveness of "reinsertion" plans set up by state officials, the inadequacy of which were already underlined by the murder of Brulin, who was forced out into the streets far from his home in the northeast of France.

Text in Context

Bon reflects on his experience in the youth detention center in an unpublished essay titled "Ecrire en prison" ("Writing in Prison") composed in January 1997, just after Hurlin's murder. Elucidating some of the sociopolitical motivations behind his work, he writes: "The [prisoners'] texts will only take on their primary importance when seen in a social context that would, in turn, make them comment on the city." He notes that their writing, while captivating on a literal level, is also "saturated with moral signifiers" (13). Indeed, the texts offer readers a rare glimpse into the minds of those who have little or no voice in mainstream cultural discourse. For *Prison* is, above all, a book that seeks to bear witness to the experience of the workshop participants in both the prison and a variety of urban situations. The fictionalized writing workshop constitutes a forum in which their voices are not only heard but also placed in a context that underlines their broader social implications—their "moral signifiers," to use Bon's phrase. The hybrid format chosen by the author allows the reader to grasp the difficulties posed by that context and, at the same time, to read lengthy and, in many cases, unedited samples of their texts.

Like many other writers who have confronted the prison milieu, Bon composed a text based on his experience that is, overall, a call for a form of social justice. *Prison* constitutes an attempt to view crime, criminality, and punishment from many perspectives; indeed, the multiplicity of voices is the book's distinguishing characteristic. Without condoning crime or deviant behavior, Bon emphasizes that many factors contribute to criminality and that inmates face hostile and dangerous environments both in and out of prison. The difficulties faced by transient young people are most apparent in the retelling of the story of Frédéric Hurlin in the book's tone-setting first chapter. Not only was Hurlin murdered for a "trivial motive," but Bon also sees the murder as a highly preventable occurrence. In describing his reaction to the murder, Bon comments on "The responsibility that it implies for our society in general" and rails against the prison administration for releasing a young man into the streets in the middle of winter with no money, no warm clothes, and no train ticket home. Furthermore, he argues that the conditions in the squat in which Hurlin sought shelter implicate society as a whole, noting in his letter to Frédéric Miremont's attorney that the death reminded him "so brutally of the harshness of the city, and the precariousness of their [the inmates'] living conditions outside the walls of the prison" (24 May 1998). The case of Frédéric Hurlin is emblematic of Bon's treatment of his experience with inmates in his fiction and serves as a thematic springboard for his depiction of young people in modern France who are so transient that they appear to the narrator to be simply "lost on the face of the Earth" (*Prison* 63). Bon emphasizes that prison is just one of the many places—along with city streets, random stairways, and stolen cars—to which their errant paths may lead them.

[CONCLUSION]

Literary controversies come and go, but the fracas surrounding James Frey's *A Million Little Pieces* in early 2006 was a sight to behold. The book tells the story of "James Frey," a twenty-three-year-old drug addict, alcoholic, and criminal who endures a brutal recovery from his addictions in a rehabilitation center in Minnesota. The text achieved great notoriety two years after its initial publication, when literary kingmaker Oprah Winfrey selected it for her book club in late 2005. That endorsement led to a surge in sales of Frey's book and set the stage for the noisiest literary controversy in the mainstream media in recent years.

The controversy centered around significant inconsistencies between the author's real life and *A Million Little Pieces*, which had been published and aggressively promoted as a factually accurate memoir. Discrepancies between Frey's lived experience and events depicted in his book were first exposed by an investigative Web site in early 2006.[1] That initial report focused primarily on the author's falsifications of his criminal history, most notably that he was "wanted in three states" (205) and was going to face "a few months" in prison in Ohio for some of his transgressions (420). In reality, Frey's most egregious brush with the law was when he was briefly detained for driving under the influence of alcohol and for having an open beer can in his car. For that the author was forced to spend a few hours in an Ohio police station. Frey's lived experience is indeed a far cry from what happens to the narrator-protagonist of *A Million Little Pieces*. While driving drunk and high on crack, "Frey" hits a policeman with his car and then resists arrest, kicking and punching the officers who try to subdue him. "Frey" eventually gets hauled away and is accused of felony mayhem, among many other crimes, after the brawl (250).

Subsequent television interviews revealed even more discrepancies between Frey's life and his "memoir," leading one prominent commentator to suggest Frey be kicked out of the "kingdom of Oprah."[2] Indeed, a number of journalists and commentators expressed dismay at Frey's abuse of his creative license, linking his fabrications to a pervasive lack of accountability, honesty, and responsibility in contemporary American society.[3] Frey and his publishers would have done themselves a great service by simply labeling his text "autofiction" rather than "memoir."[4] However, more precise labeling and more honest marketing would have certainly rendered Frey's violent story of addiction and recovery much less compelling. For, as is the case with the prison novels examined in this study, the primary interest in Frey's brutal, bloody narrative resides very much in the fact that the author seems to have lived through the trauma depicted therein. In the end, Frey turned out to be much like a latter-day Jean Genet, with at least one important difference: Frey did all he could to put a stop to his literary banishment—including threats of lawsuits and multiple apologetic and confessional appearances on television—whereas Genet probably would have reveled in such infamy.

The controversy surrounding *A Million Little Pieces* underlines the fundamental importance of the contract between text and reader in the critical and interpretative enterprise. Generic labels like "fiction," "nonfiction," "memoir," and "novel" remain important and meaningful in the public imagination, creating specific expectations about truth, verifiability, and referentiality among readers. In the case of books labeled and promoted as nonfiction, breaches of contract raise legitimate questions about authorial integrity and artistic responsibility. As I mentioned in the introduction to this book, manipulation on the level of discourse and manipulation on the level of story are entirely different endeavors, and the generic limitations of nonfiction prohibit the latter—for scrupulous producers of nonfiction, that is. The stakes of altering actuality for art's sake are especially high when manipulations serve to comment on matters of social and ideological import such as crime and punishment. When readers are led to believe that the book before them is based entirely in lived experience, even minor changes can skew the portrayal of society's most marginal and disadvantaged citizens, not to mention the depiction of their treatment by the forces of law and order.

The authors examined in this study do not follow quite the same path as did James Frey, but their formal choices bear some striking similarities. They do, for instance, through a variety of strategies, complicate the text-reader contract such that the line between fiction and nonfiction is blurred. Their artful formal decisions give readers the clear understanding that their prison novels are based partially, if not wholly, on their personal experiences in the carceral realm. The authors studied here differ from Frey, however, in that they use textual and paratextual hints (some more subtle than others) to suggest that their narratives portray fictionalized versions of their own experiences. Serge, Genet, Sarrazin, and Bon therefore benefit from the documentary effect created by certain textual and paratextual markers and, at the same time, can creatively alter their stories to render them more compelling. Their critiques of the prison system and of society are therefore doubly strengthened: first, by careful manipulation of their autobiographical story lines and source material; and second, by maintaining the pretension, and in some cases the outright illusion, of documentation.

Today, novels are but one of many strategic resources available to intellectuals to document life in prison. Indeed, investigations into conditions and relations behind bars are an important and recurring phenomenon in contemporary society, a status they have maintained since incarceration became the primary form of punishment in the late 1700s in Europe, England, and America. Although hardly a novelty in the Western world, documentary and testimonial accounts about prison life are increasingly characterized by innovation and variation, from formal and thematic standpoints.[5]

An interesting recent example of such a trend toward formal innovation is Joe Richman's radio program, *Prison Diaries*, which first aired on National Public Radio's *All Things Considered* in 2001.[6] Richman, like Bon, sought to create a medium that allowed his audience to have direct exposure to the voices of prisoners, transforming inmates into witnesses. To that effect, Richman provided two inmates, one prison guard, and one judge with tape recorders so that they could record not only their thoughts but also the sounds that envelop them in their daily lives. The individuals were thus able to provide their testimonies without the mediation of a narrator or a third-party interviewer.

Although Richman's project constitutes a creative and innovative attempt to give audiences access to allegedly unadulterated testimony, the lessons learned from Bon's narrative can be applied to *Prison Diaries*. Investigation into Richman's methods reveals that his final products—four neatly packaged, twenty-two-minute audio segments—were assembled from more than two hundred hours of audiotape.[7] Such extensive editing and narrative construction inevitably distances the final product from the raw truth the methods of documentation were intended to provide, and it is safe to say that the editor's preconceived notions of what prison life is like—acquired from film, literature, or popular legend—can play a significant role in determining what information is included in the final segments and what is left for the archives. Moreover, ideological biases can play a role in the selection and juxtaposition of audio segments. The lengthy recordings made by the inmates, the prison guard, and the judge necessarily differ from the tightly narrated stories presented to the radio audience.

Richman's and Bon's projects are not only innovative from a formal standpoint but also serve as examples of recent attempts to document the carceral realm from the perspective of those who work in prison. Indeed, the most prominent exposé about prison to be released in France in recent years is Véronique Vasseur's *Médecin-chef à la prison de la Santé* (2000), a gripping account of the author's experience as head doctor at La Santé prison in Paris. Vasseur cites a wide variety of horrors that are a part of daily life at La Santé, such as skin ailments not seen "on the outside" since World War II, widespread filth and vermin, and rampant beatings and sexual abuse among the prisoners. Beyond bad physical conditions of incarceration, she highlights organizational deficiencies that result in overcrowding, severe mismanagement of financial resources, and routinely depleted stocks of medicine. As her plea to Elisabeth Guigou (the French justice minister from 1997 to 2000) on the final page of the book indicates, Vasseur's goal in writing *Médecin-chef* was to garner more resources for the improvement of the quality of life behind bars for both prisoners and medical staff. Like the authors examined in this study, Vasseur sought to use her authority as a witness for a specific sociopolitical critique. Initially, it appeared her strategy had been successful: the doctor's testimonial account set off a firestorm of political controversy in the Hexagon, resulting in a barrage of inquiries by the media and the government into French prisons.[8] More than five years after the publication of *Médecin-chef*, however, Vasseur lamented that, in spite of the initial uproar provoked by her book, prison conditions in France have yet to be improved in any meaningful way.[9]

With interest in prison likely to continue to burgeon in academic and media circles, and as efforts to document the carceral milieu grow ever more sophisticated and polemical, the interpretative and critical enterprise becomes all the more important. For in a culture saturated with media, close analysis of narrative is an increasingly necessary endeavor. Readers should be equipped with the tools needed to grasp how narrative construction is used to manipulate what is presented as true to life. Close study of representations of prison, especially those with documentary pretensions, is becoming increasingly necessary in an era in which simple editing techniques are used to rearrange "reality" to reach a specific, often sensational or ideological, end.

[NOTES]

Introduction

1. The modes of expression mentioned here are not simply clichés of prison life; they recur frequently in sociological studies, historical studies, and fictional depictions of prison. Wall tapping, according to Judith Scheffler, is "the most ancient of all systems of prison communication" (xxxiv), and served as inspiration for the title of her anthology of women's prison writings, *Wall Tappings*. In *The Promise of Punishment*, Patricia O'Brien cites graffiti as an important form of expression for inmates in nineteenth-century France. For more information on prisoners' means of expression, which include argot and tattooing, see O'Brien 77–88. Wall tapping and communication through a prison's plumbing system are evoked in Victor Serge's *Les hommes dans la prison* (*Men in Prison*, 1930), one of the novels studied in detail in this book. The difficult encounters that take place during visiting hours are depicted in many novels and films (Albert Camus's *L'étranger* [*The Stranger*, 1942] is one example). Testimony left behind before an execution is a reference to Victor Hugo's allegedly "found" text, *Le dernier jour d'un condamné* (*The Last Day of a Condemned Man*, 1829). In original editions of that text, Hugo suppressed his own name and included a fictional prefatory note that evoked the possibility of "a bundle of yellowing papers of various sizes" that were found after the execution and contained the narrative of the condemned man.

2. Sociologist Erving Goffman in his groundbreaking book *Asylums* writes that inmates attempt to cope with their incarcerations by telling stories: "the inmate tends to develop a story, a line, a sad tale—a kind of lamentation and apologia—which he constantly tells to his fellows as a means of accounting for his present low estate" (67). In *The Prison Community*, Donald Clemmer writes that inmates who violate their parole struggle to rationalize and justify their reincarceration to their peers: "Regardless of the stories they may have ready to account for their return to prison, the irrefutable fact that they are there, signifies their failure" (101).

3. In an essay titled "A Day in Folsom Prison" in *Soul on Ice*, Eldridge Cleaver notes that it seems like "every convict" wants to write (45).

4. Camus, *La chute* 17. The term in the original French is "juge-pénitent."

5. Goffman uses the term "total institution" in *Asylums*, which describes such institutions as follows: "Their encompassing or total character is symbolized by the barrier to social intercourse with the outside and to departure that is often built right into the physical plant, such as locked doors, high walls, barbed wire, cliffs, water, forests, or moors" (4).

6. For detailed information on the development of the prison as the primary mode of punishment in France, see Jacques-Guy Petit's *Ces peines obscures* (These Mysterious Punishments). Penal prison appears explicitly in the correctional and penal codes drawn up by the Constituent Assembly in 1791 (Faugeron, Petit, and Pierre 24).

7. The nineteenth century was a period of significant prison reform in France, and O'Brien writes that much of the impetus and inspiration for those reform efforts was rooted in Enlightenment cosmopolitanism: "During the Revolutionary, Napoleonic, and Restoration periods, the experiences of foreign countries regarding penal developments were widely discussed and debated" (40). For more information see O'Brien 40–42. O'Brien identifies four major waves of reform in the eighteenth and nineteenth centuries in France: "The four major spurts in penal reforms directly followed the four revolutions in the period under consideration—1789,

1830, 1848, 1871" (20). For information on the influence of international penal and correctional trends on the Constituent Assembly see Petit 61–67.

8. The twentieth century marked a point of resurgence for the publication of texts written by prisoners. Historian Michelle Perrot remarks that in the vast archives of printed resources related to the prison system of the nineteenth century, the major lacunae are texts by the prisoners themselves. She writes that it was not until the 1970s that it became common to hear the voices of prisoners (Faugeron, Petit, and Pierre 11–12). Similarly, Petit writes that although writers and specialists wrote a great deal about prison during the nineteenth century, prisoners themselves (with the exception of political prisoners) wrote very little (470). In *La relation carcérale* (Carceral Relations), sociologist Corinne Rostaing also comments on the recent trend toward the increased publication of prison narratives as well as burgeoning media coverage of prison conditions (1–3).

9. The phenomenon of prison officials, employees, and volunteers testifying to the inner workings of prisons exists on both sides of the Atlantic. See, e.g., Dr. Véronique Vasseur's controversial exposé, *Médecin-chef à la prison de la Santé* (Head Doctor at La Santé Prison); journalist Ted Conover's gripping rendering of his undercover experience as a guard at Sing Sing prison, *Newjack*; or Jean Trounstine's account of her experience teaching in a women's prison, *Shakespeare behind Bars*.

10. For an introductory treatment of prison and execution films, see pages 117–40 of Nicole Rafter's *Shots in the Mirror: Crime Films and Society*. Documentary films and media reports about prison are made with great frequency. For a fine example of a recent documentary film, see *The Farm: Life inside Angola Prison*. Joe Richman's 2001 National Public Radio series *Prison Diaries*, which featured audio recordings made by inmates themselves while locked in their cells, is an example of an attempt to document prison life through testimony.

11. Throughout this study I use the designation "prison novel" to refer to documentary novels about prison. I explain the narrative specificities of this subgenre below.

12. Translations of Rostaing's text are mine.

13. As Michael Ignatieff writes, "[This] sober motto from Seneca" was carved in stone over the doorway of the Amsterdam Rasp House (53). See Ignatieff 44–79 for more information on Howard's role in the British penitentiary movement.

14. For information on early French reform efforts, which I return to below, see Petit 29–31, 34, and 50.

15. Petit suggests that a French Benedictine monk, Jean Mabillon (1632–1707), may be considered the precursor of those who conceived of the notion of solitary confinement in penitentiaries (65–67).

16. The scene is found in a chapter titled "Saved" in *The Autobiography of Malcolm X*. For more information see 172–73. Examples of intellectual inmates can be found in twentieth-century cinema as well, such as Norman Jewison's *The Hurricane* (1999). Based on the life story of Rubin "Hurricane" Carter, Jewison's film depicts the former boxer as an enlightened and intellectual inmate whose passions include, among others, Émile Zola.

17. The connection between art and prisoners goes beyond the radical alienation of Beckett's work. Trounstine, for instance, recounts her experience working with women prisoners in drama classes and asserts her belief in redemptive power of art in inmates' troubled lives.

18. In 1907, thirteen years after his release, London overcame his discouragement and published two autobiographical essays about his experience in jail, "'Pinched': A Prison Experience" and "The Pen: Long Days in a County Penitentiary." He also wrote a novel set in prison called *The Star Rover* (1915).

19. Wilde composed *De Profundis* while in Reading Prison, and Gramsci composed his prison notebooks between 1929 and 1935. Isidore Abramowitz based his anthology, *The Great Prisoners: The First Anthology of Literature Written in Prison* (1946), on the link between incarceration and creative inspiration. He includes excerpts from the writings of a host of well-known figures, such as Saint Paul, Boethius, Richard Lovelace, and François Villon, among many others. We should also note that writing workshops for inmates have proliferated on both sides of the Atlantic in recent

decades, some for the very purpose of giving a voice in mainstream culture to marginalized citizens. In the United States, e.g., the PEN Prison Writing program has been encouraging the establishment of such workshops since 1971. In France, Michèle Sales, Frédéric Boyer, and François Bon are among writers who have conducted writing workshops with inmates.

20. See, e.g., "Villon's Epitaph" (which in some editions is referred to as the "Ballade of the Hanged"). For a history of Villon's incarcerations see pages 35–53 of Jean-Marc Varaut's *Poètes en prison*. *The Complete Works of François Villon* contains a brief and informative biography of Villon by his translator, Anthony Bonner, as well as an introductory essay by William Carlos Williams.

21. Chantal Thomas also notes that "*Justine* was the product of many years of solitude in prison" (580).

22. Verlaine describes his various incarcerations in *Mes prisons*, beginning with a "cachot" in which he was placed because he misconjugated the verb "to read" in Latin while a young student. Verlaine also writes of his religious experiences and makes note of poetry written in specific cells and under particular circumstances.

23. Two essays in Norval Morris and David J. Rothman's *Oxford History of the Prison* deal with early confinement and prison narratives. Edward M. Peters's "Prison before the Prison" (3–43) contains an excellent, cogent analysis of prisons in the ancient and medieval worlds and cites a number of texts as sources, such as Aeschylus's *Prometheus Bound*, Plato's *Phaedo*, and a number of stories from the Bible, with particular emphasis on the story of the prophet Jeremiah. For an overview of more modern Western literature of confinement (both literal and metaphoric) see W. B. Carnochan's "The Literature of Confinement" (381–406).

24. In *Imagining the Penitentiary*, John Bender argues that the form and content of some of the earliest English novels (such as *Moll Flanders*) influenced penal reformers later in the eighteenth century, leading to the invention of the penitentiary: "I shall argue that attitudes toward prison which were formulated between 1719 and 1779 in narrative literature and art—especially in prose fiction—sustained and, on my reconstruction, enabled the conception and construction of actual penitentiary prisons later in the

eighteenth century" (1). H. Bruce Franklin, in *Prison Literature in America*, highlights the historical and national specificity of American prison literature, linking the prison and prison literature to chattel slavery and oppression of African Americans in the United States. Franklin also edited an excellent anthology, *Prison Writing in 20th-Century America*. In Italian studies, Ellen Nerenberg's *Prison Terms* focuses on the "representation of prisons and its relation to the articulation of gender during and after Fascism" (7). Nerenberg does not limit her study to prisons per se but also examines those "outside the juridical domain" such as barracks, the convent, the brothel, and the home.

25. Anna Norris's *L'écriture du défi* (The Writing of Defiance) performs the important task of continuing, updating, and expanding scholarly work on French women's prison narratives and cultural perceptions of female criminals. She includes a useful and informative overview of sociological and criminological studies of female criminals.

26. Other book-length studies of the literature of incarceration have been published in recent decades. In her book-length essay *Les écrivains en cage*, Françoise d'Eaubonne examines how imprisonment changed the artistic perspective of some noteworthy writers, including Villon, Sade, Silvio Pellico, Dostoyevsky, Wilde, Verlaine, and Genet. Varaut's *Poètes en prison* studies noteworthy poets in the French tradition who have been in prison (such as Villon, Marot, Chénier, Verlaine, Genet, and Desnos). Varaut does largely biographical analysis of the writers' work. Dennis Massey, in *Doing Time in American Prisons,* provides rapid overviews of noteworthy American novels about prison. Ioan Davies, a sociologist by trade, describes his book, *Writers in Prison,* as an "attempt to understand how the incarcerated imagination has become part of Western ideas and literature" (7). His book attempts to cover a great deal of literary and philosophical ground, examining writers as diverse as Boethius, Primo Levi, and Breyten Breytenbach and analyzing the prison in both literal and metaphoric terms. His study briefly touches on the work of Victor Serge and Jean Genet. Finally, D. Quentin Miller compiled a set of excellent essays in a volume titled *Prose and Cons* (2005). That groundbreaking tome explores prison literature published in the United States.

27. See N. Morris and Rothman for an excellent collaborative overview of the history of prisons from the ancient world to the late twentieth century. More analysis about the historiography of the prison is provided later in this introduction.

28. The prison conditions described in the following are based on the study of a number of sociological and historical sources, but above all I have relied upon the work of O'Brien, Perrot, Petit, Foucault, Sykes, Clemmer, Goffman, Rostaing, and Vasseur. While the use of American sociological texts to describe conditions in French prisons may seem problematic, it is a practice conducted in the realm of sociology, reflecting the international nature of the evolution of the practice of punishment. For example, Rostaing, a French sociologist, cites American studies in her book on French women's prisons, *La relation carcérale*.

29. For more information on the process of entry into prison and the daily life of inmates, see Goffman, *Asylums* 3–74; Sykes 63–83; and Rostaing 107–44.

30. Sykes notes: "Prisons are apt to present a common social structure" (xiii). O'Brien writes that a "distinct prison subculture developed as an important component of the modern prison system" (77).

31. Goffman defines "stigma" as a "special kind of relationship between [an] attribute and [a] stereotype" (*Stigma* 4). A stigma involves an attribute (such as a physical or a personality trait) and the social (and personal) perception of that attribute. For more information on the specifics of Goffman's definition, see chapter 1 of *Stigma*.

32. Perrot writes: "There is a discourse of crime that reveals the obsession of a society" ("Delinquency" 219). She points out how penal codes help to define normality, deviance, and delinquency and in some cases even have created crimes (such as drunkenness) and classes of criminals. For more information see her article, "Delinquency and the Penitentiary System in Nineteenth-Century France."

33. Badinter concludes that the reality of the prison changed very little over the course of the pre–World War I Third Republic, although the discourse of prison policies reflected noble "republican" val-

ues that allegedly sought to humanize the process of punishment. Another important study is Henri Gaillac's *Les maisons de correction*, which contains much valuable information on agricultural colonies and the treatment of young criminals. There are also histories of individual prisons, such as Michael Fize's *Une prison dans la ville: Histoire de la prison-modèle de la Santé, 1867–1983* and Jean Chédaille's *Fontevraud de toutes les pénitences: Histoire d'une prison de 1804–1963*.

34. Rothman and Ignatieff analyze how power is distributed and asserted over marginal populations. In a new preface published in a 1990 edition of his study, Rothman writes that the prison garnered much attention in the 1970s due to growth in the field of social history: "The underlying concerns of social history, its preoccupation with the relationships between social classes and the institutions that promoted or subverted social order, including the family, the church, and the workplace, helped bring attention to formal institutions of control, particularly the prison and the mental hospital" (xiv). He goes on to state that social historians of his era began to concentrate on the "fate of the lower classes" (xiv), spurring an interest in those confined in a variety of institutions (including prisons) that preserved social, political, and economic order. Ignatieff links the rise of the penitentiary and penal reform movements in England from the late eighteenth to the mid-nineteenth century to the consolidation of state power over not just criminals but also the insane and, above all, the working classes. He describes his investigation by stating that "a study of prison discipline necessarily becomes a study, not simply of prisons, but of the moral boundaries of social authority in a society undergoing capitalist transformation" (1). Ignatieff writes that the penitentiary reform movement in England in the 1770s and 1780s was informed by psychological assumptions, religious beliefs, and philosophical arguments. He argues that those social and intellectual trends, combined with political and economic forces, led to the rise of the penitentiary and to changes in modes of social control and hygienic practices in the hospital, the asylum, and the factory.

35. Foucault has received much well-deserved praise for his influential history of the birth of the prison. Some historians, while acknowl-

edging his influence, criticize him for paying too much attention to the discourses of the prison rather than examining prisons as they actually existed. Rothman writes: "Perhaps his most glaring deficiency, however, was an unwillingness to distinguish rhetoric from reality. For Foucault, motive mattered more than practice" (xv). Jacques-Guy Petit (72) writes that Foucault did not adequately account for specificities in the development of the penal and correctional codes during the Revolutionary period, such as the debates between 1789 and 1791.

36. Other prominent sociological studies of prison life include Donald Clemmer's *The Prison Community*; Terrence and Pauline Morris's *Pentonville: A Sociological Study of an English Prison*; and Corinne Rostaing's *La relation carcérale*.

37. The translation is mine.

38. See Petit 29–31, 34, and 50. A number of prominent figures outside France advocated penal reform during that era as well, including Cesare Beccaria, John Howard, and Jeremy Bentham. A great deal of international intellectual exchange took place on the issue of the treatment of criminals particularly in the late eighteenth and early nineteenth centuries. For an introduction to eighteenth-century texts on penal theory see James Heath's *Eighteenth-Century Penal Theory*. For more information on the specific intellectual influences on the Constituent Assembly and the 1791 penal codes, see Petit 33–72.

39. Blame was cast on prisons for being schools for crime and for giving life to a new class of hardened recidivists who became the bête noire of nineteenth-century penal reformers and legislators. For an overview of reform efforts in the late eighteenth and early nineteenth centuries, see Petit 183–260.

40. While the names of Tocqueville and Beaumont are surely better known to those outside the field of penal history, historians of the prison cite Charles Lucas as the most influential of the nineteenth-century reformers in France. For information on Lucas's career see Petit 214–18. Frédéric-Auguste Demetz is widely cited as well, in particular for his contribution to the creation of the agricultural colony for young delinquents at Mettray. See also Badinter 25–26 and O'Brien 30–32.

41. We should be careful to note that there was a penitentiary move-ment in England at this time as well that dated back to the 1770s. For more information see Ignatieff.

42. The importance of Hugo's writing as an antecedent of twenti-eth-century critiques of capital punishment should also be noted. More than a century after the publication of his *The Last Day of a Condemned Man*, a text that purports to show the difficulties of a sort of "Everyman" who is awaiting the guillotine, Sartre pub-lished his short story "The Wall," which highlights the absurdity and cruelty inherent in punishment by death. Two decades later, Camus's powerful essay "Reflections on the Guillotine" included harrowing depictions of the state of the decapitated body after its allegedly merciful processing by the guillotine. Camus too saw the practice as useless and harmful to society: "The death penalty is to the body politic what cancer is to the individual body, with perhaps the single difference that no one has ever spoken of the necessity of cancer" (*Reflections* 6).

43. For more information on Hugo's fictionalization of Gueux's life story, see Woollen xi–xvi.

44. The translation is mine. The text originally appeared in *Esprit* in March 1971 and has been republished, along with other docu-ments pertaining to the GIP, in Artières, Quéro, and Zancarini-Fournel, *Le groupe d'information sur les prisons: Archives d'une lutte, 1970–72.*

45. "Documentary effect" implies that prison novels go beyond Ro-land Barthes's notion of the "reality effect" and beyond "mime-sis" (as employed by Erich Auerbach). In *Telling the Truth: The Theory and Practice of Documentary Fiction*, Barbara Foley uses the designation "documentary effect" as well (25).

46. Elzbieta Sklodowska notes a similarly important quality of testi-monial texts, as they bear trademarks of narrative construction: "it would be naïve to assume a direct homology between text and his-tory. The discourse of a witness cannot be a reflection of his or her experience, but rather a refraction determined by the vicissitudes of memory, intention, ideology. The intention and the ideology of the author-editor further superimposes the original text, creating more ambiguities, silences, and absences in the process of selecting

and editing the material in a way consonant with norms of literary form" (qtd. in Gugelberger, *The Real Thing* 34).

47. A similar distinction between form and content can be made when studying the difference between fiction and nonfiction films. As Carl Plantinga, basing his observations on Hayden White's writing on historiography, notes in *Rhetoric and Representation in Nonfiction Film*, "What White says of narrative history also applies to the historical nonfiction film. In narrative films, ordering is not merely chronological sequencing, but investing events with dramatic movement and emotional force according to the perspective of the discourse. . . . Although nonfiction stories have their roots in actual events, the stories are not merely 'found,' 'uncovered,' and 'identified.' Invention also plays a part in the operations of the historian and the documentarian" (133). The description of that type of manipulation in a nonfictional work was best captured by British filmmaker and producer John Grierson, who is widely cited by film critics and historians for having coined the term "documentary" in reference to that subgenre of nonfiction films. Grierson defines the documentary as the "creative treatment of actuality" (qtd. in Plantinga 10).

48. This rule, of course, can be broken by an unscrupulous producer of nonfiction. I agree with film theorist Carl Plantinga, who, commenting on the nature of the duties of the documentary filmmaker, writes: "Responsibility requires that the filmmaker give up an element of freedom in the name of accuracy, for to preserve truth in discourse, one's assertions, to the best of one's knowledge, must be accurate. But this does not require that the discourse not manipulate projected world data in myriad ways, both structurally and stylistically" (125). The same can be said of producers of nonfictional texts.

49. Other twentieth-century French novels in which imprisonment is a central theme include Tristan Bernard's *Aux abois* (At Bay, 1933), Jean Genet's *Notre-Dame-des-Fleurs* (*Our Lady of the Flowers*, 1944), José Giovanni's *Le trou* (The Hole, 1958), Alphonse Boudard's *La cerise* (The Cherry, 1963), Anne Huré's *En prison* (In Prison, 1963), Serge Livrozet's *La rage des murs* (The Walls' Rage, 1974), Frédéric Boyer's *En prison* (1992), Luc Lang's *Mille*

six cent ventres (Sixteen Hundred Stomachs, 1998), and Natalie Kuperman's *Rue Jean-Dolent* (Jean Dolent Street, 2000).

50. A similar distinction exists in prison films. For example, Alan Parker's *Midnight Express* (1978) is wholly concerned with the struggle of one American prisoner (Billy Hayes) to survive brutal conditions—which are amply highlighted—in a Turkish prison. It is overtly stated at the beginning of the film that Hayes's saga is based on a true story. Conversely, although the action of Stuart Rosenberg's *Cool Hand Luke* (1967) takes place almost entirely in a prison (and on the chain gang), the film is not primarily concerned with documenting specific aspects of carceral life. Rather, its main focus—as its title indicates—is on the habits and persona of a rebel, Lucas "Luke" Jackson, who happens to have been incarcerated as a result of his nonconformist behavior.

51. On the social function of fiction and nonfiction films I am indebted to the argument of Carl Plantinga, who contends that "fictions and nonfictions . . . perform distinct social functions, and are viewed by the spectators with reference to a different set of expectations and conventions" (11). I argue that, like spectators, readers approach fictions and nonfictions with different expectations and conventions. The same can be said of the expectations created by the contract established by a documentary fiction, given the fact that a documentary fiction imitates some of the formal techniques of a nonfictional text. In *Telling the Truth*, Foley argues that the contract between text and reader is a social one "wherein writer and reader share an agreement about the conditions under which texts can be composed and comprehended" (40). The documentary novel, as Foley defines it, constitutes a "distinct fictional kind" that has a referential component but that ultimately creates a fictive pact with the reader, such as Defoe's *Moll Flanders*, Richardson's *Pamela*, or Joyce's *A Portrait of the Artist as a Young Man* (25–26). Prison novels do not fit into the specific model of the "documentary novel" described by Foley, as they deliberately attempt to confuse and manipulate readers to believe that what they are reading is *not* fiction. Foley also argues, from a Marxist perspective, that the forms of asserting documentation change over the course of history, from the eighteenth century onward. For more

information on specific categories of the documentary novel as she defines it and how they have changed over the course of three centuries, see Foley 9–41.

52. In her book on the form and function of documentary war nar ratives, *Representing War*, Evelyn Cobley writes: "Documentary accounts consequently lend themselves to extended analyses of description and narration rather than of plot." For more information on the generic specificity of such narratives, see Cobley 3–28.

53. In *L'ère du témoin* (The Era of the Witness), Annette Wieviorka notes the democratization of testimony in the latter half of the twentieth century. She comments on the proliferation of ethnographically slanted testimonies about people's ordinary lives (127).

54. Beverley remarks that the word *testimonio*, like the French word *témoignage*, translates literally as "testimony, as in the act of testifying or bearing witness in a legal or religious sense" (26).

55. Beverley writes: "Each individual testimonio evokes an absent polyphony of other voices, other possible lives and experiences" (28). The discursive and formal characteristics of *testimonio* that I have evoked (marginalization of the narrator, ideological urgency, and polyphony) are widely accepted in scholarly circles and have been highlighted by Beverley, George Yúdice, Barbara Harlow, and Elzbieta Sklodowska, among others. There are significant structural differences between *testimonios* and prison novels, most notably that in *testimonio* a compiler assembles for publication a story told by a "subaltern" narrator, further diminishing the immediacy between narrator and story that is present in prison novels. For an introduction to debates on the form and function of *testimonio*, see Gugelberger.

56. For example, in *Souvenirs d'un médecin de la préfecture de police et des prisons de Paris (1914–1918)*, Bizard notes that in La Santé prison, political prisoners are kept in separate quarters and are given very special treatment. For more information see Bizard 138–40. In *Robben Island and Prisoner Resistance to Apartheid*, Fran Lisa Buntman writes: "Political imprisonment plays a vital role in shaping resistance movements and their methods" (2).

57. For information on the history of penal colonies in France, see O'Brien 258–96.

58. Scholars in sociology and history have made this same distinction. Rostaing writes that she does not address the question of concentration camps in her work on women's prisons because "The prison is not the concentration camp, whose intended purpose is to dehumanize man" (ix). While a degree of dehumanization does result from incarceration in prison, it is not a fundamental goal of imprisonment. For similar reasons, historians Norval Morris and David J. Rothman did not include a chapter on concentration camps in their *Oxford History of the Prison*: "in their design and horror . . . [concentration camps] are outside the history of the prison. The genocidal practice that went on within the camps did not take their inspiration from the conduct of criminal punishment" (xiii).

59. Areas of high (twenty-four-hour) surveillance were created for prisoners awaiting capital punishment partly in order to prevent them from committing suicide while awaiting the death penalty. For a description of such a space in La Santé prison see Bizard 141–49. Other inmates treat the condemned with exceptional respect and reverence. Depictions of such behavior are found in a number of literary and cinematic works. Harcamone, the object of the author-narrator's obsession in *Miracle de la rose*, is an example—albeit extreme—of such respect and admiration. Oscar Wilde's "The Ballad of Reading Gaol" depicts how an entire prison focuses on the rhythms of a condemned man's final days. For a cinematic depiction of special treatment accorded to inmates awaiting the death penalty, see André Cayette's 1952 film, *Nous sommes tous des assassins*.

60. This same ineffability and unrepresentability has been highlighted by Berlin's very abstract Holocaust memorial (dedicated in 2005), which consists of twenty-seven hundred stone slabs distributed over five acres. Primo Levi also comments on the inadequacy of witnessing, but for him it is not due to the nature of testimony but rather due to precisely *who* is doing the telling. In one of his most powerful autobiographical books, *The Drowned and the Saved*, he writes that one who lives to tell the tale is not the event's "true

witness." It is those who did not live, "those who saw the Gorgon, have not returned to tell about it or have returned mute, but they are ... the complete witnesses, the ones whose deposition would have a general significance. They are the rule, we are the exception" (83–84). Silence and the ineffable are topoi that are common—central, even—to many Holocaust narratives, and they are absent from prison novels.

61. Beyond stylistic concerns and documentary intentions, Serge makes explicit his debt to Dostoyevsky's account. One of the detainees in *Men in Prison* describes the bleak environment in the prison by simply stating, "*The House of the Dead*" (25).

62. I examine the genesis of *La cavale* in greater detail in chapter 3. For more information about Sarrazin's avowed original intentions for her first novel, see her third autobiographical novel, *La traversière* (1966), pages 21–22.

1. Everyman in Prison

1. Serge was a productive writer and wrote many thousands of pages on a host of literary, historical, and political subjects. Much of his work remains in manuscript form. His bibliography includes seven published novels—*Les hommes dans la prison* (*Men in Prison*, 1930), *Naissance de notre force* (*Birth of Our Power*, 1931), *Ville conquise* (*Conquered City*, 1932), *S'il est minuit dans le siècle* (*Midnight in the Century*, 1939), *Les derniers temps* (*The Long Dusk*, 1946), *L'affaire Toulaev* (*The Case of Comrade Tulayev*, 1948), and *Les années sans pardon* (*The Unforgiving Years*, 1971)—as well as two—*Les hommes perdus* (Lost Men) and *La tourmente* (Turmoil)—that were lost due to Soviet censorship. He also wrote studies on the Russian Revolution and its aftermath, including *L'an I de la révolution russe* (*Year One of the Russian Revolution*, 1930) and *Destin d'une révolution* (*Russia Twenty Years After*, 1937). Furthermore, Serge wrote a biography of Trotsky, studies on Lenin and Stalin, a book of poetry titled *Résistance* (*Resistance*), and several short stories. For a complete bibliography of published and unpublished works, see Susan Weissman's excellent intellectual biography, *Victor Serge: The Course Is Set on Hope*

319–36. Her text, which filled a significant lacuna in the study of Serge's life and work, describes in detail his intellectual development as well as the difficult circumstances in which he lived and wrote. Serge's place in intellectual and literary history is currently enjoying a minor resurgence with the publication of Weissman's book as well as new editions of his three first novels. One of Serge's best late novels, *The Case of Comrade Tulayev*, has been released in a new edition that includes an introduction by Susan Sontag (New York Review of Books, 2004).

2. "Pour le seul tiroir," Serge writes in his *Carnets*. Wherever possible, quotes are from published translations and pagination is included from both English and French editions. All other translations are mine.

3. Throughout this chapter, pagination for *Les hommes dans la prison* refers first to the English translation, *Men in Prison* (designated by the initials *MP*), followed by the pagination in the original French edition of *Les hommes dans la prison* (designated by the initials *HP*) published by Rieder (1930).

4. That Istrati wrote the preface to *Les hommes dans la prison* is unsurprising given the affinity between the writers. Istrati and Serge met in 1927, and Serge wrote the second volume of Istrati's trilogy on the Soviet Union (Weissman 121–22). The volume, which was signed by Istrati, was called *Soviets 1929*. For more information on that text see Weissman 121–26.

5. For reasons unexplained, this passage was deleted from Sedgwick's translation. The original reads as follows: "Le 'Je' me répugne comme une vaine affirmation de soi-même, contenant une grande part d'illusion et une autre de vanité ou d'injuste orgueil. Toutes les fois qu'il est possible, c'est-à-dire que je puis ne pas me sentir isolé, que mon expérience éclaire par quelque côté celle d'hommes avec lesquels je me sens lié, je préfère employer le "nous," plus général et plus vrai. . . . [C]elui qui parle, celui qui écrit est essentiellement un homme qui parle pour tous ceux qui sont sans voix."

6. His first use of the pseudonym Victor Serge came during his brief Spanish sojourn while writing for *Tierra y libertad* in 1917 (*Mémoires* 61). Serge left Spain in July of that year, and while attempting to reach Russia he was arrested in France for violating his

court-ordered exile. He spent fifteen months in a French concentration camp and eventually arrived in Russia in early 1919. From 1921 to 1925 he worked toward fomenting proletarian revolution in Germany and Austria. Both endeavors failed, and he returned to the USSR. He began writing *Les hommes dans la prison* in 1926. For more information on Serge's travels and various political commitments, see Weissman 52–73.

7. In that same period Serge also wrote a historical work, *L'an I de la Révolution russe* (*Year One of the Russian Revolution*), and two other documentary novels, *Naissance de notre force* (*Birth of Our Power*) and *Ville conquise* (*Conquered City*).

8. A number of historians argue that there is a link between social control of the working classes and the establishment of the prison system in eighteenth- and nineteenth-century Europe. Petit, e.g., writes: "Since the sixteenth and seventeenth centuries, in almost all of Europe, rasphouses, workhouses, *hôpitaux généraux*, *maisons de force*, then *dépôts de mendicité* and other similar institutions confine the poor, beggars, and vagabonds—the various layers of the at-drift population and those deemed near delinquency" (160). Rusche and Kirchheimer see a link between the use of penal labor and the rise of mercantilism. For them, the use of penal labor is derived from an understanding of the "potential value of a mass of human material completely at the disposal of the administration" (24). For more details, see their book, *Punishment and Social Structure*.

9. The fact that capital punishment represents a polemical issue in the novel is not at all surprising given the resurgence in guillotine usage in the 1910s (72 victims) and the 1920s (114) versus the comparatively blood-free first decade of the century, during which 36 people were beheaded (Bessette 104).

10. He notes that the twenty-four-hour surveillance cells are painted differently from the one in which he was placed (*MP* 82; *HP* 115).

11. In a chapter titled "Burial and Victory" Serge again links the prison cell to a type of tomb: "You can feel the creeping numbness, the memory of life growing weak. Burial. Each hour is like a shovelful of earth falling noiselessly, softly, on this grave" (*MP* 57; *HP* 86).

12. In his reading of *Les hommes dans la prison*, Brombert notes that

Serge "aims at transcending personal suffering to reach out to the larger community. . . . Collective tragedy is conceived by him as an apprenticeship in solidarity" (178). Brombert equivocates in his generic interpretation of the novel: on one occasion he refers to it as a "semi-fictionalized autobiographical account" (177), but later he remarks that Serge "describe[s] a non-fictional experience" (182).

13. *Memoirs from the House of the Dead* opens with a brief introduction that situates the embedded prison narrative of Alexander Petrovich. That narrative follows same arrest-to-release structure of the other testimonial texts I have cited.

14. For more information on the history of La Santé prison, see Michel Fize's *Une prison dans la ville: Histoire de la prison-modèle de la Santé, 1867–1983*. Fize has also condensed his work into an article-length publication titled "Histoire de la 'prison modèle' de la Santé, 1867–1914."

15. In 1910, "la Santoche," as it was derisively dubbed by its inmates, held 1,300 prisoners, 300 more than its design intended; in 1913 the number had swelled to 1,560. La Santé's failure to live up to its architect's ambitions as a model prison was best illustrated by the high-profile escape-turned-suicide of an anarchist inmate named Lacombe in April 1913. A government-led investigation into the suicide claimed that the death highlighted the egregious understaffing and overcrowding of the prison: approximately sixty guards were charged with the task of watching more than fifteen hundred prisoners (Fize, *Ville* 170–71, 179; see 158 for more information on jargon in use at La Santé).

16. André Dumas writes: "All the Melunais, and even the foreigners who tour Melun, deplore that the most beautiful location in the city—the best situated from every viewpoint, in the cheerful vicinity of the banks of the Seine, between the Motte-aux-Cailles prairies and the Vaux promenade—is occupied by a prison, which throws an unfortunate shadow on the general appearance of the town" (qtd. in Plancke 137). The prison was officially established in 1811, and its purpose was to house male and female prisoners from five departments (Plancke 126). Soon thereafter, the female

inmates were moved to Clairvaux, and Melun was used strictly for male convicts (Clayette 37).

17. In *Melun à la Belle Epoque*, René-Charles Plancke interpolates a lengthy article written by André Dumas, who describes in detail the city's *maison centrale*. Originally published in 1907—just a few years before Serge was incarcerated there—Dumas's text is titled "La vie d'une prison: La maison centrale de Melun." Far fewer texts are written about Melun's *maison centrale* than about La Santé, no doubt because La Santé is situated in the middle of France's capital city. See, e.g., Léon-Clément Bizard's *Souvenirs d'un médecin de la préfecture de police et des prisons de Paris (1914–1918)* or Pierre Montagnon's *Quarante-deux rue de la Santé: Une prison politique, 1867–1968*.

18. Plancke provides the following information about meals: "830 grams of bread, a thin soup, a ration of dried vegetables, and a fatty pâté [pitance grasse] usually make up the menu that well-behaved prisoners can improve through purchases at the cantine" (131–32).

19. As Fize notes in his history of La Santé, "Three principles that characterized nineteenth-century prisons and still exist (with slight differences) in our era are as follows: precise organization of the inmates in the space of the prison; detailed planning of their time; and a strongly hierarchical prison administration" (*Ville* 118).

20. Dumas confirms the details of the process of entry at the Melun prison: "An hour later [after entry], his hair, his beard, and his mustache have fallen. He wears the prison uniform. His civilian identity has vanished. Nothing distinguishes him anymore from the other convicts. The detainee is a prisoner for good" (qtd. in Plancke 129). Goffman writes that such harsh and degrading inductions are a standard phenomenon in total institutions. He notes that the initial moments of socialization in such closed worlds "may involve an 'obedience test' and even a will-breaking contest" (*Asylums* 17). Using many of the same examples as Serge, Goffman describes the process of entry (he calls it "mortification") and writes that when inmates are stripped of their names they lose their most precious possession. Physical alteration plays an integral role in the transformation of the inmates for efficient bureaucratic pro-

cessing. Goffman asserts that such changes are indispensable for the administrative functioning of the carceral world: "Admission procedures might better be called 'trimming' or 'programming' because in thus being squared away the new arrival allows himself to be shaped and coded into an object that can be fed into the administrative machinery of the establishment, to be worked on smoothly by routine operations" (16). Disempowering and dehumanizing the inmate are central objectives of such procedures. As the narrator states upon his initial arrest, the prisoner "feels as if he has been stripped of part of himself, reduced to an impotence inconceivable an hour before" (*MP* 8; *HP* 31).

21. Serge's protagonist mentions the use of the Auburn method ("the last word in prison economy" [*MP* 114; *HP* 153]) and describes his tasks performed in the printing workshop, a space Dumas also describes (Plancke 132). A number of other noteworthy facets of daily life depicted in *Les hommes dans la prison* have also been mentioned separately by historians and sociologists. Details include the anxiety and feeling of strangulation experienced after arrest (*MP* 1–3; *HP* 23–25); the existence of a class system among the prisoners based on money and influence (45; 72); how much money the prisoners make by working while detained (123; 164–65); the presence and danger of tuberculosis (129; 172); the tendency of prisoners to observe each other to determine who will survive the brutalities of incarceration (127; 169); and the unexpected, oppressive anguish before release into the free world (248; 304).

22. According to historian Jacques-Guy Petit, the phenomenon dates to the early nineteenth century: "Built progressively, according to the needs of crime suppression, the growth of the workforce, and local supplies of buildings, the *maisons centrales* of the first three-quarters of the century do not fit together according to a harmonious blueprint" (46). Critic Bill Marshall concurs: "The disciplinary processes depicted in Serge's text, like the architectural edifices, are hybrids in that the modernized system contains vestiges of older, more traditionalized practices" (39).

23. Remarkably, Fize notes nearly the exact same meals and quantities: "We know that each prisoner at La Santé was allotted 750 grams of bread, a liter of bouillon with vegetables, or 125 grams

of meat, depending on the day. That food was spread out over two meals. At the 9 a.m. meal, prisoners received vegetable soup, at the evening meal, served at 4 p.m., 3 deciliters of beans, lentils or rice (with butter or lard), and Sundays, 100 grams of de-boned meat and potatoes. For the detainees in the cellular system (considered a system that weakened prisoners more), that proportion of meat was also served on Thursday" ("Histoire" 712).

24. Information provided by Fize partially corroborates the information in *Les hommes dans la prison*: "We know that the prisoners of La Santé had at their disposal a library that contained an impressive number of books (around 4,700 in the year 1895)" (*Ville* 132). He elaborates on the books in the book collection, many of which were annotated by the prisoners: "We know that, apart from the travel books and novels (Walter Scott, Fenimore Cooper) which were highly sought out by the prisoners, the moral, religious, history, and science books were, on the other hand, in very little demand" (133).

25. For example, see Jacques Becker's fictional film, *Le trou* (1960), or Ted Conover's testimonial account, *Newjack*. In both works, prisoners take whatever meager physical objects they find at their disposal and use them as weapons as well as tools to subvert their captors' intentions.

26. As is the case with the process of entry and other procedures common to modern prisons, the descriptions of inmate behavior in *Les hommes dans la prison* complement observations made in sociological and historical texts. The phenomenon of jargon has been widely commented upon by historians and sociologists. Patricia O'Brien, e.g., in *The Promise of Punishment*, writes: "The use of argot, hardly unique in the modern prison, is an immemorial practice associated with corporate groups. Inmates constituted a type of community, albeit a fluid one, and argot was a means of special communication" (79).

27. Words such as "la came" (an abbreviated form of the word "camelote," which stands for contraband texts [*HP* 192]), "un brifeton" (clandestine written messages between inmates [204]), and "un cipal" (short for "garde municipal" [126]) are introduced and explained.

2. A Pariah's Paradise

1. I examine how this pact is initiated below. Lejeune, in his oft-quoted essay "The Autobiographical Pact," writes that referential texts such as scientific or historical texts "claim to provide information about a 'reality' exterior to the text, and so to submit to a test of *verification*. Their aim is not simple verisimilitude, but resemblance to the truth. Not 'the effect of the real,' but the image of the real" (*On Autobiography* 22). Lejeune continues, stating that a referential pact is implicit or explicit, and the accuracy of the text is fundamentally, and paradoxically, not of paramount importance: "it is essential that the referential pact be *drawn up*, and that it be *kept*; but it is not necessary that the result be on the order of strict resemblance. The referential pact can be, according to the criteria of the reader, badly kept, without the referential value of the text disappearing (on the contrary)" (22–23).

2. Throughout this chapter, pagination for Sartre's *Saint Genet* refers first to the English translation followed by pagination in the French edition (published as volume 1 of Genet's *Œuvres complètes*).

3. Examples include Genet "singing" his long-lost childhood agricultural penal colony (76; 104) and the staircase in which he, as an adult prisoner, shares cherished intimacy with his fellow Fontevrault inmates (59; 82). Throughout this chapter, pagination for *Miracle de la rose* refers first to the English translation *Miracle of the Rose* followed by the pagination in the original French.

4. That temporal and spatial ambiguity is examined below in the section titled "Narration: An Eyewitness Approach."

5. In Frechtman's translation it is a "rejected kiss" (73). On the Proustian aspects of *Miracle*, critic Richard Coe, in *The Vision of Jean Genet* remarks, "At times the Proustian parallel is so exact that one almost suspects parody" (74).

6. Another "miracle" involving a rose and Harcamone occurs early in the novel. During a sequence in which the narrator witnesses Harcamone's passage through the prison, "Genet" imagines a "miracle" in which Harcamone's chains are transformed into white roses. The narrator clips one of the roses from the chain of his "idol," whose hair resembles a crown of thorns. The narrator ex-

presses a sort of religious ecstasy during that scene. For more information see *Miracle* (16–17; 25–26).

7. The narrator of *Notre-Dame* states, e.g., "The odor of prison is an odor of urine, formaldehyde, and paint. I have recognized it in all the prisons of Europe" (85–86; 49).

8. Genet's first play, *Haute surveillance* (*Deathwatch*), is delimited by the frame of a prison, even though a documentary representation of prison conditions and relations is not among its primary ambitions. Although the rules of the prison administration are evoked superficially through the commands of a prison guard, and the play makes an explicit reference to Weidmann, a real-life criminal-hero also evoked in both *Miracle de la rose* and *Notre-Dame-des-fleurs*, the play is not distinguished by a high degree of documentary realism. Indeed, the second sentence of its opening stage directions emphasizes the oniric: "The entire play unfolds as in a dream" (*The Maids and Deathwatch* 181; *Haute surveillance* 103). A play in one act, *Haute surveillance* depicts the petty rivalries, hierarchies, and glorification of violence that appear to be endemic to a seedy criminal underworld represented by three prisoners—Maurice, Yeux-Verts ("Green Eyes"), and Lefranc—who are forced to share a prison cell. Spectators witness the violence (Maurice is killed by Lefranc at the end of the play) that results as these characters jockey for power and seek prestige according to the norms and inverted values of the criminal universe they inhabit.

9. Prison imagery figures prominently in other works by Genet, including his poems "Le condamné à mort," "Marche funèbre," "La galère," and "Le parade," each of which, with varying degrees, uses carceral imagery and depicts inmates faced with specific aspects of confinement. Genet also wrote a filmscript about Mettray's history (which remains unpublished) titled *Le langage de la muraille: Cent ans jour après jour* (The Language of the Wall: A Hundred Years, Day after Day), for which he did a great deal of research. For more information on this script and its overriding political themes, see E. White 70–72, 605–7. For the use of prison and confinement imagery in Genet's oeuvre in general, see Witt 155–98.

10. The original quote from *Moi aussi* (Me, Too) is as follows: "De

la 'vérité' du nom principal (c'est-à-dire de l'identité du nom du personnage-narrateur et de celui de l'auteur . . .), le lecteur a tendance à déduire, sinon la vérité des faits (comme devant tout témoignage, il peut avoir des doutes), du moins le fait que l'auteur les donne pour vrais."

11. Frechtman's translation of "bagne d'enfants" as "children's hell" is accurate in that it captures the negative connotations of the term *bagne* but inaccurate in that it misses the true denotative meaning of the term, the English equivalent of which is "penal colony."

12. Beyond the inclusion of his own name in the text, the process of remembering, and the process of documenting his own transformation, other confessional elements in *Miracle* are worthy of note. In telling the story of his childhood at Mettray, "Genet" examines his behavior and attempts to explain it to his imagined readers. The narrator, for instance, delves into possible reasons why he threw a bowl of soup at an authority figure just a few moments after his detention at Mettray began: "In the mess-hall, a few moments after my arrival—I was in a state of nervous tension that evening (or perhaps I did it to prove I was very daring)—I threw a plate of soup in the face of the head of the family" (63–64; 88). Interspersed with real, verifiable biographical information, those revelations take on a confessional quality. Other revelations, reminiscent of Rousseau's disingenuousness in his own *Confessions*, appear false. Explaining his motivations to steal, for instance, "Genet" accentuates his supposed goodness: "When I was poor, I was mean because I was envious of the wealth of others, and that unkindly feeling destroyed me, consumed me. I wanted to become rich in order to be kind, so as to feel the gentleness, the restfulness that kindness accords (rich and kind, not in order to give, but so that my nature, being kind, would be pacified). I stole in order to be kind" (61; 84). The notion that the narrator stole in order to be "kind" (*bon*) and to resemble more closely the bourgeois population that has rejected him is hard to believe, especially given his embrace of the underworld of the prison and the subversion of traditional notions of the sacred found throughout the text.

13. For a useful overview of the vast body of critical work on Genet (up to 1980), see Webb. Alongside Coe's book, prominent studies

include McMahon, Thody, and Plunka. Recent work on the theme of the prison in Genet includes El Basri's Bachelardian study of the mythical space of prison in Genet's prose and theater. Recent articles specifically on *Miracle de la rose* include Champagne's Lévinassian study and Boyle's Foucauldian reading. Edmund White's *Genet* is still the most thorough biography on Genet. More recent biographical works include Barber and Reed.

14. Lejeune writes in "Autobiography, Novel, and Proper Name" that the referential strength of the author's name in the text is so strong that, for most readers, it would even nullify the significance of a subtitle "novel" (*On Autobiography* 47).

15. Weidmann, in particular, was a particularly notorious real-life figure, as he was the last man to be publicly executed in France and photos of his dead body were widely disseminated in magazines throughout the country. For more information see Camus's *Reflections on the Guillotine* 9.

16. Sartre, *Saint Genet* 453 (French). In *A Thief's Journal*, Genet writes about a team burglary in which he participated (87).

17. In his history of Fontevrault prison, Jean Chédaille corroborates White's observation. Citing as his authority the exhaustive research of Jean Poulain, the former adjunct director of the cultural center of Fontevrault, Chédaille writes that Genet "never had his name in the records of Fontevrault. Against all evidence, it is there, however, that he situates the action of his book" (5).

18. "To tell the truth, it is necessary to lie."

19. The narrator appears to be forthright with his readers by mentioning that memories of Mettray included in the narrative are carefully selected, prioritized, and sometimes even falsely constructed. He notes: "And all the memories that crowd on me are obscurely chosen, in such a way that my stay at Mettray seems to have been only a long mating broken by bloody turmoils in which I saw colonists whack each other and become a mass of bleeding flesh, red or pale" (78–79; 108). At times the memories are difficult to evoke, and moments at Mettray are not easy for the narrator to describe. On one occasion he laments, "It will be rather difficult for me to portray the characters in this book" (105; 143). Similarly, he writes, "I rack my brains trying to find some device, some artifice

that would enable me to convey to you the peculiar feel of certain moments at Mettray" (169; 231). Moreover, the narrator mentions that he is a bit reluctant to share all of the mysteries of Mettray with his readers: "I do not claim to be giving you full knowledge of all the mysteries (and to be unveiling them) that were dormant in the colony. There were lots of other things as well. I'm searching. They sometimes occur to me, but they flit through my mind without leaving traces. Without a trace on paper. You have to wait, they will appear at the end of the book" (225–26; 304–5).

20. See Cohn 118.

21. Short for Théodule, "Dudule" can be used for ridicule and teasing. Thanks go to Jean-Max Guieu for providing this information.

22. In the English translation the speeches are not italicized, but they are separated from the rest of the text by quotation marks. The official discourse will be examined in a section below titled "Mettray and Fontevrault, According to 'Genet.'"

23. The translation is mine. Frechtman translates "me rappeler" as "render" (152).

24. Here again, the italics do not appear in the English translation, but the text is placed within quotation marks.

25. He writes, e.g., "But first, here is why I was sent to the punishment cell, where I began to write this account" (34; 49).

26. A similar ambiguous temporal slip occurs in the middle of one of the narrator's nostalgic remembrances of Mettray: "I realize that I loved my Colony with my flesh, just as, when it was reported that the Germans were preparing to leave, France realized, in losing the rigidity they had imposed on her, that she loved them" (227; 307). If the Nazis had already made their departure arrangements, as the narrator's subversive observation indicates, it would certainly appear that the narrative was composed after 1943.

27. Tension between fiction and nonfiction is further revealed through Genet's use of metacommentary throughout *Miracle de la rose*. The narrator, e.g., attempts to define from a generic standpoint the kind of story he is telling on a number of occasions. Early in the narrative, when speaking of his past activity as a burglar, he writes: "If I were writing a novel, there might be a point in describing the gestures I made, but the aim of this book is only to relate the ex-

perience of freeing myself from a state of painful torpor" (27; 39). His explicit denial of the composition of a novel—together with the inclusion of the author's name in the text—initially seems to indicate that the work is a nonfiction. However, in spite of that denial and his repeated use of the word "book" to designate his work, "Genet" makes a revelatory slip in describing the contents of his narrative. While commenting on Harcamone's death sentence toward the end of *Miracle*, the narrator writes: "Novels are not humanitarian reports. Indeed, let us be thankful that there remains sufficient cruelty, without which beauty would not be" (200; 271). The narrator's observation implies that his "novel" is enriched aesthetically by depictions of the cruelties of prison life. That slip, while oblique, forces the reader to confront conflicting information regarding the manner in which the story should be read. Is it, or is it not, a "novel"? Examined in the light of other indicators of fictionality in the text, that slippage further encourages interpretation of *Miracle de la rose* as a work of fiction. Generic designations are not the only form of metaliterary references that point toward fictionality. The narrator's past at Mettray, e.g., is repeatedly depicted in the light of both adventure novels and popular novels. Upon his entrance to Mettray, the narrator notes: "We walked up the road. The trees were getting denser, Nature was growing more mysterious, and I should like to speak of her the way islands occupied by pirates and savage tribes are sometimes spoken of in adventure stories [romans d'aventures]" (97; 133). "Genet" demonstrates that he has read a variety of *romans*, and he even expects his readers to call upon their knowledge of such texts in order to better their understanding of his own story. For example, in describing youths who have been exposed to sex too early in their lives, the narrator writes: "But in order to see these children more clearly, call up the dreams provoked by your reading of pulp fiction [romans populaires]" (123; 168). The narrator therefore not only attempts to fill in the blanks in his life story with that which is fictional and oniric (e.g., his imaginary sexual fantasies, his dreams about Harcamone, and reenacted speeches by Dudule and the bishop), but he encourages his readers to do the same. Within such a system of metaliterary commentary, the narrator's references to his own story as his "adventure" (25, 149; 36, 203) take on a specific, fictional denotation. By using such terminology, the narrator fictionalizes his own life and the lives of his characters, thereby demonstrating a belief in the interchangeability of the fictional and the real. For example, "Genet" characterizes the individuals in his life story as would a writer of fiction. When mentioning his experience at Mettray, he comments on the members of the penal administration, writing that as they lived their lives "They were writing my story. They were my characters" (104; 143).

28. For historical information on Mettray I have relied on Gaillac's authoritative *Maisons de correction, 1830–1945*. Gaillac includes a chapter on the creation of Mettray titled "Une réalisation exemplaire" (An Exemplary Achievement), pp. 80–85. See also O'Brien 109–39.

29. For Gaillac, that praise was well deserved. He lauds the dedication of the Mettray founders and writes that their work enabled thousands of children to avoid prison. He writes that he respects the founders and the guards alike. Gaillac acknowledges with regret that some of the guards were deviants and that Mettray devolved into a "bagne d'enfants" (85).

30. Agricultural colonies were moreover one among a number of solutions proffered by reformers to isolate young delinquents from the dangers and promiscuity of adult prisons. Other solutions included the creation of "maisons d'éducation correctionnelle" (houses of corrective education) and the placement of young delinquents in apprenticeships in groups that would protect and sponsor them, which were dubbed "sociétés de patronage" (Gaillac 27).

31. A critique by the inspectors general De Lurieu and Roman (published in 1852) stated that they were very skeptical of the plan to reverse demographic trends and make agricultural families out of inveterate city-dwellers (Gaillac 74).

32. Front-page newspaper reports about the colonies were quite common in the 1930s, and a number of films, both fictional and nonfictional, were made in the 1930s and 1940s about the experience of young delinquents in the justice system. For more information see Gaillac 291 and 300–302.

33. A fine example of Genet's willingness to reject both patriotism and

religion is found in his derisive comments about soldiers in the trenches, the manner in which they are coddled by society, and a parallel Genet makes between them and the colonists at Mettray (whom a bishop refers to as "stray lambs" [152; 206]). He writes: "In the early days of the war, old ladies with pale blue hearts entered into conversation by talking about 'our little soldiers . . . our little braves'! They, in the trenches, jerked off at night with their mudcaked hands. God's little lambs, sitting in the pews with their hands in their pockets, did likewise" (152; 206–7).

34. Further alienating his audience, he cheers the destruction wrought upon their society by World War II (389). Genet accentuates his separation by calling the bourgeois weak for embracing neither pure evil nor pure virtue and by lambasting them for enjoying art about criminals but rejecting real-life delinquency (390).

35. Genet mentions Alexis Danan, Edouard Helsey, and Albert Londres, criticizing their work and putting into question their observations on the colonies. See *Miracle* 105 (143) and 163 (222).

36. All of these details can be corroborated in Gaillac's *Maisons de correction*. For the use of hammocks and the practice of naval exercises, see p. 80; for the lack of walls, see p. 81; for the use of "families," see p. 74.

37. Genet errs here, as the correct spelling of the second founder's name is "Courteilles" and, according to Gaillac, he was a viscount, not a baron (23).

38. Much is made of the sanguine character of Mettray colonists in historical accounts, especially during the revolutionary upheaval of 1848. See, e.g., Foucault, *Discipline and Punish* 295 and Gaillac 84. Both cite Guillaume Marie-André Ferrus's 1850 work, *Des prisonniers, de l'emprisonnement et des prisons* (On Prisoners, Imprisonment, and Prisons), as their source.

39. See, e.g., the scene in which the narrator "marries" his lover Divers at Mettray (68–70; 94–96). O'Brien also writes that reformers and investigators deplored the "horrible contagion" of homosexuality among the juvenile prisoners (136–37).

40. This scene takes place while the narrator is in Fontevrault prison, but Genet's description is intended to make it clear to the reader that the brutal methods learned at Mettray are readily remembered by recidivist inmates later in life.

41. For more information on details of the hierarchy of colonists at Mettray, see Plunka 79–80.

42. The official spelling of the name, which has changed over the years, is "Fontevrauld" (Chédaille 6), but for the sake of simplicity and clarity I use the spelling found in *Miracle de la rose*. For more information on the history of Fontevrault as a prison, see Chédaille.

43. See Chédaille 33 for more information on inmate population numbers over the course of Fontevrault's history.

44. The narrator also states that each inmate "within himself" had the proud soul of a monk of old (134; 182).

45. Moreover, the narrator finds a parallel between his remembrances of Bulkaen and Harcamone and the monastic rituals that he assumes took place in Fontevrault: "The dead Bulkaen and Harcamone are now within me, in crypts which are as strange (to my eyes) as the dark, windowless capitular room of the abbesses of Fontevrault. . . . They must have engaged in indescribable ceremonies around the tombs of the Plantagenets, of Richard the Lionhearted. There the monks and nuns celebrated a forgotten liturgy which I faithfully continue" (164; 223).

46. An example of a definition provided for the imagined readers is found in dialogue about black market activities in Fontevrault: "T'as pas un bout de brutal? (du pain)" (136). "Brutal" would be the slang term for bread (*du pain*). Frechtman's translation simply reads: "You wouldn't have a hunk of bread, would you?" (100).

47. As part of his description of the daily routine of the inmates, Ménard writes that they were forced to salute the guards upon crossing their path in the morning (23).

48. Sarrazin is designated as such on the front cover of the first U.S. edition of *The Runaway* (Grove, 1967).

3. A Recidivist's Tale

1. Throughout this chapter, pagination for *La cavale* refers first to the U.S. edition of *The Runaway*, and second to the Poche edition of *La cavale*. Similarly, citations from *L'astragale* refer first

to the U.S. edition of *Astragal*, and second to the Poche edition of *L'astragale*. All other translations are mine.

2. Sarrazin's biographer, Josane Duranteau, makes this assertion (*Sarrazin* 165).

3. Duranteau writes: "Albertine had Julie build a 'cell' at La Tanière that imitated the ones found in prisons" (Introduction 61). Sarrazin referred to their country lodging as La Tanière (The Hideaway). The house was owned by their "Uncle" Maurice, a longtime friend of the couple.

4. *La traversière* has not yet been translated into English. *Traversier* is an adjective in French signifying "that which runs across." The feminine form of the adjective is *traversière*, and Sarrazin transforms it into a noun. The title evokes "crossings," for the narrator-protagonist (*la traversière*—i.e., she who crosses) must adjust to a new life on the outside.

5. Only Sarrazin's three novels were published during her lifetime. Her correspondence and personal journals were published by Julien after her death. Her correspondence with Julien was published in *Lettres à Julien, 1958–1960*, and their clandestine correspondence was published in *Biftons de prison*. The latter contains twenty-six *biftons*, or notes, that the couple exchanged in secret between 1958 and 1960.

6. The first date provided early in the book is 23 April (22; 24), and the book ends about twenty months later, just after Christmas (480; 506).

7. Sarrazin's three novels were published over the course of two years. Pauvert released *La cavale* and *L'astragale* simultaneously in 1965, and *La traversière* appeared the following year. Gallimard also bid on Sarrazin's first two novels, but according to information included in her correspondence, Sarrazin had already agreed to publication with Pauvert (Duranteau, Introduction 50). Simone de Beauvoir, who had read Sarrazin's manuscripts, was instrumental in setting up a connection between the Gallimard publishing house and Sarrazin. Sarrazin mentions Beauvoir in a number of her letters. For more information, see *Lettres de la vie littéraire* 22 and 35.

8. In her commentary on Sarrazin's journal, Duranteau agrees: "Daily

life does not figure into this 1959 Prison Journal, which she herself called 'The Times' and where she abandons herself to a serene meditation on herself, on her destiny, on love, life, death" (*Passe* 104).

9. Julien serves as the figure of the beloved in her journal. A number of the passages are directly addressed to him.

10. Duranteau describes their situation: "At Amiens prison, she takes up her journal again, whereas Julien begins work in a factory, and takes care of the formalities of their marriage. . . . They get married on February 7, 1959, in Amiens. After having just enough time to say 'I do' at city hall, the prisoner is taken back to her cell" (*Sarrazin* 104). That scene is hardly reminiscent of the one found in the novel in which the couple drinks champagne in a private apartment with their police escort. For more details on the fictionalized ceremony and celebration, see part 2, chapter 11.

11. For more information on the Chessman case see Machlin and Woodfield. See also Chessman's testimonial text, *Cell 2455, Death Row.*

12. The prison at Melun and Fontevrault prison, examined in the first and second chapters of this study, are examples of such *maisons centrales.*

13. Such use of prisoners as laborers has existed since the late sixteenth century; and work in prison has been viewed, often erroneously, by reformers as a means of rehabilitating unruly and undisciplined inmates into law-abiding citizens. See note 7 of chapter 1 for more information.

14. See note 1 in the introduction.

15. Sarrazin places her protagonist in situations that make her appear to be above the daily morass in which the other inmates find themselves trapped. Elissa Gelfand in *Imagination in Confinement* notes that the inmates with whom Anick shares the prison space are fundamentally her "Other": "Sarrazin/Anick uses the other faceless entity as a foil whenever she wishes to demonstrate her superiority. Prison's bringing together 'asocial' and 'undesirable' women vindicates Sarrazin's self-aggrandizement" (233). Her protagonist is unwilling to entertain the prospect of integrating herself into the society of women prisoners, however much they may resemble mainstream society on the outside: "I am neither logical nor bal-

anced, nor am I the sociable type, and I have no hope of becoming so; I feel quite uncomfortable among my little sisters in stir, who have their own way of reshaping society" (82; 86).

16. The death penalty was abolished in France in 1981.

17. Goffman refers to this process as "mortification" (*Asylums* 16). For more information on the traumatic process of entry, see 12–35.

18. Gelfand's central thesis on *La cavale* is as follows: "With *La Cavale* Sarrazin proves that female criminals, by their understanding of limitation, are the antithesis of marginal 'monsters': far from being antisocial and maladjusted, they are women in society, like all others" (*Imagination* 238). Gelfand's observation about Sarrazin's banalization of the figure of the female criminal is an astute one. Indeed, Anick does underline the fact that women in prison re-create a version of the society that exists on the outside. One striking example of a social process that exists on the outside (and that is imitated on the inside) surfaces when Anick informs her cellmates that she is going to attempt an escape. She notes: "Naturally, everyone asks how at the same time: The silence that follows is like the silence that envelops the model housewife when she is about to disclose the secret of her creamed duck" (68; 70). Sarrazin's depiction of women runs against currents in many criminological studies on female criminal-prisoners. For more information see Gelfand's *Imagination* 214–21 and, more recently, Norris 99–140.

19. Translation has been altered for clarity. Markmann's translation states: "the Bic is my piece."

20. As Gelfand notes, "Sarrazin's desire to be perceived as a writer, not a prisoner, finds its vehicle in *La Cavale*" (*Imagination* 230).

21. After Albertine's death, Julien filed a wrongful-death suit in the courts and eventually won. The doctors implicated in the incident were found guilty of involuntary homicide. For more information see Duranteau, *Sarrazin* 15–25.

4. Corrected Inmates, Corrected Texts

1. Jean-Paul Vigneaud, "Pour un motif futile," *Sud Ouest*, 10 Dec. 1996, http://www.sudouest.com/. I would like to thank *Sud Ouest* for their permission to reprint the article here in a translated and

abridged form. Because Bon's *Prison* has not yet been translated into English and a great deal of the material treated here has never been published, all translations in this chapter are mine.

2. François Bon, interviews conducted with the author in person and via e-mail from April 2000 to February 2001.

3. I would like to thank François Bon for his generosity in providing me with his unpublished source material. Without his help, the composition of this chapter would not have been possible. "Parfois je me demande" includes, according to Bon, the young detainees' entire body of work. In a book that discusses his methodology for conducting writing workshops, *Tous les mots sont adultes* (All Words Are Adult), Bon notes that, as a rule, he saves all the texts produced in his sessions with the workshop participants (17). The formatting is generously spaced, and many of the texts are structured in unrhymed verse. Total word count is just under thirty-seven thousand words.

4. At Bon's request, I have deleted Miremont's text from my book.

5. Bon interviews.

6. In *Les prisons de la misère* (Prisons of Poverty), sociologist Loïc Wacquant comments on one of the most volatile and widely mediatized subjects in turn-of-the-century France: the intersection of youth, violence, immigration, and urban life (9). See also Sobanet and Terrio, which includes information about Bon's writing workshop.

7. Bon interviews.

8. See chapter 9 of John Corner's *The Art of Record* for more information on *Roger and Me* and the controversy surrounding Moore's manipulation of chronology.

9. See, e.g., Haberman. I revisit this controversy in greater detail in the conclusion.

10. Bon interviews.

11. In telling the story of Jean-Claude Brulin, Molinier writes: "The head guard informs the author that 'Brulin was stabbed.'"

12. For English translations see "Récit" in the *Collins-Robert French Dictionary*, 5th ed. (New York: Collins, 1998). In "Discours du récit," Genette acknowledges that there are a number of widely accepted meanings of the term, the most applicable of which for

Bon's text would be "la succession d'événements, réels ou fictifs, qui font l'objet [d'un] discours, et leurs diverses relations d'enchainement, d'opposition, de répétition" (71). That meaning is mentioned in both the *Grand Larousse* and the *Grand Robert*, as both dictionaries define the term as a piece of writing that depicts either real or imagined events. The *Grand Robert*'s primary definition is as follows: "Relation orale ou écrite (d'événements vrais ou imaginaires)." The *Grand Larousse* defines the term thus: "Oeuvre littéraire relatant des faits réels ou imaginaires."

13. DRAC is the Direction régionale des affaires culturelles.

14. Bon interviews.

15. The fourth chapter does not depict or treat in any way the Gradignan writing workshop and is only linked thematically to the remainder of the work. The source material provided to me by the author is not used in that chapter. According to Bon, he conducted several writing workshops in prisons, and this fourth chapter appears to be based on an experience other than the one conducted in the youth detention center near Bordeaux. In a letter to Frédéric Miremont's legal representation, Bon writes that the re-creation of the carceral environment in *Prison* results not just from his experience in Gradignan but from other experiences with the French penal administration as well (24 May 1998). Study of this fourth chapter is not pertinent to our analysis.

16. The entire original texts reads: "Et pourquoi je suis en prison, c'est qu'il me fallait de l'argent pour le commerce que je voulais ouvrir. Et lors d'un bizness avec un copain ça c'est mal passé et on en est venu aux mains et on a trébuché et il m'a tiré vers lui et le couteau que je portais est tombé de ma poche et il l'a ramassé et sur la peur je l'ai retourné plusieurs fois sur lui mais avant qu'on en vienne aux mains il m'avait menacé moi et ma famille alors quand je l'ai vu qu'il s'était emparé de mon couteau c'était moi ou lui mais aujourd'hui c'est moi qui me retrouve en prison et si c'était moi qui était mort c'est lui que vous auriez trouvé à ma place car il m'avait menacé et il avait juré que c'était moi ou lui et comme je le connaissais il était capable de le faire et sur la peur voilà le geste que j'ai fait et jamais je pourrai me le pardonner" ("Parfois" 80).

17. In a letter to Odile Dhavernas, Bon describes his method in com-

posing Tignasse's fictional monologues: "It is not a case in which elements of the text were communicated to me by Miremont [i.e., "Tignasse"], but rather it is a completely fictive reconstruction based on diverse sources of knowledge" (25 Oct. 1999).

18. As we have seen with his manipulation of the grammar and spelling of the prisoner's text above, Bon does not even follow that principle in the first chapter. However, readers without access to "Parfois je me demande" would not be able to see that that text had been altered.

19. At Bon's request, I have altered all inmates' names found in "Parfois je me demande."

20. The name of his housing project served as the title for his text ("Parfois" 137–38).

21. Bon interviews.

22. There are three texts by Lionel J. ("Parfois" 44, 58, 148), two by Tahar (45, 46), and one by Mark C. (168–69).

23. The documentary effect is enhanced not only by that striking level of detail but also by the fact that the passage is italicized, which generally signifies a direct quote from an inmate's workshop text. The passage, however, is not found in "Parfois je me demande," which would seem to indicate that it was written entirely by Bon.

24. Both of these stories surface in *Prison* unitalicized. Bon's decision not to italicize the two texts by Tahar is a curious one. Without italics or quotations marks, the narratives appear to be the product of the author's imagination, when they are, in fact, based on real events.

25. In the original text in "Parfois je me demande," they want to go to Paris to get the papers.

Conclusion

1. For more information on the initial exposé, see the article "A Million Little Lies" at http://www.thesmokinggun.com/. The exposé also mentions previously published newspaper articles that questioned the veracity of Frey's memoir.

2. *New York Times* columnist Maureen Dowd said this in an appearance on Winfrey's show on 26 January 2006.

3. See, e.g., Rich.
4. *A Million Little Pieces* was placed, like Serge's *Les hommes dans la prison*, in the HV section of the Library of Congress's classification system, the section normally reserved for social pathology and criminology. See chapter 1 of this study for more information.
5. For example, in the realm of nonfiction, Christophe Lambert's *Derrière les barreaux* (Behind Bars) was published in 1999. Lambert was a prison guard for thirty-one years, and his account documents his attempts to buck unethical trends in the system and fight—on a day-to-day basis—for prisoners' rights. In 2001, sociologist Anne-Marie Marchetti published *Perpétuité: Le temps infini des longues peines* (Life: The Unending Time of Lengthy Sentences), a text based on interviews with twenty-seven male and female prisoners. Her project serves as yet another attempt to extract testimony from inmates, as her main goal is to determine how people cope with day-to-day existence when faced with a lifetime of imprisonment. Ted Conover's *Newjack* also constitutes an innovative attempt to document conditions in the carceral realm. A freelance writer and journalist, Conover worked "undercover" for nearly a year in New York's Sing Sing prison with the goal of experiencing prison firsthand to see how it transforms staff and inmates alike. His fascinating account details how prison guards are trained, how they work, and how their work affects their lives outside of prison.
6. The program remains accessible at http://www.npr.org/programs/ atc/prisondiaries/.
7. See Strum for information on Richman's method.
8. The result of the government's study was a scathing indictment of the penal system in the form of two reports published in mid-2000 by the Senate and the National Assembly. See, e.g., the Assemblée Nationale report no. 2521, published 28 June 2000, available at http://www.assemblee-nationale.fr/.
9. Vasseur stated in a 2005 interview with the French magazine *Le nouvel observateur* that nothing has changed. *Le nouvel observateur* has dedicated a section of its website to prison conditions. For more information see http://tempsreel.nouvelobs.com/speciales/prisons/. In one polemical essay dated 15 February 2007 they declare French penal institutions "prisons of shame."

[BIBLIOGRAPHY]

Abramowitz, Isidore. *The Great Prisoners: The First Anthology of Literature Written in Prison*. New York: Dutton, 1946.

Améry, Jean. *At the Mind's Limits*. Trans. Sidney and Stella P. Rosenfeld. Bloomington: Indiana UP, 1980.

Apollinaire, Guillaume. *Alcools*. Paris: Gallimard, 1913.

Artières, Philippe, Laurent Quéro, and Michelle Zancarini-Fournel, eds. *Le groupe d'information sur les prisons: Archives d'une lutte, 1970–72*. Paris: IMEC, 2003.

Bachelard, Gaston. *The Poetics of Space*. Trans. Maria Jolas. Boston: Beacon, 1969.

Badinter, Robert. *La prison républicaine*. Paris: Fayard, 1992.

Barber, Stephen. *Jean Genet*. London: Reaktion, 2004.

Bataille, Georges. *La littérature et le mal*. Paris: Gallimard, 1957.

Beaumont, Gustave de, and Alexis de Tocqueville. *On the Penitentiary System in the United States and Its Application in France*. Trans. Francis Lieber. Carbondale: Southern Illinois UP, 1964.

Bender, John. *Imagining the Penitentiary: Fiction and the Architecture of the Mind in Eighteenth-Century England*. Chicago: U of Chicago P, 1987.

Berchtold, Jacques. *Les prisons du roman (XVIIe–XVIIIe siècle)*. Geneva: Droz, 2000.

Berg, Louis. *Revelations of a Prison Doctor*. New York: Minton, Balch, 1934.

Bernard, Tristan. *Aux abois*. Paris: Union générale d'éditions, 1988.

Bessette, Jean-Michel. *Il était une fois la guillotine*. Paris: Editions Alternatives, 1982.

Beverley, John. *Testimonio: On the Politics of Truth*. Minneapolis: U of Minnesota P, 2004.

Bizard, Léon-Clément. *Souvenirs d'un médecin de la préfecture de police et des prisons de Paris (1914–1918)*. Paris: Grasset, 1925.

Blumenthal, Ralph. "Confined in Prisons, Literature Breaks Out." *New York Times* 26 Aug. 2000: B9.

Bon, François. *C'était toute une vie*. Paris: Verdier, 1995.

———. *La douceur dans l'abîme: Vies et paroles de sans-abri*. Paris: La Nuée Bleue, 1999.

———. "Ecrire en prison." Unpublished reflection on the writing workshop. January 1997. Copy in author's possession.

———. Letter to Maître Odile Dhavernas (attorney representing Frédéric Miremont). 14 December 1998. Copy in author's possession.

———. Letter to Maître Odile Dhavernas "Concernant l'atelier d'écriture tenu en 96–97." 25 October 1999. Copy in author's possession.

———. Letter to *Sud Ouest* newspaper "Au sujet de *Prison*." 4 July 1999. Copy in author's possession.

———. Letter to the legal representation of Frédéric Miremont. 24 May 1998. Copy in author's possession.

———. "Parfois je me demande: Un atelier d'écriture au CJD Gradignan." Unpublished manuscript. Copy in author's possession.

———. *Prison*. Paris: Verdier, 1997.

———. *Tous les mots sont adultes: Méthodes pour l'atelier d'écriture*. Paris: Fayard, 2000.

Boudard, Alphonse. *La cerise*. Paris: Plon, 1963.

Boyer, Frédéric. *En prison*. Paris: P. O. L., 1992.

Boyle, Claire. "Autobiography: The Dangers of Knowledge and Genet's Suspect Reader." *French Studies* 59.2 (2005): 189–202.

Brombert, Victor. *The Romantic Prison: The French Tradition*. Princeton: Princeton UP, 1978.

Bunker, Edward. *The Animal Factory*. New York: Viking, 1977.

———. *No Beast So Fierce*. Harpenden: No Exit, 1993.

Buntman, Fran Lisa. *Robben Island and Prisoner Resistance to Apartheid*. Cambridge: Cambridge UP, 2003.

Camus, Albert. *La chute*. Paris: Gallimard, 1956.

———. *L'étranger*. Paris: Gallimard, 1942.

———. *The Fall*. Trans. Justin O'Brien. New York: Knopf, 1957.

———. *Reflections on the Guillotine*. Trans. Richard Howard. Michigan City IN: Fridtjof-Karla, 1960.

Carco, Francis. *Les hommes en cage*. Paris: Albin Michel, 1936.

Carlen, Pat. *Women's Imprisonment: A Study in Social Control*. London: Routledge and Kegan Paul, 1983.

Carlier, Christian. *Fresnes la prison: Les établissements pénitentiaires de Fresnes, 1895–1990*. Fresnes: Ecomusée de Fresnes, 1991.

———. *Histoire du personnel des prisons française du XVIIIe siècle à nos jours*. Paris: Ouvrières, 1997.

Cau, Jean. *La pitié de Dieu*. Paris: Gallimard, 1961.

Cayrol, Jean. *Lazare parmi nous*. Paris: Seuil, 1950.

Certeau, Michel de. *L'invention du quotidien*. Paris: Gallimard, 1990.

Chambers, Ross. *Facing It*. Ann Arbor: U of Michigan P, 1998.

Champagne, Roland. "Jean Genet in the Delinquent Colony of Mettray: The Development of an Ethical Rite of Passage." *French Forum* 26.3 (2001): 71–90.

Un chant d'amour. Dir. Jean Genet. 1950.

Chédaille, Jean. *Fontevraud de toutes les pénitences: Histoire d'une prison de 1804–1963*. Saintes: Les Chemins de la Mémoire, 2002.

Chessman, Caryl. *Cell 2455, Death Row*. Westport CT: Greenwood, 1969.

Chevigny, Bell Gale, ed. *Doing Time: 25 Years of Prison Writing*. New York: Arcade, 1999.

Churchill, Winston S. *Winston S. Churchill: His Complete Speeches, 1897–1963*. Vol. 2, *1908–1913*. Ed. Robert Rhodes James. New York: Chelsea House, 1974.

Cleaver, Eldridge. *Soul on Ice*. New York: McGraw-Hill, 1968.

Clemmer, Donald. *The Prison Community*. New York: Holt, 1958.

Cobley, Evelyn. *Representing War: Form and Ideology in First World War Narratives*. Toronto: Toronto UP, 1993.

Coe, Richard. *The Vision of Jean Genet*. London: Peter Owen, 1968.

Cohn, Dorrit. *The Distinction of Fiction*. Baltimore: Johns Hopkins UP, 1999.

Un condamné à mort s'est échappé (ou Le vent souffle où il veut). Dir. Robert Bresson. 1956.

Conover, Ted. *Newjack: Guarding Sing Sing*. New York: Random House, 2001.

Cool Hand Luke. Dir. Stuart Rosenberg. Warner Bros., 1967.

Corner, John. *The Art of Record: A Critical Introduction to Documentary*. Manchester: Manchester UP, 1996.

Crosland, Margaret. *Women of Iron and Velvet*. New York: Taplinger, 1976.

Davies, Ioan. *Writers in Prison*. Oxford: Basil Blackwell, 1990.

Derrida, Jacques. *Glas*. Paris: Galilée, 1974.

Doré, Gustave, and Blanchard Jerrold. *London: A Pilgrimage*. New York: Dover, 1970.

Dostoevsky, Fyodor. *Memoirs from the House of the Dead*. Trans. Jessie Coulson. Oxford: Oxford UP, 1983.

Dunne, Tom. "A Polemical Introduction: Literature, Literary Theory, and the Historian." *Writer as Witness*. Ed. Tom Dunne. Cork: Cork UP, 1987. 1–9.

Duranteau, Josane. *Albertine Sarrazin*. Paris: Editions Sarrazin, 1971.

———. Introduction. *Lettres de la vie littéraire*. By Albertine Sarrazin. Paris: Pauvert, 1974. 1–9.

D'Eaubonne, Françoise. *Les écrivains en cage*. Paris: Balland, 1970.

El Basri, Aïcha. *L'imaginaire carcéral de Jean Genet*. Paris: L'Harmattan, 1999.

Erhel, Catherine, and Catherine Leguay. *Prisonnières*. Paris: Stock, 1977.

Esslin, Martin. *The Theater of the Absurd*. New York: Doubleday, 1961.

The Farm: Life inside Angola Prison. Dir. Jonathan Stack and Liz Garbus. A&E, 1998.

Faugeron, Claude, Jacques-Guy Petit, and Michel Pierre. *Histoire des prisons en France (1789–2000)*. Paris: Privat, 2002.

Favard, Jean. *Les prisons*. Paris: Flammarion, 1994.

Felman, Shoshana, and Dori Laub. *Testimony*. New York: Routledge, 1992.

Fize, Michel. "Histoire de la 'prison modèle' de la Santé, 1867–1914." *Revue de science criminelle et de droit pénal comparé* October–December 1983: 707–13.

———. *Une prison dans la ville: Histoire de la prison-modèle de la Santé, 1867–1983*. Paris: Centre national d'études et de recherches pénitentiaires, Ministère de la justice, 1983.

Foley, Barbara. *Telling the Truth: The Theory and Practice of Documentary Fiction*. Ithaca: Cornell UP, 1986.

Foucault, Michel. *Discipline and Punish: The Birth of the Prison*. Trans. Alan Sheridan. 2nd ed. Vintage: New York, 1995.

———. "Space, Knowledge, and Power." *The Foucault Reader*. Ed. Paul Rabinow. New York: Pantheon, 1984. 239–56.

———. *Surveiller et punir: Naissance de la prison*. Paris: Gallimard, 1975.

Franklin, H. Bruce. *Prison Literature in America*. New York: Oxford UP, 1978.

———, ed. *Prison Writing in 20th-Century America*. New York: Penguin, 1998.

Frey, James. *A Million Little Pieces*. New York: Anchor Books, 2003.

Gaillac, Henri. *Les maisons de correction, 1830–1945*. Paris: Cujas, 1991.

Gelfand, Elissa D. "Albertine Sarrazin: A Control Case for Femininity in Form." *French Review* 51.2 (1977): 245–51.

———. "Albertine Sarrazin: The Confined Imagination." *L'esprit créateur* 19.2 (1979): 47–57.

———. *Imagination in Confinement: Women's Writings from French Prisons*. Ithaca: Cornell UP, 1983.

Genet, Jean. *Le bagne*. Paris: L'Arbalète, 1993.

———. "L'enfant criminel." In *Oeuvres complètes*, vol. 5. Paris: Gallimard, 1979. 379–93.

———. *Haute surveillance*. Paris: Gallimard, 1949.

———. *Journal du voleur*. Paris: Gallimard, 1949.

———. *The Maids and Deathwatch*. Trans. Bernard Frechtman. New York: Grove, 1962.

———. *Miracle de la rose*. Paris: L'Arbalète, 1946.

———. *Miracle of the Rose*. Trans. Bernard Frechtman. London: Penguin, 1971.

———. *Notre-Dame-Des-Fleurs*. In *Oeuvres complètes*, vol. 2. Paris: L'Arbalète, 1951.

———. *Our Lady of the Flowers*. Trans. Bernard Frechtman. Intro. Jean-Paul Sartre. London: Faber and Faber, 1963.

———. *A Thief's Journal*. Trans. Bernard Frechtman. Paris: Olympia, 1954.

Genette, Gérard. "Discours du récit." *Figures III*. Paris: Seuil, 1972. 65–282.

Giles, Jane. *Un chant d'amour: Le cinéma de Jean Genet*. Paris: Macula, 1993.

Goffman, Erving. *Asylums: Essays on the Social Situation of Mental Patients and Other Inmates*. New York: Doubleday, 1961.

———. *The Presentation of Self in Everyday Life*. New York: Doubleday, 1959.

———. *Stigma: Notes on the Management of a Spoiled Identity*. Englewood Cliffs NJ: Prentice Hall, 1963.

Goodman, Nelson. *Ways of Worldmaking*. Indianapolis: Hackett, 1978.

Gorkín, Julián. "Les dernières années de Victor Serge 1941–1947." Afterword to *Mémoires d'un révolutionnaire*. Paris: Club des éditeurs, 1957. 377–86.

Gugelberger, Georg M., ed. *The Real Thing: Testimonial Discourse and Latin America*. Durham: Duke UP, 1996.

Haberman, Clyde. "Getting Rich by Making Stuff Up." *New York Times* 17 Jan. 2006: B1.

Hallinan, Joseph. *Going Up the River: Travels into a Prison Nation*. New York: Random House, 2001.

Hanrahan, Mairéad. *Lire Genet: Une poétique de la différence*. Montréal: PUM, 1997.

Hardt, Michael. "Prison Time." *Yale French Studies* 91 (1997): 64–79.

Heath, James. *Eighteenth-Century Penal Theory*. Oxford: Oxford UP, 1963.

Himes, Chester. *Yesterday Will Make You Cry*. New York: Norton, 1998.

Howells, Christina M. "Derrida and Sartre: Hegel's Death Knell." *Derrida and Deconstruction*. Ed. Hugh J. Silverman. Routledge: New York, 1989. 169–81.

Hugo, Victor. *Claude Gueux*. Paris: Larousse/VUEF, 2002.

———. *Le dernier jour d'un condamné*. Paris: Gallimard, 1970.

———. *The Last Day of a Condemned Man and Other Prison Writings*. Trans. Geoff Woollen. Oxford: Oxford UP, 1992.

Huré, Anne. *En prison*. Paris: Julliard, 1963.

Ignatieff, Michael. *A Just Measure of Pain: The Penitentiary in the Industrial Revolution, 1750–1850*. London: Penguin, 1978.

Kennelly, Brian Gordon. *Unfinished Business: Tracing Incompletion in Jean Genet's Posthumously Published Plays*. Amsterdam: Rodopi, 1997.

Knapp, Bettina. *Jean Genet*. Boston: Twayne, 1989.

Kreitzer, Larry. *Prometheus and Adam: Enduring Symbols of the Human Situation*. New York: UP of America, 1994.

Kropotkin, Peter. *In Russian and French Prisons*. Trans. Paul Avrich. New York: Schocken, 1971.

Kuperman, Natalie. *Rue Jean-Dolent*. Paris: Gallimard, 2000.

Lambert, Benjamin. *La cavale d'Albertine: Mémoire*. Paris: Nizet, 1994.

Lambert, Christophe. *Derrière les barreaux*. Paris: Michalon, 1999.

Lang, Luc. *Mille six cent ventres*. Paris: Fayard, 1998.

Leavey, John P., Jr. *GLASsary*. Lincoln: U of Nebraska P, 1986.

Lehrer, Jim. *The Special Prisoner*. New York: Random House, 2000.

Lejeune, Philippe. *Moi aussi*. Paris: Seuil, 1986.

———. *On Autobiography*. Trans. Katherine Leary. Minneapolis: Minnesota UP, 1989.

Levi, Primo. *The Drowned and the Saved*. Trans. Raymond Rosenthal. New York: Summit, 1988.

———. *Survival in Auschwitz*. Trans. Stuart Woolf. New York: Macmillan, 1993.

Lévi-Strauss, Claude. *Tristes tropiques*. Paris: Plon, 1955.

London, Jack. "The Pen: Long Days in a County Penitentiary." Franklin, *Prison Writing* 49–57.

———. "'Pinched': A Prison Experience." Franklin, *Prison Writing* 38–49.

———. *The Star Rover*. New York: Macmillan, 1915.

Londres, Albert. *Au bagne*. Paris: A. Michel, 1924.

———. *Dante n'avait rien vu*. Paris: Le Serpent à Plumes, 2000.

Machlin, Milton, and William Read Woodfield. *Ninth Life*. New York: Putnam, 1961.

Mailhot, Laurent. *Albert Camus ou l'imagination du désert*. Montreal: PUM, 1973.

Malcolm X. *The Autobiography of Malcolm X*. With Alex Haley. New York: Ballantine, 1964.

Mandel, Barrett J. "Full of Life Now." *Autobiography: Essays Theoretical and Critical*. Ed. James Olney. Princeton: Princeton UP, 1980. 49–72.

Marchetti, Anne-Marie. *Perpétuité: Le temps infini des longues peines*. Paris: Plon, 2001.

Marshall, Bill. *Victor Serge: The Uses of Dissent*. New York: Berg, 1992.

Massey, Dennis. *Doing Time in American Prisons: A Study of Modern Novels*. New York: Greenwood, 1989.

McMahon, Joseph H. *The Imagination of Jean Genet*. New Haven: Yale UP, 1963.

Ménard, Bertrand. *Encore 264 jours à tirer: Pénitencier de Fontevrault*. Paris: Cheminements, 1994.

Midnight Express. Dir. Alan Parker. Columbia TriStar, 1978.

Miller, D. Quentin, ed. *Prose and Cons: Essays on Prison Literature in the United States*. Jefferson NC: McFarland, 2005.

Molinier, Christian. "Les mots désincarcérés." *Le matricule des anges* 23 (June–July 1998). http://www.lmda.net.

Montagnon, Pierre. *Quarante-deux rue de la Santé: Une prison politique, 1867–1968*. Paris: Pygmalion, 2001.

Morris, Norval, and David J. Rothman, eds. *The Oxford History of the Prison: The Practice of Punishment in Western Society*. Oxford: Oxford UP, 1998.

Morris, Terence, and Pauline Morris. *Pentonville: A Sociological Study of an English Prison*. London: Routledge and Kegan Paul, 1963.

Motte, Warren F. "Sarrazin's Articulation." *French Literature Series* 20 (1993): 103–17.

Naish, Camille. *A Genetic Approach to Structures in the Work of Jean Genet*. Cambridge: Harvard UP, 1978.

Nerenberg, Ellen. *Prison Terms: Representing Confinement during and after Italian Fascism*. Toronto: Toronto UP, 2001.

Norris, Anna. *L'écriture du défi: Textes carcéraux*. Birmingham: Summa, 2003.

Nous sommes tous des assassins. Dir. André Cayette. Studiocanal Image, 1952.

O'Brien, Patricia. *The Promise of Punishment: Prisons in Nineteenth-Century France*. Princeton: Princeton UP, 1982.

Ong, Walter J. "The Writer's Audience Is Always a Fiction." *PMLA* 90 (1975): 9–21.

Pellico, Silvio. *My Prisons*. New York: Oxford UP, 1963.

Perrot, Michelle. "Delinquency and the Penitentiary System in Nineteenth-Century France." Trans. Elborg Forster. *Deviants and the Abandoned in French Society*. Ed. Robert Forster and Orest Ranum. Baltimore: Johns Hopkins UP, 1978. 213–45.

———. *L'impossible prison: Recherches sur le système pénitentiaire au XIXe siècle réunies par Michelle Perrot*. Paris: Seuil, 1980.

Petit, Jacques-Guy. *Ces peines obscures*. Paris: Fayard, 1990.

Plancke, René-Charles. *Melun à la Belle Epoque*. Le Mée-sur-Seine: Editions Amattéis, 1992.

Plantinga, Carl. *Rhetoric and Representation in Nonfiction Film*. Cambridge: Cambridge UP, 1997.

Plunka, Gene A. *The Rites of Passage of Jean Genet*. Cranbury: Associated UPs, 1992.

Prince, Gerald J. "Introduction to the Study of the Narratee." Trans. Francis Mariner. *Essentials of the Theory of Fiction*. Ed. Michael J. Hoffman and Patrick D. Murphy. Durham: Duke UP, 1988. 213–33.

Prison Diaries. Ed. Joe Richman and Wendy Dorr. *All Things Considered*. National Public Radio. http://www.npr.org. 23 Apr. 2006.

Rafter, Nicole. *Shots in the Mirror: Crime Films and Society*. Oxford: Oxford UP, 2000.

Redonnet, Marie. *Jean Genet le poète travesti*. Paris: Grasset, 2000.

Reed, Jeremy. *Jean Genet: Born to Lose*. London: Creation Books, 2005.

Rich, Frank. "Truthiness 101: From Frey to Alito." *New York Times* 22 Jan. 2006. http://www.nytimes.com/.

Riffaterre, Michael. *Fictional Truth*. Baltimore: Johns Hopkins UP, 1990.

Rostaing, Corinne. *La relation carcérale: Identités et rapports sociaux dans les prisons de femmes*. Paris: PUF, 1997.

Rothman, David J. *The Discovery of the Asylum*. Boston: Little, Brown, 1990.

Rusche, Georg, and Otto Kirchheimer. *Punishment and Social Structure*. Trans. M. I. Finkelstein. New York: Russell and Russell, 1968.

Sarrazin, Albertine. *Astragal*. Trans. Patsy Southgate. New York: Grove, 1967.

———. *L'astragale*. Paris: Pauvert, 1965.

———. *Biftons de prison*. Paris: Pauvert, 1977.

———. *La cavale*. Paris: Pauvert, 1965.

———. *Dit*. Paris: Editions Sarrazin, 1973.

———. *Journal de Fresnes*. Paris: Le Passe-peine, 1976.

———. *Journal de prison 1959*. Paris: Editions Sarrazin, 1972.

———. *Lettres à Julien, 1958–1960*. Paris: Pauvert 1971.

———. *Lettres de la vie littéraire*. Paris: Pauvert, 1974.

———. *Lettres et poèmes*. Paris: Pauvert, 1967.

———. *Le passe-peine 1949–1967*. Paris: Juillard, 1976.

———. *Romans, lettres et poèmes*. Préf. Hervé Bazin. Paris: Pauvert, 1967.

———. *The Runaway*. Trans. Charles Lam Markmann. New York: Grove, 1967.

———. *La traversière*. Paris: Pauvert, 1966.

Sartre, Jean-Paul. *Saint Genet, Actor and Martyr*. Trans. Bernard Frechtman. New York: Braziller, 1963.

———. *Saint Genet, comédien et martyr*. Vol. 1. Jean Genet, *Œuvres complètes*. Paris: Gallimard, 1951.

Scarfe, Francis. *André Chénier: His Life and Work, 1762–1794*. Oxford: Oxford UP, 1965.

Schaeffer, Jean-Marie. *Qu'est-ce qu'un genre littéraire*. Paris: Seuil, 1989.

Scheffler, Judith A. *Wall Tappings*. 2nd ed. New York: CUNY Feminist P, 2002.

Sellin, Thorsten. Introduction. *On the Penitentiary System in the United States and Its Application in France*. By Gustave de Beaumont and Alexis de Tocqueville. Trans. Francis Lieber. Carbondale: Southern Illinois UP, 1964. xv–xl.

Serge, Victor. *L'affaire Toulaev*. Paris: Seuil, 1948.

———. *Les années sans pardon*. Paris: La Découverte, 2003.

———. *Carnets*. Paris: Actes Sud, 1985.

———. *Les derniers temps*. Paris: Grasset, 1951.

———. *Les hommes dans la prison*. Paris: Rieder, 1930.

———. *Littérature et révolution*. Paris: Maspero, 1976.

———. *Mémoires d'un révolutionnaire de 1901 à 1941*. Paris: Seuil, 1951.

———. *Memoirs of a Revolutionary*. Trans. Peter Sedgwick. Iowa City: U of Iowa P, 2002.

———. *Men in Prison*. Trans. Richard Greeman. New York: Doubleday, 1969.

———. *Naissance de notre force*. Paris: Climats, 2004.

———. *Le rétif*. Ed. Yves Pagès. Paris: Monnier, 1989.

———. *S'il est minuit dans le siècle*. Paris: Grasset, 1939.

———. *Ville conquise*. Paris: Climats, 2004.

Sobanet, Andrew, and Susan Terrio. "Silence in the Court and Testimony behind Bars: Juvenile Defendants and the French Judicial System." *French Cultural Studies* 16.1 (2005): 21–39.

Solzhenitsyn, Aleksandr. *One Day in the Life of Ivan Denisovich*. Trans. H. T. Willetts. New York: Noonday, 1991.

Spens, Iona, ed. *Architecture of Incarceration*. London: Academy, 1994.

Spiegelman, Art. *Maus*. New York: Pantheon, 1997.

Starobinski, Jean. "The Style of Autobiography." *Autobiography: Essays Theoretical and Critical*. Ed. James Olney. Princeton: Princeton UP, 1980. 73–83.

Strum, Charles. "Messages from Prison, Whispered in Our Ears." *New York Times* 7 Jan. 2001: Arts & Leisure, 35.

Sykes, Gresham M. *The Society of Captives*. Princeton: Princeton UP, 1958.

Teeters, Negley K. *World Penal Systems*. Philadelphia: Pennsylvania Prison Society, 1944.

Thody, Philip. *Jean Genet: A Study of His Novels and Plays*. New York: Stein and Day, 1968.

Thomas, Chantal. "Pleasure, Perversion, Danger." *A New History of French Literature*. Ed. Denis Hollier. Cambridge: Harvard UP, 1994. 579–84.

Trounstine, Jean. *Shakespeare behind Bars*. New York: St. Martin's P, 2001.

Valladares, Armando. *Against All Hope*. Trans. Andrew Hurley. New York: Knopf, 1986.

Varaut, Jean-Marc. *Poètes en prison: De Charles d'Orléans à Jean Genet*. Paris: Perrin, 1989.

Vasseur, Véronique. *Médecin-chef à la prison de la Santé*. Paris: Le Cherche Midi, 2000.

———. "Pourquoi je signe." *Le nouvel observateur* 14 Nov. 2005. http://tempsreel.nouvelobs.com/.

Verlaine, Paul. *Mes prisons*. Paris: Mille et une nuits, 2003.

Vey, Jean-Louis. *Jacques Becker ou la fausse évidence*. Lyon: Aléas, 1995.

Vigneaud, Jean-Paul. "Pour un motif futile." *Sud Ouest* 10 Dec. 1996: SOURCE database.

Villon, François. *The Complete Works of François Villon*. Trans. Anthony Bonner. New York: Bantam, 1960.

———. *Oeuvres*. Ed. André Mary. Paris: Garnier, 1962.

Wacquant, Loïc. *Les prisons de la misère*. Paris: Raisons d'agir, 1999.

Webb, Richard C. *Jean Genet and His Critics: An Annotated Bibliography, 1943–1980*. Metuchen: Scarecrow, 1982.

Weissman, Susan. *Victor Serge: The Course Is Set on Hope*. London: Verso, 2001.

White, Edmund. *Genet: A Biography*. New York: Knopf, 1993.

White, Hayden. *The Content of the Form*. Baltimore: Johns Hopkins UP, 1987.

Wiesel, Elie. "The Holocaust as Literary Inspiration." *Dimensions of the Holocaust*. Ed. Elliot Lefkovitz. Evanston: Northwestern UP, 1977. 5–19.

Wieviorka, Annette. *L'ère du témoin*. Paris: Plon, 1998.

Wilde, Oscar. "The Ballad of Reading Gaol." *De Profundis*. London: Penguin, 1973. 229–52.

Williams, Philip F., and Yenna Wu. *The Great Wall of Confinement: The Chinese Prison Camp through Contemporary Fiction and Reportage*. Berkeley: California UP, 2004.

Witt, Mary Ann Frese. *Existential Prisons: Captivity in Mid-Twentieth-Century French Literature*. Durham: Duke UP, 1985.

Woollen, Geoff. Introduction. *The Last Day of a Condemned Man and Other Prison Writings*. By Victor Hugo. Trans. Geoff Woollen. Oxford: Oxford UP, 1992. vii–xx.

[INDEX]

condemned prisoners. *See* capital punishment, prisoners awaiting

confessional autobiography, claims of, in works by Genet, 79–80

confinement narratives *vs.* prison novels, 21

conflation of real people into fictional characters, in works by Bon, 147, 168–69, 172

contract between text and reader: and James Frey controversy, 184–85; in works by Bon, 152, 154, 155, 163, 165; in works by Genet, 25; in works by Sarrazin, 111; in works by Serge, 35. *See also* referential pact

Count of Monte Cristo, allusions to, 2, 3

Courteilles, Viscount Brétignières de, 92, 217n37

creative license, of Bon, 171

creativity and incarceration, 6, 192n19; in works by Sarrazin, 123

daily lives of prisoners. *See* routines of prisoners

Danan, Alexis, 73, 85, 217n35

death penalty. *See* capital punishment, prisoners awaiting

Deathwatch (Haute surveillance) (play) (Genet), 211n8

debilitating effect of prison, in works by Sarrazin, 109, 118–

19, 126–28, 131–32, 134–39. *See also* dehumanization of inmates

Defoe, Daniel, 8

dehumanization of inmates, in works by Serge, 30. *See also* debilitating effect of prison

Demetz, Frédéric, 85, 91–92

Le dernier jour d'un condamné (The Last Day of a Condemned Man) (Hugo), 13, 189n1, 198n42

description in documentary novels: by Bon, 172; by Sarrazin, 117

documentary effect, 23, 28; and autobiographical inclinations, 15, 198n45; and fictionalization, 33–35, 185; in works by Bon, 154–55; in works by Genet, 64, 77, 96–98; in works by Sarrazin, 124–26; in works by Serge, 33–35, 49–62

documentary fiction: in works by Genet, 73–74; in works by Serge, 50–52

Doré, Gustave, *Newgate: Exercise Yard* (engraving), 58

Dostoyevsky, Fyodor, 3; *Memoirs from the House of the Dead*, 24, 50, 206n13

dramatization of inmates' writings, 151–52

drug trafficking in prisons, in works by Sarrazin, 126

Dumas, Alexandre, 3

Dumas, André, 55, 206n16

editing. *See* source material, manipulation of
entry of new prisoners: in works by Bon, 164–65; in works by Genet, 70, 93–94, 98; in works by Sarrazin, 118, 132; in works by Serge, 56–57
episodic structure of *Prison*, 149
escape attempts, in works by Sarrazin, 108–9, 117–18, 121–22
Esslin, Martin, on San Quentin production of *Waiting for Godot*, 5
L'étranger (The Stranger) (Camus), 17, 189n1

The Fall (La chute) (Camus), 2
family members, 161–62
fantasy as escape from reality: in works by Bon, 160; in works by Genet, 70–71, 160
female prisoners, in works by Sarrazin, 101–2, 139–40, 221n8
feminist portrayal of single-sex institutions, 28
fictional elements, in works by Bon, 160–61, 171–72
fictionality, 23–24; and manipulation of source materials, 17; in works by Bon, 157–58; in works by Genet, 75–76, 79–80, 80–82, 82–83, 92, 213n17, 214n26, 214n27; in

works by Serge, 32, 35. *See also* third-person omniscient narration
fiction and autobiography, line between, in works by Sarrazin, 109–10, 115
fiction and documentation, tension between: in works by Bon, 152–53; in works by Genet, 79–80, 99, 214n27; in works by Sarrazin, 114–15
fiction and nonfiction, blurring of: in prison novels, 185; in works by Bon, 146, 147, 152, 154–55, 164–65; in works by Genet, 74–75
fiction as documentary tool: in prison narratives, 4; in works by Bon, 146
films: *Un chant d'amour (A Song of Love)*, 67–68; *Cool Hand Luke*, 200n50; *The Hurricane*, 192n16; *Midnight Express*, 200n50; nonfiction, 199nn47–48; about prison, 3, 191n10, 192n16, 200nn50–51; *Roger and Me*, 154
first-person narration: in works by Bon, 180; in works by Sarrazin, 103, 114; in works by Serge, 30, 42
first-person plural narration, Serge on, 40–41
Fontevrault prison: and Genet, 64, 68–69, 74–76, 84, 94, 213n17; history of, 94–96
food for prisoners: in works by

Gibran, Khalil, 147
Gogois-Myquel, Christiane,
 103, 112
graffiti, 1, 189n1; in works by
 Genet, 98; in works by Serge,
 41
grammatical errors as sign of
 authenticity, 159–60, 224n18
Gramsci, Antonio, *Prison Notebooks*, 6, 192n19
Groupe d'information sur les
 prisons (GIP), 14–15
guards: in works by Bon, 174; in
 works by Serge, 41–43, 47

Haute surveillance (Deathwatch)
 (play) (Genet), 211n8
*Head Doctor at La Santé Prison
 (Médecin-chef à la prison de
 la Santé)* (Vasseur), 187–88
Helsey, Edouard, 217n35
Himes, Chester, 8; *Yesterday
 Will Make You Cry*, 2, 3
Holocaust survivor narratives
 vs. prison narratives, 21–22,
 34, 202n60
holy space, prison as, in works
 by Genet, 72–73, 90–92, 96,
 134. *See also* penitentiary
 movement
homelessness in prisoners' writings, 148
*Les hommes dans la prison
 (Men in Prison)* (Serge), plot
 summary of, 36–39
Howard, John, 5
Hugo, Victor: and allusions to

Jean Valjean, 2, 3; *Claude
 Gueux*, 13–14; *Le dernier
 jour d'un condamné (The
 Last Day of a Condemned
 Man)*, 13, 189n1, 198n42;
 legacy of, 3, 28
humor, in works by Sarrazin,
 133–34, 136
Hurlin, Frédéric, 144, 158, 181.
 See also "Jean-Claude Brulin" (fictional character)
hybrid structure, in works by
 Bon, 146, 149–50, 157–58,
 166–68, 180–81

ideology in prison novels, 4,
 18–19; by Bon, 154; as characteristic of, 15; and editing
 choices, 187; by Genet, 87–
 89; lack of, by Sarrazin, 129–
 31; by Serge, 31, 35, 37–39.
 See also sociopolitical issues
imagery of prisons, 2; in works
 by Genet, 67–68, 211n9
imprisonment-as-burial motif,
 in works by Serge, 48,
 205n11
incarceration, nature of, 2–3
industrialization of prisons, in
 works by Serge, 45–46
inmates, relations between, in
 works by Bon, 174. *See also*
 solidarity among prisoners
inmates' writing, in works by
 Bon, 147, 149–50, 165
invention and fictionality of
 prison novels, 23

isolation. *See* solitary confinement

Istrati, Panaït, 30, 31–32, 204n4

jargon used by prisoners: in works by Genet, 98; in works by Serge, 61, 209n27

"Jean-Claude Brulin" (fictional character), 160–63. *See also* Hurlin, Frédéric

"Jean Valjean" (fictional character), allusions to, 2, 3

Jewison, Norman, *The Hurricane* (film), 192n16

Justine (Sade), 192n21

juvenile offenders: in works by Bon, 147, 151; in works by Genet, 89–90

juvenile penal colonies, 28. *See also* Mettray penal colony

Lamartine, Alphonse de, 85

The Last Day of a Condemned Man (Le dernier jour d'un condamné) (Hugo), 13, 189n1, 198n42

Laub, Dori, 22

Levi, Primo, *Survival in Auschwitz*, 34, 50

Lévi-Strauss, Claude, and Serge, 29–30

libraries, prison, in works by Serge, 60–61, 209n24

London, Jack, 3, 6, 192n18

Londres, Albert, 217n35

Lucas, Charles, 85, 92, 197n40

lyrical prose passages, in works by Genet, 64

Mabillon, Jean, 192n15

maisons centrales (central prisons), in works by Sarrazin, 121. *See also* Fontevrault prison; Melun prison

Malcolm X, 5

Malesherbes, Chrétien Guillaume de Lamoignon de, 12

manipulation of experience, in works by Serge, 41

marginalized groups: in Bon's workshops, 147; and power structure, 9, 196n34; and testimonial literature, 20, 28

Marxism, 28; in works by Serge, 31–32

Médecin-chef à la prison de la Santé (Head Doctor at La Santé Prison) (Vasseur), 187–88

meditation and reflection: prison as opportunity for, 5–6; in works by Bon, 174. *See also* holy space, prison as; penitence; penitentiary movement

Melun prison, 55, 206n16

Mémoires d'un révolutionnaire (Memoirs of a Revolutionary) (Serge), 33–34, 40

Memoirs from the House of the Dead (Dostoyevsky), 24, 50, 206n13

oppression, witness to, in works
by Serge, 34, 48
Our Lady of the Flowers
(Notre-Dame-des-fleurs)
(Genet), 66–67, 73, 211n7
outcasts: in works by Bon, 159;
in works by Genet, 84, 86–
89, 94–99; in works by Sarrazin, 220n15

paratextual information: and
fictionalization, 19, 185; in
works by Bon, 155–57; in
works by Sarrazin, 110–12;
in works by Serge, 32–33
Parker, Alan, *Midnight Express*
(film), 200n50
Paul, Saint, allusions to, 2, 3
Pellico, Silvio, 3, 50
penal colonies *vs.* confinement
narratives, 4, 21. *See also*
Mettray penal colony
penal practices, 2–3; in works
by Serge, 53–59
penitence, avoidance of by Sarrazin, 132–33. *See also* holy
space, prison as; meditation
and reflection
penitentiary movement, 5, 12–
13, 192n15; echoes of in
works by Genet, 92; influence
of early novels on, 193n24
La Petite Roquette prison, 116;
and Sarrazin, 124
Philadelphia system, 54
physical setting: as documentation in works by Genet, 96–

97; in works by Bon, 162; in
works by Sarrazin, 119–20;
in works by Serge, 52–53,
59–60
Pilorge (criminal), 73
La pitié de Dieu (Mercy of God)
(Cau), 17, 101–2, 114, 117
Plantagenet dynasty and Fontevrault prison, 95–96
plumbing, communication
through: in works by Sarrazin, 125; in works by Serge,
61, 189n1, 209n27
point of view, change of. *See*
narrative voices, changes in
political prisoners, 21, 201n56
politicization, 9. *See also* sociopolitical issues
power structures, resistance to:
prison as a vehicle to question, 10–11, 196n34; in
works by Sarrazin, 132; in
works by Serge, 35, 37, 46–
47, 48–49
power structures among prisoners, in works by Genet, 93–94
Prison (Bon), 15; chapter 1,
144–46, 157–64; chapter 2,
164; chapter 6, 171–73; overview of, 27–28; summary of,
150–52
prisoners as enemies, in works
by Serge, 48
Prisoners Exercising (painting)
(Van Gogh), 58
prisoners' round exercise. *See*
forced marching

prison narratives, 3, 191n8;
French tradition of, 6–7, 14
Prison Notebooks (Gramsci), 6,
192n19
prison novel, characteristics of,
7–8, 15–21, 172
prison reform: history of, 3, 11–
13, 190n7; in works by Serge,
57–58
prison structure, in works by
Serge, 30, 45–46, 47
prison system, modern: critiques
of and documentary effect,
185–86; systematic deprivation in, 9–10; in works by
Bon, 178; in works by Sarrazin, 109, 119
prison system, resistance to, in
works by Sarrazin, 137–38
privacy, limitation of, in works
by Sarrazin, 126–27
Proust, Marcel, *A la recherche
du temps perdu (Remem-
brance of Things Past)*, 25,
64–65, 71
publication information, ambiguity of: in works by Bon,
156; in works by Genet, 83;
in works by Sarrazin, 111,
112, 219n7
punishment in prison novels, 22

readership: and Bon, 171, 173–
75, 180; and Genet, 87–88,
96–100, 217n34
realist fiction *vs.* documentary
fiction, 17

recidivism, in works by Bon,
180
"récit" in subtitle in work by
Bon, 155, 156–57, 222n12
referentiality, 18–19; in works
by Genet, 63–64, 73–74; in
works by Sarrazin, 116; in
works by Serge, 53, 60–61,
208n21
referential pact, in works by
Genet, 63–64, 77–78. *See
also* contract between text
and reader
reflection. *See* meditation and
reflection
reintegration into mainstream
society: in works by Bon,
178–80; in works by Sarrazin, 107
*Remembrance of Things Past (A
la recherche du temps perdu)*
(Proust), 25, 64–65, 71
Richman, Joe, *Prison Diaries*
(radio program), 186–87
"Roman" in subtitle in work by
Sarrazin, 111
Rosenberg, Stuart, *Cool Hand
Luke* (film), 200n50
Rousseau, Jean-Jacques, 12
routines of prisoners: in works
by Bon, 153, 172–74; in
works by Genet, 91, 98; in
works by Sarrazin, 106, 107,
114, 117; in works by Serge,
45–46, 52, 56, 59–60
rules and processes, in works by
Bon, 162

The Runaway (La cavale) (Sarrazin). See *La cavale (The Runaway)*

sacred space, prison as. *See* holy space, prison as
Sade, marquis de, *120 journées de Sodome,* 7; *Justine,* 192n21
sanitation: in works by Genet, 89–90; in works by Sarrazin, 120
La Santé prison, 187; and Genet, 82–83; and Serge, 53, 54–55, 206nn14–15, 208n23
Sarrazin, Albertine: *L'astragale (Astragal),* 103, 105–6, 139–40; autobiographical discourse in works by, 110; avoidance of penitence in, 132–33; and Cau, 102; and contract between text and reader, 111; critiques of prison system by, 110, 119; and de Beauvoir, 219n7; debilitating effect of prison in works by, 109, 118–19, 126–28, 131–32, 134–39; documentary details in works by, 124–26; escape attempts by, 108–9, 117–18, 121–22; female prisoners and, 101–2, 139–40, 221n18; fiction and documentation in works, tension between, 109–10, 114–15; forced labor of, 123–24, 137–38, 220n13; and Genet,

110; journals of, 101–2, 116, 141; lack of ideology by, 129–31; lack of solidarity with, 105, 106; *Lettres de la vie littéraire (Letters from Literary Life),* 103–4; as media phenomenon, 103–4; and narrator as character, 103, 111–13, 114, 115–16; otherness in works by, 220n15; overview of works by, 99–100; physical settings in works by, 119–20; prison system in works by, resistance to, 137–38; routines of prisoners in, 106, 107, 117–18, 122–23; and self-preservation, 132–35, 136; and Serge, 109, 110, 118, 127; transformation of, 137–38; *La traversière,* 103, 106–7, 116, 119n4; and writing as act of defiance by, 140–41. See also *La cavale (The Runaway)*
Sartre, Jean-Paul, 14, 101–2
schedule for prisoners. *See* routines of prisoners
self-conscious narrator, in works by Genet, 76–83
self-preservation, in works by Sarrazin, 121–22, 132–35
Serge, Victor, 29–62; actuality of, 30–32; anti-capitalist sociopolitical agenda of, 31, 35, 37–39, 43–48; architecture of French prisons and, 58–59, 208n22; autobiograph-

*Listening In: Music, Mind,
and the Modernist Narrative*
By Eric Prieto

Essays in Aesthetics
By Gérard Genette
Translated by Dorrit Cohn

Fuzzy Fiction
By Jean-Louis Hippolyte

In Praise of Flattery
By Willis Goth Regier

*Jail Sentences: Representing
Prison in Twentieth-Century
French Fiction*
By Andrew Sobanet